MOCK TEST SERIES for Olympiad

English | Mathematics
Science | General Knowledge
Cyber | Logical Reasoning

3 Class

Comprehensive MCQ with detailed solutions covering all the Olympiad Exams.

- **Corporate Office :** 45, 2nd Floor, Maharishi Dayanand Marg, Corner Market, Malviya Nagar, New Delhi-110017
  Tel. : 011-49842349 / 49842350

Typeset by Disha DTP Team

Printed at Repro Knowledgecast Limited, Thane

DISHA PUBLICATION

For further information about the books from DISHA,

Log on to **www.dishapublication.com** or email to **info@dishapublication.com**

CONTENTS

English

Mathematics

Science

General Knowledge

Logical Reasoning

Cyber

ENGLISH
MOCK TEST 1–5

OLYMPIAD

Mock Test

Name : __________

Max. Marks : 35

Number of Questions : 35

Time : 1 Hour 30 Minutes

There is no negative marking in the test.

Section I
Word and Structure Knowledge

1. Choose a word for image given below.

(a) Axe (b) Sickle

(c) Hammar (d) Scythe

2. A person whose job is making and repairing wooden objects is called a ________.

(a) plumber (b) carpenter

(c) blacksmith (d) mechanic

DIRECTIONS (Qs. 3 to 5): Choose the correct spelling.

3. (a) Dezive (b) Desire
   (c) Desiar (d) Dezire

4. (a) Fondation (b) Foundasion
   (c) Foundation (d) Fundation

5. (a) Wodden (b) Wooden
   (c) Wudden (d) Woodden

DIRECTIONS (Qs. 6 to 8): Choose the odd one out.

6. (a) Slippers (b) Sandals
   (c) Shoes (d) Gloves

Space for Rough Work

7. (a) Table (b) Chair
   (c) Bed (d) Carpet
8. (a) Mango (b) Onion
   (c) Cucumber (d) Capsicum
9. (a) Eye : See
   (b) Ear : Hear
   (c) Knife : Clean
   (d) Nose : Smell
10. (a) Rose : Flower
    (b) Car : Mechanic
    (c) Hammer : Tool
    (d) Crow : Bird

DIRECTIONS (Qs. 11 to 19): Choose the most appropriate word to fill the blanks.

11. We were stuck ______ the traffic jam.
    (a) at (b) in
    (c) into (d) on
12. The show begins ________ 11 o'clock in the morning.
    (a) by (b) within
    (c) at (d) from
13. We plan to see him ______ two and three in the afternoon tomorrow.
    (a) in (b) at
    (c) between (d) by
14. The wings of the ______ are very beautiful.
    (a) butterflies (b) butterfly's
    (c) butterfly (d) butterflys
15. The cat was sitting ______ the table.
    (a) from (b) in
    (c) before (d) under
16. Aditya _________ improve his handwriting.
    (a) want (b) had
    (c) should (d) may

Space for Rough Work

17. You aren't from Brazil, _______ ?

    (a) do you (b) are you

    (c) don't you (d) doesn't you

18. Rain has stopped now. The match _________ resume shortly.

    (a) can (b) being

    (c) is (d) might

19. _______ are you going to Mumbai?

    (a) What (b) Where

    (c) How (d) Who

DIRECTIONS (Qs. 20 & 21): Read statement I and II. Choose correct answer from the given options.

20. **Statement I:** Doctor is to patient as teacher is to garden.

    Statement II : Horse is to stable as fish is to aquarium.

    (a) Only statement I is correct.

    (b) Only statement II is correct.

    (c) Both the statements I and II are correct.

    (d) Both the statements are incorrect.

21. **Statement I:** Anita write a letter.

    Statement II : Boys play football in the ground.

    (a) Only statement I is correct.

    (b) Only statement II is correct.

    (c) Both the statements are correct.

    (d) Both the statements are incorrect.

Section II
Reading

DIRECTIONS (Qs. 22 to 26): Read the passage given below and answer the questions from the options given below.

Space for Rough Work

The Hungry Lion

Once upon a time there was no one left in the jungle to eat. When the lion came to know of it, he got very angry. It knew that it will have to go to some other jungle to find food. But it was not easy to go and live in another jungle. There will be some other lion there, who would not allow it to stay there. It will have to fight with that lion to drive it away. It was not easy. But the lion had no choice. So it decided to start off another day. It started off its journey next day in the morning. It was a long journey. But it managed somehow. After all it was the king of a jungle.

22. Why was lion angry?

(a) Because there was another lion

(b) Because there was no food to eat

(c) Because it had lost its way

(d) Because the rabbit had fooled him

23. Why was the lion forced to leave the jungle?

(a) Because there was no one left to eat

(b) Because another lion had come

(c) Because he did not like the jungle

(d) Because he wanted to go to the town

24. It was not easy to live in another jungle because______

(a) the other jungle would be dirty.

(b) the other jungle was full of snakes.

(c) there would be another lion.

(d) there was no food there.

Space for Rough Work

25. The journey was ______.

(a) very short (b) very long
(c) tough (d) easy

26. Lion is the ______.

(a) prince of a jungle
(b) queen of the jungle
(c) princess of the jungle
(d) king of the jungle

Section III
Spoken and Written Expressions

DIRECTIONS (Qs. 27 to 31): Read the following sentences and fill in the blanks from the options given below.

27. Jane: I was planning a trip to Germany during the summer vacation.

Davis: ________________

(a) What are you saying? What happened?
(b) What a coincidence! Even I was discussing the same trip yesterday.
(c) This house is mine.
(d) No, I had gone there yesterday.

28. Do you have any hobby?

____

(a) Yes, I like playing chess and reading.
(b) My mom is not well.
(c) The postman has delivered this parcel.
(d) My school is too far.

29. What do you do?

____

(a) This pen belongs to me.
(b) I am into property business.
(c) My dad bought this car for me.
(d) I don't like going for an outing.

Space for Rough Work

30. Sales Girl : Good morning, Sir. May I help you?

Customer : ________

(a) I am going for a picnic.

(b) No, my mom has told me not to go there.

(c) Yes, do you have split AC's?

(d) He's too clumsy!

31. In which class do your children study?

____

(a) I have two cars.

(b) My son is in 2nd standard and my daughter is in 4th standard.

(c) My dad has just left for work

(d) This is really too much!

Section IV
Achievers Section

32. If good is to better, then cool is to ________.

(a) coldest (b) cooler

(c) warm (d) bad

33. If pen is to pens, then tooth is to ________.

(a) tooths (b) toothes

(c) teeth (d) mouth

34. ________ are you so happy today?

(a) When (b) Where

(c) Why (d) Who

35. My children ________ white rabbits.

(a) like (b) likes

(c) is liking (d) was liking

Space for Rough Work

OLYMPIAD

Mock Test

Name : __________

Max. Marks : 35

Number of Questions : 35

Time : 1 Hour 30 Minutes

There is no negative marking in the test.

Section I
Word and Structure Knowledge

DIRECTIONS (Qs. 1 to 3): Choose a word for the images given below.

1.

(a) Jackfruit (b) Beetroot
(c) Broccoli (d) Sweet Potato

2.

(a) Fawn (b) Calf
(c) Mare (d) Cub

3.

(a) Orchid (b) Jasmine
(c) Marigold (d) Palash

DIRECTIONS (Qs. 4 to 6): Choose the correct spelling.

4. (a) Achieve (b) Acheive
(c) Achive (d) Acheeve

5. (a) Acoros (b) Acoross
(c) Accross (d) Across

6. (a) Calendar (b) Calender
(c) Calander (d) Calnadar

Space for Rough Work

DIRECTIONS (Qs. 7 to 11): Choose the odd one out.

7. (a) Bowl (b) Plate
   (c) Glass (d) Knife

8. (a) Lettuce (b) Carrots
   (c) Bananas (d) Mushrooms

9. (a) An (b) Any
   (c) Many (d) Some

10. (a) Sandwich (b) Juice
    (c) Milk (d) Lemonade

11. (a) Grave (b) Cheerful
    (c) Happy (d) Overjoyed

DIRECTIONS (Qs. 12 & 13): Choose the correct answer from the given options.

12. **Statement I :** Hens live in a coop.

    Statement II: Dogs live in a kennel.

    (a) Only statement I is correct.
    (b) Only statement II is correct.
    (c) Both statements are correct.
    (d) Both statements are incorrect.

13. **Statement I :** Baby of fish is called fry.

    Statement II: Baby of pig is called puppy.

    (a) Only statement I is correct.
    (b) Only statement II is correct.
    (c) Both statements are correct.
    (d) Both statements are incorrect.

DIRECTIONS (Qs. 14 to 20): Choose the most appropriate word to fill the blanks.

14. If hexagon is to six then octagon is to _______.

    (a) four (b) six
    (c) eight (d) ten

Space for Rough Work

15. If dog is to bitch then bear is to ______.

(a) sow (b) tom

(c) jack (d) bull

16. Yuvraj hit the ball ______ the stands for a six.

(a) before (b) in

(c) into (d) after

17. We have been living in Delhi _____ 2010.

(a) around

(b) after

(c) approximately

(d) since

18. Oh! That garage is _____ fire. Call for help.

(a) on (b) in

(c) by (d) to

19. A _____ of cattle is crossing the road.

(a) herd (b) nerd

(c) geek (d) flock

20. Those _____ are going for a party.

(a) women (b) women's

(c) womans (d) woman's

Section II
Reading

DIRECTIONS (Qs. 21 to 25): Read the passage carefully and then answer from the options given below.

Harry was very happy today. His parents were taking him out to a picnic. They were going out to the deer park. Harry was very excited. He called up all his friends to tell them about it. All his friends were also very excited about it. They also wanted to come along. Harry wanted to take five of his friends with him. He went

Space for Rough Work

to ask his Dad about it, who agreed. They had a big car. In the morning all of them got together at Harry's place and left for picnic. They took cricket bat, football and other outdoor games with them.

21. Why was Harry happy?
    (a) Because it was his birthday
    (b) Because his father bought him new bat
    (c) Because his father was taking him out for picnic
    (d) Because he came first in class

22. Where was Harry going for picnic?
    (a) India Gate
    (b) Nearby park
    (c) Deer park
    (d) Botanical Garden

23. How many friends did Harry want to take with him?
    (a) Two (b) Five
    (c) Eight (d) One

24. What did they take with them?
    (a) Outdoor games
    (b) Chess, Ludo
    (c) Chips and burgers
    (d) Vegetables

25. The antonym of big is _______.
    (a) small (b) large
    (c) tall (d) short

Section III

Spoken and Written Expression

DIRECTIONS (Qs. 26 to 30): Read the following sentences and fill in the blanks from the options given below.

Space for Rough Work

26. Hello, Karen. How are you feeling today?

Karen: ____________________

(a) He is sleeping.

(b) Much better, thanks for your concern.

(c) She is playing in the park

(d) I don't know, I will go.

27. Hello, Harry. It's my birthday today. I am throwing a party at my place. Will you come?

Harry: ______________________

(a) Thanks for inviting me. Many many happy returns of the day. Yes I will come.

(b) What did you say? Its very tough to understand.

(c) His dad is very busy today.

(d) I will buy flowers for decoration.

28. Do you know, what is the date today?

(a) Of course, today is 30th March.

(b) What did he say?

(c) My mom is a very good cook.

(d) Yes, its very tough to tell.

29. Tom: Ms. Jannet, is it your first trip to California?

Jannet: __________________

(a) That picture is so beautiful.

(b) I'll like to have a cup of tea.

(c) Yes, everything is new to me. California is lovely.

(d) The doctor is just coming.

Space for Rough Work

30. The scenery out there is so beautiful.

(a) How much do we have to walk?

(b) Yes, the scenery is beautiful.

(c) Will you give me your car?

(d) I don't like to go there.

Section IV

Achievers Section

DIRECTIONS (Qs. 31 to 35): Read the following sentences and fill in the blanks from the options given below.

31. Srinagar is __________ beautiful.

(a) almost (b) extreme

(c) enough (d) extremely

32. Abhishek is as __________ as his father.

(a) shorter (b) tall

(c) taller (d) tallest

33. My examination result is _______ than yours.

(a) worst (b) good

(c) best (d) better

34. Naresh wanted to make quick profits, so he took a/an _______.

(a) envelope

(b) cold shoulder

(c) down to earth

(d) big step

35. The sun __________ in the east.

(a) has rise (b) rise

(c) rises (d) was rise

Space for Rough Work

OLYMPIAD

Mock Test

Name : ________

Max. Marks : 35

Number of Questions : 35

Time : 1 Hour 30 Minutes

There is no negative marking in the test.

Section I
Word and Structure Knowledge

DIRECTIONS (Qs. 1 to 10): Fill in the blanks with correct answer.

1. I missed the train __________ I was late.
   (a) but (b) actually
   (c) still (d) because

2. Rima met Ruchi ________ she was in Mumbai.
   (a) that (b) when
   (c) under (d) inside

3. Abstract noun of child is __________.
   (a) children (b) childs
   (c) baby (d) childhood

4. He went _________ his friend's house.
   (a) at (b) to
   (c) in (d) on

5. I am going to stay _______ home this weekend.
   (a) at (b) to
   (c) in (d) on

Space for Rough Work

6. ________ sun rises in the east.

(a) A (b) An

(c) The (d) None of these

7. He works in ________ post office.

(a) a (b) an

(c) the (d) none of these

8. ________! You have done a good job.

(a) Yippee

(b) Congratulations

(c) Hurrah

(d) Oh God

9. There is a garden ________ the backyard.

(a) in (b) at

(c) on (d) none of these

10. I have kept my books ________ the table.

(a) on (b) upon

(c) over (d) all of these

DIRECTION (Qs. 11): Find the synonym of the word in capital letters.

11. DETERMINED

(a) Adamant (b) Flexible

(c) Divided (d) Resolute

DIRECTION (Qs. 12): Find antonym of the word in capital letters.

12. REWARD

(a) Punishment

(b) Unsafe

(c) Defeat

(d) Cruel

DIRECTIONS (Qs. 13 to 16) : Choose the correct spelling.

13. (a) Quilified (b) Quaelified

(c) Qualified (d) Qualifide

14. (a) Reciprocale (b) Reciprocal

(c) Reaciprocal (d) Reciproacal

Space for Rough Work

15. Which one of the following words has been misspelled?
    (a) Select (b) Tough
    (c) Believe (d) None of these
16. Rewrite given sentence using possessive: Jack has a car.
    (a) This is Jack car.
    (b) This is Jack's car.
    (c) This car belongs to Jack.
    (d) All of these

DIRECTIONS (Qs. 17 & 18): Choose the opposite gender of the given words from the options.

17. COW
    (a) Ox (b) Bull
    (c) Oxen (d) Buffalo
18. DRAKE
    (a) Chicken (b) Duckling
    (c) Duck (d) None of these

DIRECTIONS (Qs. 19 to 21): Identify the odd one out.

19. (a) Ceiling fan (b) Table fan
    (c) Fridge (d) Cooler
20. (a) Lion (b) Tiger
    (c) Leopard (d) Monkey
21. (a) Pakistan
    (b) Bangladesh
    (c) Myanmar
    (d) South Africa

Section II
Reading

DIRECTIONS (Qs. 22 & 23): Read the passage carefully and answer the questions that follow.

Mohandas Karamchand Gandhi was born on 2 October, 1869. He was a prominent leader of India during the Indian independence movement. He pioneered Satyagraha – resistance

Space for Rough Work

to tyranny through mass civil disobedience. He believed in the policy of truth and non-violence, which helped India to gain independence and inspired movements for civil rights and freedom across the world. Gandhiji is often referred to as Mahatma Gandhi or "Great Soul" and also as Bapu. He is officially honoured in India as the "Father of the Nation". His birthday is celebrated as Gandhi Jayanti in India. This day is a national holiday. His birthday is celebrated as the International Day of Non-Violence worldwide.

22. What was the policy of Gandhiji?
    (a) Truth
    (b) Non-violence
    (c) Both (a) and (b)
    (d) None of these

23. Which one of the following days is celebrated as International Day of Non-Violence worldwide?
    (a) 14th November
    (b) 2nd October
    (c) 15th August
    (d) None of these

Section III
Spoken and Written Expression

DIRECTIONS (Qs. 24 to 29): Fill in the blanks with the most suitable option.

24. Dev: Do you know Sahil?

    Akshat: ____________________

    Dev: He is very tall and he's got quite short, brown hair.
    (a) I recognize the name but I can't picture him. What does he look like?
    (b) Where is he from?
    (c) How old is he?
    (d) Yes, he is my best friend.

25. Rahul: What is your brother like?

Atul: ______________________ He can't talk in front of people.

(a) He is very generous.

(b) He is very tall.

(c) He likes eating hamburger.

(d) He is incredibly shy.

26. Amar: Who is that girl over there?

Vikas: ______________________

(a) Which one? The girl with long hair?

(b) She is wearing the blue jeans.

(c) Do you know her?

(d) Are they standing there?

27. Raju: Juliet asks a lot of questions in the class. Her teachers are fed up with her questions.

Ajay: ______________________.

Raju: Yes, she is very curious.

(a) Does she know English?

(b) Is she helpful?

(c) Does she like her teachers?

(d) Is she curious?

28. Tom: Daniel is very ambitious.

Adam: How do you know?

Tom: ______________________

(a) He wants to play football for his country.

(b) He doesn't like studying.

(c) He always plays truant.

(d) He usually gets bad marks.

29. Roma: Will you take my photograph Neetu?

Neetu:______________________

(a) No, I left it somewhere.

(b) The flowers are so beautiful!

(c) Of course, it's my pleasure.

(d) Thank you so much.

Space for Rough Work

Section IV

Achievers Section

DIRECTIONS (Qs. 30 to 33): Read the following sentences and fill in the blanks from the options given below.

30. A sentence whose meaning is unclear is called ______________.

    (a) not clear (b) ambiguous

    (c) dark (d) all of these

31. A person who is very polite is called ____________________.

    (a) proud (b) humble

    (c) rude (d) none of these

32. If Chennai is to India, then Brisbane is to ________________.

    (a) Sri Lanka (b) New Zealand

    (c) Australia (d) None of these

33. If tiger is to cub, then deer is to ______________________.

    (a) calf (b) foal

    (c) fawn (d) none of these

DIRECTIONS (Qs. 34 & 35): Make a meaningful word from jumbled letters given below.

34. OWYRR

    (a) ROYWR (b) WRORY

    (c) WORRY (d) None of these

35. PRISESUR

    (a) SURPRIES (b) SURPRISE

    (c) SURPREIS (d) None of these

Space for Rough Work

OLYMPIAD Mock Test

Name : ___________

Max. Marks : 35

Number of Questions : 35

Time : 1 Hour 30 Minutes

There is no negative marking in the test.

Section I
Word and Structure Knowledge

DIRECTIONS (Qs. 1 to 5): Make a meaningful sentence by arranging the words.

1. In, garden, the, Steve's, is, mother
   (a) Steve's mother in the garden.
   (b) Steve's mother is in the garden.
   (c) Steve's mother is the garden in.
   (d) None of these
2. What, in, did, see, he, water, the
   (a) What did see he in the water?
   (b) What did he see water?
   (c) What did he see in the water?
   (d) None of these
3. Make noun from the word 'Happy'.
   (a) Happyies (b) Happines
   (c) Happyful (d) None of these
4. Which one of the following is a material noun?
   (a) Children (b) City
   (c) Gold (d) Childhood
5. What is 'This'?
   (a) This is a noun.
   (b) This is a pronoun.
   (c) This is a verb.
   (d) This is a conjunction.

Space for Rough Work

DIRECTIONS (Qs. 6 to 17): Fill in the blanks with correct answer.

6. Delhi is the capital of India. __________ is a beautiful city.
   (a) It (b) He
   (c) These (d) She
7. He saw a girl. _____ girl was beautiful.
   (a) A (b) An
   (c) The (d) None of these
8. If hockey is to goal, then cricket is to _______.
   (a) bat (b) ball
   (c) run (d) none of these
9. If grain is to kilogram, then milk is to _______.
   (a) metre
   (b) litre
   (c) kilogram
   (d) none of these
10. I congratulate you _______ the occasion of your birthday.
   (a) on (b) in
   (c) at (d) but
11. He has been playing _______ two hours.
   (a) for (b) with
   (c) to (d) from
12. Person who respects all religions is _______.
   (a) martyr (b) secular
   (c) linguist (d) convent
13. Big cities have multi-storeyed _____.
   (a) bridges (b) buildings
   (c) markets (d) roads
14. He ______ a laptop yesterday.
   (a) brought (b) buys
   (c) bought (d) buying

Space for Rough Work

15. She lives in London ________ Hudson Avenue.

(a) in (b) on

(c) at (d) over

16. She is wise ________ a beautiful girl.

(a) or (b) but

(c) as well as (d) though

17. He will not play in the next match ________ he is injured.

(a) because (b) so

(c) yet (d) but

DIRECTIONS (Qs. 18 & 19): Find the synonym of the word written in capital letters.

18. APPEAL

(a) Cheat (b) Commit

(c) Request (d) Stop

19. CHASE

(a) Hunt (b) Frustrate

(c) Torture (d) Taunt

DIRECTIONS (Qs. 20 & 21): Find the antonym of the word written in capital letters.

20. SLAVERY

(a) Free (b) Relax

(c) Freedom (d) All of these

21. INTRINSIC

(a) Extrinsic (b) Extra

(c) Extreme (d) All of these

DIRECTIONS (Qs. 22 & 23): Choose the correct spelling from the options.

22. (a) Civilisd (b) Civiliseed

(c) Civilissed (d) Civilised

23. (a) Rumour (b) Rumore

(c) Rumar (d) Rumear

DIRECTIONS (Qs. 24 & 25): Choose the opposite gender of given words from the options.

24. Gander

(a) Goose (b) Gosling

(c) She-Gander (d) None of these

Space for Rough Work

25. Poet

(a) Poetry (b) Poetes

(c) Poetess (d) None of these

Section II
Reading

DIRECTIONS (Qs. 26 & 27): Read the passage carefully and answer the questions that follow.

The greenhouse effect is the heating of the surface of a planet or moon due to the presence of an atmosphere containing gases that absorb and emit infrared radiation. Thus, greenhouse gases trap heat within the surface-troposphere system. This mechanism is fundamentally different from that of an actual greenhouse, which works by isolating warm air inside the structure so that heat is not lost by convection. The greenhouse effect was discovered by Joseph Fourier in 1824, first reliably experimented on by John Tyndall in 1858, and first reported quantitatively by Svante Arrhenius in 1896. In the absence of the greenhouse effect and an atmosphere, the Earth's average surface temperature of 14°C (57°F) could be as low as 18°C (0.4° F), the black body temperature of the Earth. Anthropogenic Global Warming (AGW), a recent warming of the Earth's lower atmosphere, is believed to be the result of an "enhanced greenhouse effect", mainly due to human-produced increases in atmospheric greenhouse gases.

26. What harm the greenhouse gases can do?

(a) They trap heat and decrease temperature.

(b) They trap heat and increase temperature.

(c) They trap heat and thus, control the temperature.

(d) None of these

27. How greenhouse effect has enhanced?

   (a) Because of human activities

   (b) Because of natural phenomenon

   (c) Because of hot climate

   (d) None of these

Section III
Spoken and Written Expression

DIRECTIONS (Qs. 28 to 31): Fill in the blanks with the most suitable option.

28. Akaash: "You seem to be quite tired, you need rest".

   ____

   (a) No, my mom is very busy.

   (b) Dad has gone to office. He is not at home.

   (c) Yes, I am quite tired. I'll go home and rest.

   (d) I will go by my car.

29. The paper was very tough today. I could not answer all the questions.

   ____

   (a) I know it was very tough.

   (b) Ok, so you go and play.

   (c) Yes, you can stay at home and study.

   (d) No, I don't mind cooking.

30. He is a famous singer. I want to go for his concert.

   ____

   (a) Even I want to go, I like his singing.

   (b) Not at all, I can't.

   (c) Our moms are friends.

   (d) It's raining, we will need an umbrella.

Space for Rough Work

31. I can't come, there is no one at home.

____

(a) Ok, you always say this.

(b) Ok, I will manage on my own.

(c) What did you say?

(d) His house is not that far.

Section IV
Achievers Section

32. Identify the odd one out.

(a) Eagle (b) Snake

(c) Vulture (d) Crow

33. Identify the odd one out.

(a) Rabbit (b) Parrot

(c) Crow (d) Pigeon

34. A place where people worship to the God is _______________.

(a) gurudwara (b) temple

(c) church (d) all of these

35. A baby who has no one to take care is _______________.

(a) orphan (b) wanderer

(c) illegal (d) all of these

Space for Rough Work

OLYMPIAD

Mock Test

Name : ________ **Max. Marks : 40**

Number of Questions : 40 **Time : 2 Hours**

There is no negative marking in the test.

DIRECTIONS (Qs. 1 to 9): Find the suitable word.

1. Movie : Hero, Play : Actor, Concert: ______.
   (a) Piano
   (b) Symphony
   (c) Musician
   (d) Flute

2. India is one of the ________ countries in ancient monuments.
   (a) rich
   (b) more richer
   (c) richest
   (d) most richest

3. The robber threw down the knife and ______ into the darkness.
   (a) went fleeing
   (b) fled
   (c) fleed
   (d) none of these

4. He could see ____ the glass.
   (a) in (b) from
   (c) through (d) to

5. When Anup reached home, his friends came ________ to meet him.
   (a) in (b) over
   (c) inside (d) with

Space for Rough Work

6. What a wonderful _____, while this is the _______ that is being sold.

   (a) site, sight (b) cite, site

   (c) sight, site (d) cite, sight

7. There is _____ facility in sleeper trains, while the cow gave ____ to a calf today.

   (a) berth, birth

   (b) birth, berth

   (c) breth, brith

   (d) brith, berth

8. I do not have ________ chocolates with me now.

   (a) a (b) any

   (c) some (d) none

9. When we move beyond something that bothered us, we say we____________.

   (a) got over it (b) got onto it

   (c) got upon it (d) got with

DIRECTIONS (Qs. 10 to 12): Read the letter and answer the following questions.

Dear Vidya,

I have a friend. My friend lives in the same neighbourhood where I live. She is eight years old. Her name is Pihu Sharma. Pihu is cool. I like her a lot. She likes to read. She is a good reader. She is good at Math too. It is her best subject. She is smart. I like to eat lunch with her. We eat lunch together on Monday, Wednesday and Friday. Pihu is my best friend.

Best Regards,

Divya

10. How is Vidya's friend, Pihu?

    (a) Cool

    (b) Cool and Composed

    (c) Cool and Smart

    (d) Cute and Cool

Space for Rough Work

11. When do Vidya and Pihu have lunch together?
   (a) On alternate weekdays
   (b) On the first 3 weekdays
   (c) On the last 3 weekdays
   (d) All week days

12. What is Pihu good at?
   (a) Reading and Math
   (b) Reading and Talking
   (c) Talking and Playing
   (d) Playing and Reading

DIRECTIONS (Qs. 13 & 14): Complete the following sentences.

13. Siri _____ goes out to play with her friends.
   (a) often
   (b) generally
   (c) ever
   (d) none of these

14. The friends shared the sweets ________ themselves.
   (a) above (b) upon
   (c) among (d) between

DIRECTIONS (Qs. 15 & 16) : Select the answer that identifies the noun in the sentence.

15. The works of many great poets have been placed on reserve.
   (a) Many (b) Placed
   (c) Reserve (d) Great

16. The Brooklyn Bridge was opened in 1883.
   (a) Bridge (b) Was
   (c) Opened (d) In

DIRECTIONS (Qs. 17 & 18): For each sentence, identify the subject or the predicate (verb).

17. The professor handed out the syllabus on the first day of class.
   The subject is
   (a) professor (b) syllabus
   (c) class (d) Out

18. The tennis team won the state championship.
   The subject is
   (a) tennis
   (b) team
   (c) championship
   (d) won

Space for Rough Work

DIRECTIONS (Qs. 19 & 20): Choose the correct preposition.

19. I'll be ready to leave ____ about twenty minutes.
(a) in (b) on
(c) at (d) of

20. I think she spent the entire afternoon ______ the phone.
(a) on (b) in
(c) at (d) with

21. Choose the word that is most nearly the opposite in meaning to the word in capital letters.
COMMON
(a) Standard (b) Unusual
(c) Scary (d) Super

22. Find the odd pair.
(a) Books: Read
(b) TV: Watch
(c) Cricket: Game
(d) Fruit : Eat

DIRECTIONS (Qs. 23 to 26): Find the suitable word

23. Pen : Write, Clock : Time, Bat:_______.
(a) Ball (b) Cricket
(c) Play (d) Hockey

24. He saw a blind man sitting ____ the side of the road.
(a) to (b) of
(c) by (d) in

25. Didn't I just _______ that to you?
(a) proved (b) prove
(c) proving (d) move

26. The police _______ of the thief and left.
(a) hold (b) took hold
(c) held (d) holds

DIRECTIONS (Qs. 27 to 29): Fill in the blanks by choosing the right words.

27. The ill dog had to be taken to the _____, while the bag got _____ in the rain.
(a) vet, wet (b) wet, wait
(c) wet, vet (d) vet, wait

Space for Rough Work

28. This is a wonderful ______ of art, while through meditation, ____ can be brought to the world.
    (a) peas, peace
    (b) peace, peas
    (c) piece, peace
    (d) peas, piece
29. When we carefully keep a watch on a person, we ___________
    (a) keep two eyes on him.
    (b) keep an eye on him.
    (c) keep an eye over him.
    (d) keep an eye about him.
30. Find the odd pair.
    (a) Cat : Kitten
    (b) Cow : Calf
    (c) Pig : Pigeon
    (d) Horse : Colt
31. Complete the sentence with the correct spelling of the word.
    The bear went over the ________.
    (a) mountan (b) mountain
    (c) mountane (d) muotein
32. Find the odd word.
    (a) Sunflower (b) Rose
    (c) Turmeric (d) Lily
33. My teacher's name is Sheela. I like ______.
    (a) her (b) him
    (c) she (d) them
34. Given below are three sentences. One of them is incorrect. Find the incorrect sentence and mark it in your answer sheet.
    (a) I go for a walk.
    (b) My father's name are Prasad.
    (c) My name is Kishan.
    (d) I live in Delhi.

DIRECTIONS (Qs. 35 to 38): Read the letter and answer the following questions.

Letter to Rudolf, Santa's Reindeer

Dear Rudolf,

My name is Meethu. I am a baby parrot! I live with my friend in the

Space for Rough Work

great city of Mumbai in the state of Maharashtra, of course, that's in India, but I'll bet you knew that! Rudolf, some things that I might like for Christmas this year, two bags full of my favourite seedmix, lots of green chillies and another baby parrot to play with. And please don't forget to put in a good word for my friend with Santa! He is very nice. He doesn't keep me in a cage.

Lots of love,

Meethu

Direction : Choose the correct answer.

35. Meethu lives in __________.
    (a) Hyderabad
    (b) Mumbai
    (c) a cage
    (d) a tree

36. Meethu asks for __________.
    (a) two things
    (b) three things
    (c) five things
    (d) four things

37. Meethu asks Rudolf for things to
    (a) eat (b) drink
    (c) read (d) play

38. Why does Meethu like his owner?
    (a) He doesn't give him food.
    (b) He puts Meethu in a cage.
    (c) He allows Meethu to fly.
    (d) He plays with him.

39. Find one sentence to complete the dialogue.

    Geeta: Hello! I am Geeta ! What is your name?

    Lina : ____________
    (a) Hello! I am Lina.
    (b) Hello! I am going home.
    (c) Let us go home.
    (d) Hello! I am playing.

Select the answer that identifies the noun in the sentence.

40. Joe, have you met your new boss?
    (a) Have (b) Met
    (c) Boss (d) You

Space for Rough Work

MATHEMATICS MOCK TEST 1–5

OLYMPIAD

Mock Test

Name : ________

Max. Marks : 40

Number of Questions : 40

Time : 2 Hours

There is no negative marking in the test.

1. Simplify: 765 + 65 + 70 – 45 – 35.

   (a) 820 (b) 870

   (c) 780 (d) 990

2. Fill in the blank with appropriate number from the options given below.

   5 × 300 = (5 × □) × 100

   (a) 1 (b) 10

   (c) 3 (d) 4

3. $\frac{5}{7}$ of 49 is

   (a) 35 (b) 36

   (c) 46 (d) 47

4. Division of two digit smallest number by smallest even number is?

   (a) 10 (b) 5

   (c) 20 (d) 40

5. Find the fraction of unshaded part of the given figure?

   (a) $\frac{4}{7}$ (b) $\frac{5}{8}$

   (c) $\frac{3}{8}$ (d) $\frac{3}{7}$

6. What is the difference between the face and place value of 5 in the number, 45632?

   (a) 4995 (b) 4985

   (c) 4975 (d) 4945

Space for Rough Work

7. The expanded form of the number 55432 is
   (a) 50000 + 5400 + 432
   (b) 50000 + 5000 + 400 + 30 + 2
   (c) 50000 + 5000 + 4000 + 32
   (d) 8 + 7 + 6 + 0 + 5

8. Which of the following is a line?
   (a) ⟶
   (b) ⟷
   (c) ———
   (d) All of these

9. How many metres are there in 5 km 60 m?
   (a) 5600 m (b) 5800 m
   (c) 5060 m (d) 5900 m

10. Peter bought a bag for ₹ 145.75 and an instrument for ₹ 23.25. How much money did he pay ?
   (a) ₹ 170 (b) ₹ 169
   (c) ₹ 159 (d) ₹ 149

11. Total rotation of second hand of a watch in 30 minutes is
   (a) 30 (b) 40
   (c) 20 (d) 17

12. The cost of 19 pens is ₹ 247. Find the cost of 30 such pens.
   (a) ₹ 380 (b) ₹ 370
   (c) ₹ 390 (d) ₹ 320

13. Solve : 2735 + 5237 – 3756
   (a) 7972 (b) 4216
   (c) 2729 (d) 3175

14. A plane figure has four vertices and four equal sides. Which one of the following is the name of the figure?
   (a) Square
   (b) Equilateral triangle
   (c) Parallelogram
   (d) Pentagon

15. Replace the question mark with a number given in the options below.
   56 + 47 – 23 = 89 + 5 – ?
   (a) 19 (b) 18
   (c) 14 (d) 10

16. A figure does not have height, width and length. If it has a place then which one of the following is the name of the figure ?
   (a) A point
   (b) A line segment
   (c) A line
   (d) A ray

Space for Rough Work

17. Convert 734 centimetres in millimetres.

(a) 7340 (b) 73.40

(c) 0.7340 (d) All of these

18. Priya ate $\frac{2}{5}$ of a pizza. What fraction of the pizza is left?

(a) $\frac{2}{5}$ (b) $\frac{3}{5}$

(c) 3 (d) 2

19. Match the columns.

	Column-I		Column-II
(A)	45 kilometres	(1)	45000 millilitres
(B)	45 litre	(2)	4500 centimetre
(C)	45 metre	(3)	45000 grams
(D)	45 kilograms	(4)	45000 metres

	A	B	C	D		A	B	C	D
(a)	4	2	1	3	(b)	3	1	2	4
(c)	4	1	2	3	(d)	3	2	1	4

20. Smriti bought 3m 5 cm ribbon of red colour and 2 m 13 cm ribbon of blue colour. What is the total length of ribbons?

(a) 1 m 8 cm (b) 8 m 15 cm

(c) 5 m 63 cm (d) 5 m 18 cm

21. The sum of place value and face value of digit 6 in the number 4786239 is

(a) 60,060 (b) 6239

(c) 6006 (d) 6200

22. Consider the following two statements:

Statement 1: Sum of digits of a number is its expanded form.

Statement 2: Sum of place value of every digit of a number is the expanded form of that number.

Which one of the following is correct about the above statements?

(a) Statement 1 is false and 2 is true.

(b) Statement 1 is true and 2 is false.

(c) Both statements 1 and 2 are false.

(d) Both statements 1 and 2 are true.

Space for Rough Work

23. If a line with fixed length is called line segment, then a figure which has a starting point and extends in one direction is called

(a) ray (b) point

(c) line (d) all of these

24. Which of the following is a closed figure?

(a)  (b) 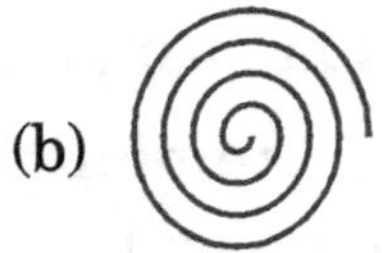

(c)  (d) 

25. Consider the following statements.

Statement 1 : We can compare 23 litre and 52 kilograms.

Statement 2 : All the faces of a cube are squares.

Now, which of the following is correct about the statements.

(a) Statement 1 is true and 2 is false.

(b) Statement 1 is false and 2 is true.

(c) Both statements 1 and 2 are true.

(d) Both statements 1 and 2 are false.

26. Which of the following are like fractions.

(a) $\frac{1}{3}$ and $\frac{3}{4}$ (b) $\frac{1}{4}$ and $\frac{4}{7}$

(c) $\frac{2}{7}$ and $\frac{3}{7}$ (d) $\frac{7}{2}$ and $\frac{2}{3}$

27. The cost of 4 pens is ₹ 67. What is the cost of 5 such pens?

(a) ₹ 83.75 (b) ₹ 82

(c) ₹ 80 (d) ₹ 75.80

28. The cost of one notebook is ₹13.25. How much money did the Miriam pay to the shopkeeper for 9 note books?

(a) ₹ 122.25 (b) ₹ 119.25

(c) ₹ 130 (d) ₹ 141.25

29. If the cost of 6 balloons is ₹ 9 and cost of 9 kites is ₹ 12, then how much you pay to the shopkeeper for 2 balloons and 3 kites?

(a) ₹ 7 (b) ₹ 4

(c) ₹ 8 (d) ₹ 3

Space for Rough Work

30. The two angles of a triangle are 45° and 56°. What is the measurement of third angle?
(a) 79° (b) 89°
(c) 99° (d) 39°

31. How many triangles are there in the figure below?

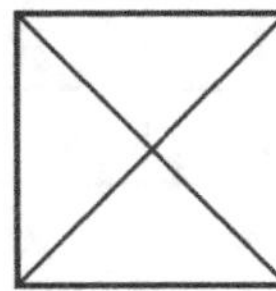

(a) 3 (b) 8
(c) 4 (d) 6

32. The shaded part of the given figure is represented by which one of the following fractions ?

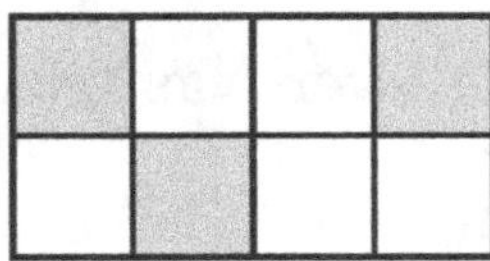

(a) $\frac{3}{8}$ (b) $\frac{7}{8}$
(c) $\frac{9}{8}$ (d) $\frac{1}{8}$

33. There are 40 questions in a question paper. If 30 questions carry 2 marks each and remaining 10 questions carry 4 marks each, then the maximum marks is
(a) 50 (b) 80
(c) 100 (d) 90

34. What comes next?
BCD, DEF, FGH, HIJ, ...
(a) KLM (b) LMN
(c) JKL (d) KLM

35. Which fraction is odd one out?

$$\frac{3}{9}, \frac{2}{6}, \frac{8}{10}, \frac{4}{12}$$

(a) $\frac{3}{9}$ (b) $\frac{2}{6}$
(c) $\frac{8}{10}$ (d) $\frac{4}{12}$

Space for Rough Work

36. David's football game starts at 10:00 a.m. and ends at 2:25 p.m. How long does David's game last?
    (a) 2 hours twenty five minutes
    (b) Three hour twenty five minutes
    (c) Four hour twenty five minutes
    (d) Four hour thirty five minutes

37. How many mugs of water with capacity 500 ml are needed to fill a 5 litre bucket?
    (a) 7 (b) 10
    (c) 8 (d) 9

38. Ritu ate $\frac{3}{7}$ and Priya ate $\frac{2}{7}$ of the sweets. How much sweets did they eat altogether?
    (a) $\frac{6}{7}$ (b) $\frac{5}{7}$
    (c) $\frac{1}{7}$ (d) $\frac{4}{7}$

DIRECTIONS (Qs. 39 & 40): Mr. Bee collected some flowers to make a bouquet. He made a list of flower is used in the bouquet as given below.

Flower	Tally marks
Rose	𝍸 |||
Lily	𝍸 𝍸 ||
Sunfower	||||
Daisy	𝍸
carnations	𝍸	

39. How many Roses he used ?
    (a) 6 (b) 7
    (c) 8 (d) 9

40. Which flower was used the most times ?
    (a) Rose (b) Sunflower
    (c) Lily (d) Daisy

Space for Rough Work

OLYMPIAD

Mock Test

Name : ________ **Max. Marks : 35**

Number of Questions : 35 **Time : 2 Hours**

There is no negative marking in the test.

1. Which one of the following digits is at the place of ten thousand in the numerals 81564 ?

   (a) 5 (b) 4
   (c) 8 (d) 2

2. The expanded form of the number 648345 is

   (a) 6 + 4 + 8 + 3 + 4 + 5
   (b) 600000 + 40000 + 8000 + 300 + 40 + 5
   (c) 60000 + 4000 + 83000 + 45
   (d) All of these

3. There is a straight street between India gate and President house. If president house is supposed to be point A and India gate is point B, then the length of street between the points is

   (a) A line
   (b) A line segment
   (c) An arrow
   (d) All of these

4. How many triangles are there in the figure below ?

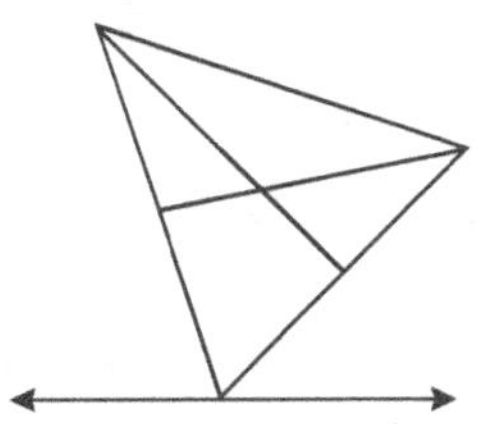

   (a) 9 (b) 8
   (c) 6 (d) 3

5. How much is 65 kg greater than 62450g?

   (a) 2 kg 500 g (b) 2 kg 400 g
   (c) 2 kg 550 g (d) 2 kg 450 g

Space for Rough Work

6. Convert 52367 ml into litres and millilitres.
   (a) 5ℓ 2367mℓ (b) 523ℓ 67mℓ
   (c) 52ℓ 367mℓ (d) 50ℓ 367mℓ

7. What is the difference between the greatest and smallest of five digit numbers ?
   (a) 80000 (b) 90000
   (c) 89999 (d) 10000

8. A bicycle covers a distance of 12 km in one hour. What is the distance covered by the bicycle in 6 hours?
   (a) 68 km (b) 42 km
   (c) 72 km (d) 56 km

9. Convert 4 km 5 metre in metre.
   (a) 4400 m (b) 4005 m
   (c) 4200 m (d) 4000 m

10. Consider the following statements:
    Statement 1: A point has place but does not have length and width.
    Statement 2: A sphere has only one flat face.
    Which one of the following is correct about the above statements?
    (a) Statement 1 is true and statement 2 is false.
    (b) Statement 1 is false and statement 2 is true.
    (c) Both statements are true.
    (d) Both statements are false.

11. How many vertices are there in the figure below?

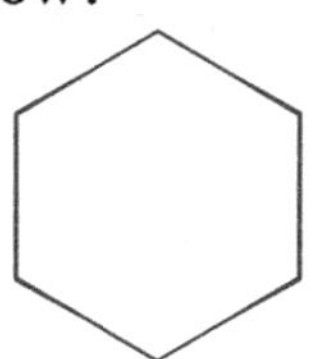

    (a) 5 (b) 4
    (c) 6 (d) 3

12. Find the smallest even number.
    (a) 1 (b) 2
    (c) 3 (d) 4

13. Consider the following statements:
    Statement 1: Product of a number by 1 is the number itself.
    Statement 2: Product of a number by 0 is always 1.
    Which one of the following is correct about the above statements?
    (a) Statement 1 is false and statement 2 is true.
    (b) Statement 1 is true and statement 2 is false.
    (c) Both statements 1 and 2 are false.
    (d) Both statements 1 and 2 are true.

Space for Rough Work

14. State whether the following statements are True or False.

(a) 1 rupee = 100 paise

(b) A year has 11 months

(c) Quarter of an hour means 15 minutes

(d) 1 m = 1000 cm

Now, choose the correct option.

(a) TTFF (b) TFTF

(c) TFFT (d) FTFT

(d) 1 m = 1000 cm

15. The cost of 12 toffees is ₹ 6. What would be the cost of 1 toffee ?

(a) 50 paise (b) 60 paise

(c) 70 paise (d) 75 paise

16. An object has length, width and height. It has 8 corners and all sides are equal. Which one of the following is the geometrical name of the object ?

(a) Cylinder (b) Cuboid

(c) Cube (d) All of these

17. Arrange in descending order.

$\frac{7}{9}, \frac{4}{9}, \frac{11}{9}, \frac{13}{9}$

(a) $\frac{13}{9} < \frac{11}{9} < \frac{7}{9} < \frac{4}{9}$

(b) $\frac{13}{9} < \frac{11}{9} > \frac{7}{9} < \frac{4}{9}$

(c) $\frac{13}{9} > \frac{11}{9} > \frac{7}{9} > \frac{4}{9}$

(d) All of these

DIRECTIONS (Q 18 to 20) : At a parking, a board shows the following information.

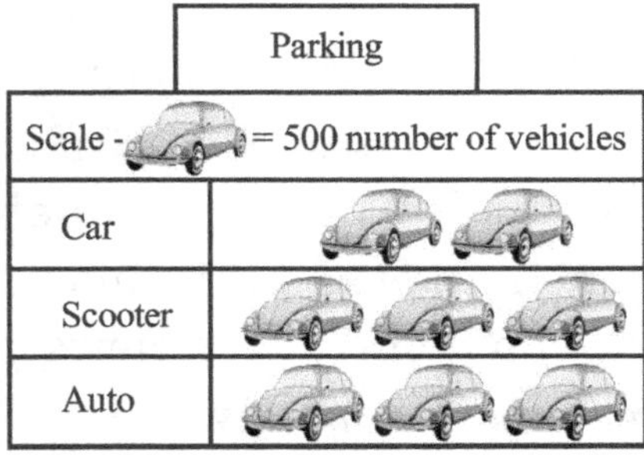

Now, answer the following questions.

18. What is the number of scooters in the parking place ?

(a) 1500 (b) 1600

(c) 1700 (d) 1800

19. How many cars are parked?

(a) 1500 (b) 500

(c) 1000 (d) 2000

20. Which two vehicles are same in number in the parking place?

(a) Car, Scooter

(b) Car, Auto

(c) Scooter, Auto

(d) None of these

21. In the year of 2013, 2000 students appeared in a competitive examination and this information was published by a news paper which is given below.

Year	Appeared students
2012	1890
2013	2000
2014	1980

How many more students appeared in the year of 2014 than 2012?

(a) 80 (b) 90

(c) 20 (d) 98

22. Which one of the following is the short form for.

50000 + 4000 + 300 + 20 + 8

(a) 45328 (b) 54328

(c) 50438 (d) None of these

23. Fill in the numbers from the options on the number line given below.

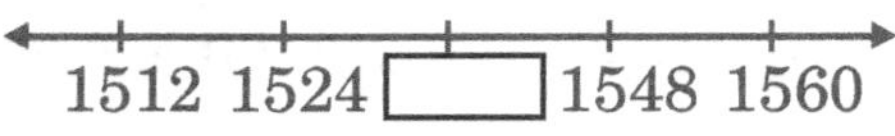

(a) 1536 (b) 1538

(c) 1532 (d) 1530

24. Cody had 1230 green apples and 8270 red apples. If 6783 green and red apples were sold, then how many apples were left ?

(a) 2718 (b) 2717

(c) 2700 (d) 2800

Space for Rough Work

25. A tap dispense 5 litres of water in 1 minute. How much water does the tap dispense in one hour ?

(a) 100 litre (b) 500 litre

(c) 300 litre (d) 200 litre

26. The cost of prepared food of a reputed hotel in the city are as follows:

Rice plate	₹ 230
Green vegetables	₹ 175
Curd	₹ 35
Coffee	₹ 25

Cody placed order for 1 rice plate, 1 plate of green vegetables and 1 cup of curd. How much money did Cody pay ?

(a) ₹ 440 (b) ₹ 467

(c) ₹ 468 (d) ₹ 470

27. The sum of 4-digit largest and 2-digit smallest numbers is

(a) 109 (b) 10009

(c) 1009 (d) 100009

28. In a town the total number of voters are 34765 and the total number of children in the age group of 10 to 14 years are 23451. If the total number of women voters are 25621, find the total number of men voters.

(a) 9100 (b) 9144

(c) 9250 (d) 2502

29. If $3 \times 4 = 12$; $12 \div 4 = ?$

(a) 3 (b) 4

(c) 12 (d) 6

30. The total number of people in a train is 880. These people are travelling in 8 coaches. Find the number of people in each coach.

(a) 110 (b) 111

(c) 112 (d) 109

31. If cost of 1 packet of toffees is ₹ 75.20, then what will be the cost of such 5 packets?

(a) ₹ 367.50 (b) ₹ 376

(c) ₹ 365 (d) ₹ 365.20

Space for Rough Work

32. There are 3960 sheets of paper in bundles. If one bundle contains 18 sheets, then how many bundles are there?
(a) 240 (b) 220
(c) 230 (d) 250

33. The difference between $\frac{3}{4}$ and $\frac{7}{4}$ is
(a) $\frac{2}{4}$ (b) $\frac{1}{4}$
(c) 1 (d) $\frac{10}{4}$

34. The maximum time for the English test paper is 45 minutes. If the test starts at 10:00 a.m. then at what time does it end?
(a) 9 : 40 a.m. (b) 10 : 45 a.m.
(c) 11 : 50 a.m. (d) 11 : 30 a.m.

35. Match the following:

Column-I	Column-II
(A) $\frac{2}{7}+\frac{3}{7}$	(1) $\frac{3}{5}$
(B) $\frac{6}{7}-\frac{2}{7}$	(2) $\frac{1}{2}$
(C) $\frac{9}{10}-\frac{3}{10}$	(3) $\frac{5}{7}$
(D) $\frac{2}{10}+\frac{3}{10}$	(4) $\frac{4}{7}$

	A	B	C	D		A	B	C	D
(a)	3	1	4	2	(b)	2	4	1	3
(c)	3	4	1	2	(d)	4	1	2	3

Space for Rough Work

OLYMPIAD

Mock Test

Name : ________

Number of Questions : 40

Max. Marks : 40

Time : 2 Hours

There is no negative marking in the test.

1. Look at the numbers in this box.

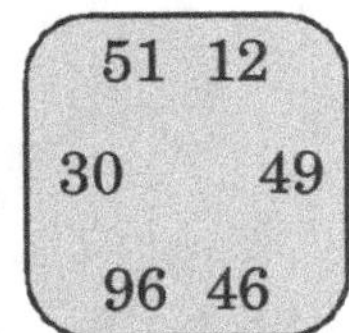

Which of the following is true about the numbers in the box?
(a) They are all greater than 50.
(b) They are all between 10 and 100.
(c) They are all less than 90.
(d) They are all less than 95.

2. 987 rounded off to nearest hundred gives
(a) 900 (b) 990
(c) 980 (d) 1000

3. Look at the number line below. What number replaces question mark on it?

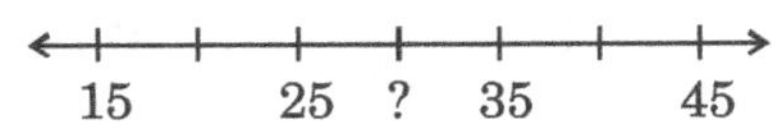

(a) 20 (b) 26
(c) 30 (d) 34

4. What number replaces question mark in the following?

Before	Between	After
80849	?	80851

(a) 80800 (b) 80850
(c) 80900 (d) 80949

Space for Rough Work

5. Which subtraction gives 102 as the answer?

(a) 100 – 2 (b) 300 – 198

(c) 400 – 202 (d) 58 – 44

6. Hindu - Arabic numeral for XXXIX is

(a) 29 (b) 41

(c) 32 (d) 39

7. 5 thousands + 6 tens – 4 ones is equal to

(a) 5640 (b) 5056

(c) 5604 (d) 5540

8. Look at the picture given below.

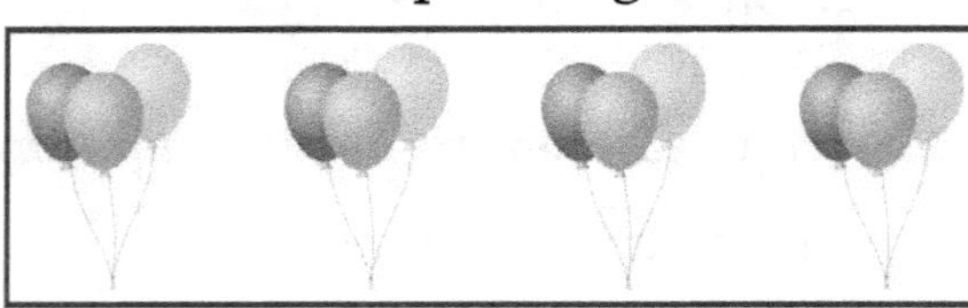

Which of the following number sentence shows above picture?

(a) 3 + 3 + 3 + 3 = 12

(b) 12 + 3 = 15

(c) 16 ÷ 4 = 4

(d) 3 + 4 = 7

9. What fraction of alphabets are consonants?

(a) $\frac{5}{26}$ (b) $\frac{1}{5}$

(c) $\frac{1}{2}$ (d) $\frac{21}{26}$

10. Estimated sum of 372 and 313 by rounding off to nearest hundred is

(a) 800 (b) 700

(c) 600 (d) 680

11. Multiply 985 by 8. The answer is the same as _______

(a) 788 + 10 + 8

(b) 700 + 80 + 8

(c) 7000 + 80 + 8

(d) 7000 + 800 + 80

12. What is (275 × 8)?

(a) 11 × 50 (b) 20 × 100

(c) 11 × 20 (d) 22 × 100

Space for Rough Work

13. Convert 52037 mℓ into ℓ and mℓ.

(a) 5kℓ 237ℓ (b) 5ℓ 203mℓ

(c) 52kℓ 370mℓ (d) 52ℓ 37mℓ

14. What is the remainder when 497 is divided by 9 ?

(a) 7 (b) 9

(c) 2 (d) 55

15. Find $\frac{1}{3}$ of the following strawberries.

(a) 8 (b) 6

(c) 12 (d) 16

16. Samiksha has 644 cream rolls. She wants to distribute them equally among her 14 friends. How many cream rolls will each get?

(a) 42 (b) 48

(c) 46 (d) 44

17. What is $\left(\frac{1}{5}-\frac{1}{5}\right)+\frac{1}{5}$?

(a) $\frac{1}{10}$ (b) $\frac{1}{20}$

(c) $\frac{1}{4}$ (d) $\frac{1}{5}$

18. Swapna made the following design using squares.

What fractional part of the design is shaded ?

(a) $\frac{5}{6}$ (b) $\frac{5}{12}$

(c) $\frac{7}{12}$ (d) $\frac{12}{5}$

19. What do 40 stamps cost, if the cost of each stamp is ₹5 and 15 paise?

(a) ₹ 200 (b) ₹ 202

(c) ₹ 415 (d) ₹ 206

Space for Rough Work

20. How many weeks are there in 210 days?

(a) 50 (b) 10

(c) 30 (d) 50

21. Six thousand eight hundred two rupees in numerals is

(a) ₹ 6820 (b) ₹ 6812

(c) ₹ 6280 (d) ₹ 6802

22. Match the Column.

Column-I	Column-II
(A) 5 hours 20 minutes	(1) 220 seconds
(B) 3 minutes 40 seconds	(2) 730 days
(C) 2 years	(3) 270 days
(D) 9 months	(4) 320 minutes

	A	B	C	D		A	B	C	D
(a)	4	2	1	3	(b)	2	4	3	1
(c)	4	1	2	3	(d)	1	3	4	2

23. Rani started studying at 5:30 p.m. and finishes at 7 p.m. How much time does she study?

(a) 2 hours

(b) 3 hours and 30 minutes

(c) 1 hour and 30 minutes

(d) 30 minutes

24. How much time will quarter past 4 takes to be half past 4?

(a) 6 hours (b) 4 minutes

(c) 15 minutes (d) 60 minutes

25. Raj was practising for his running race for the school sports day. On the first day he ran for 10 minutes, on the second day he ran for 12 minutes, on the third day he ran for 14 minutes. If he continued like this, how many minutes would he have been running on the tenth day?

(a) 24 minutes (b) 28 minutes

(c) 30 minutes (d) 32 minutes

Space for Rough Work

26. Which one of the following is a leap year?

(a) 1980 (b) 1981

(c) 1982 (d) all of these

27. Which of the following is used to measure the weight of a rock ?

(a) Balance (b) Scale

(c) Therometer (d) Compass

28. A horse's height is measured in a unit called '*hand*'. A hand measures 4 inches. What is the height (in inches) of a horse that measures 14 hands ?

(a) 36 (b) 46

(c) 56 (d) 66

29. Which of the lengths below is the shortest ?

(a) 1 millimetre (b) 1 centimetre

(c) 1 metre (d) 1 kilometre

30. 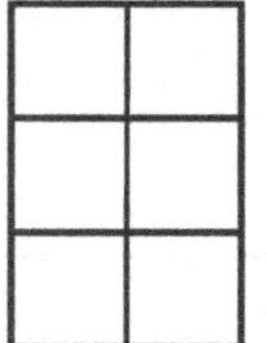

Which of the following pair of shapes could be put together to form the rectangle shown above ?

(a) 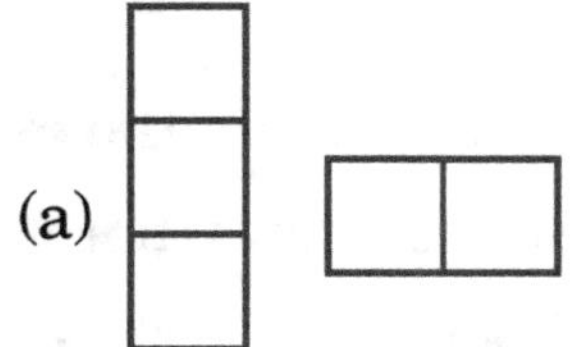

(b) 

(c) 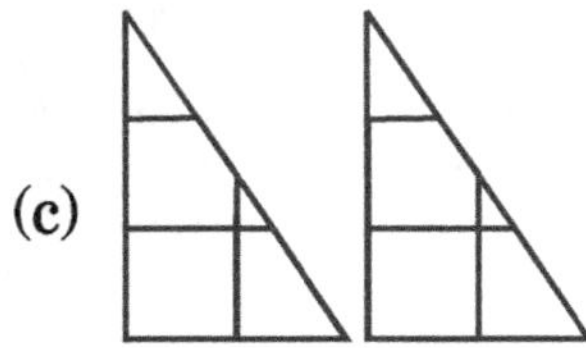

(d) 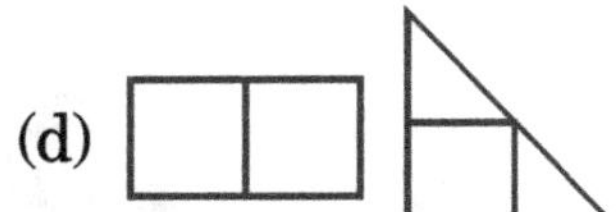

Space for Rough Work

31. Which of the following is not symmetrical?

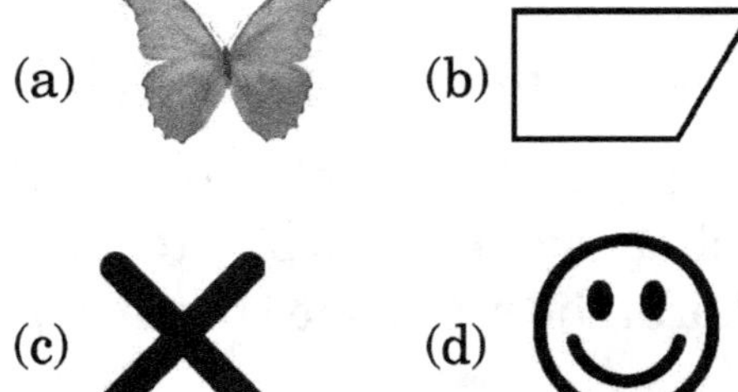

32. Srikanth is working on the graph shown below. He knows there were 30 babies born in March at KG Hospital.

Babies Born at KG Hospital

January

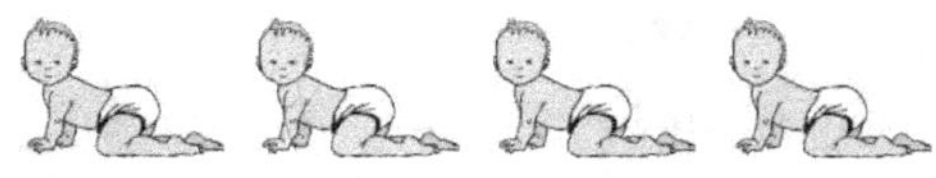

February

March

Each means 5 babies.

How many more babies does Srikanth need to add to March to finish the graph?

(a) 3 (b) 5

(c) 27 (d) 6

33. The following pictographs shows the number of icecreams sold at a bakery in a weak.

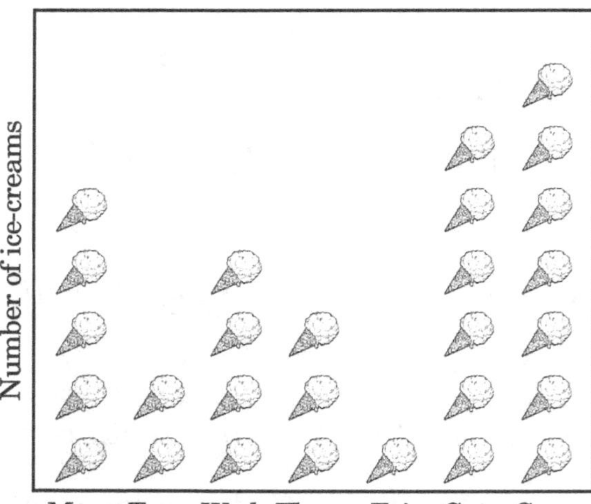

Space for Rough Work

On which day maximum number of icecreams were sold?

(a) Saturday (b) Tuesday

(c) Sunday (d) Friday

34. Mrs. Vasundhara's students asked their mothers what their favourite flower was.

Mother's Favourite Flowers

Jasmine	4 flowers
Tulip	3 flowers
Rose	7 flowers
Daisy	2 flowers
Lily	2 flowers

Key (flower) = 2 mothers

How many mothers choose daisies?

(a) 2 (b) 4

(c) 8 (d) 14

35. Mrs. Keertana asked her friends what kind of pet they have. The information follows:

Kind of Pets

Bird	2 teddy bears
Cat	6 teddy bears
Gunea pig	4 teddy bears
Fish	4 teddy bears
Dog	7 teddy bears

Key (teddy bear) = 1 pet

What kind of pet do the most of her friends have ?

(a) Bird (b) Cat

(c) Dog (d) Fish

36. How many beads should be removed from the hundred's place in the abacus shown here, if it has to represent a number between 500 and 600 ?

Space for Rough Work

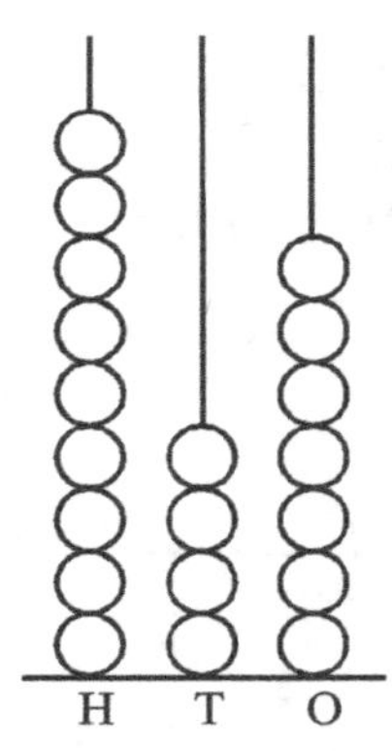

(a) 5 (b) 4

(c) 3 (d) 2

37. How much does an icecream cost ?

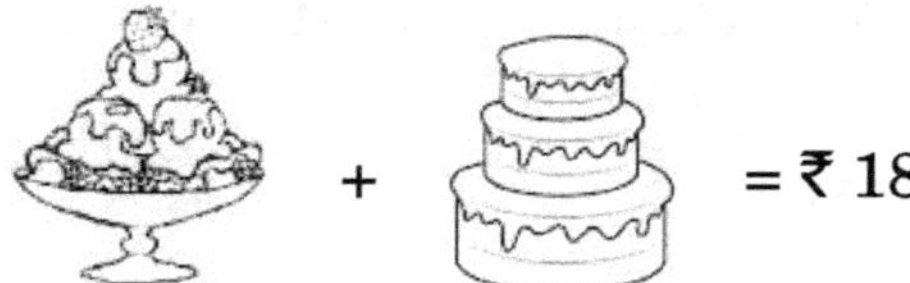

(a) ₹ 5 (b) ₹ 8

(c) ₹ 10 (d) ₹ 15

38. Miss Radhika wants to buy a videogame that costs ₹ 2205. So far she has saved ₹2147. How much more money does she need to save to buy the videogame ?

(a) ₹ 158 (b) ₹ 58

(c) ₹ 68 (d) ₹ 168

39. What is

$19 - 18 + 17 - 16 + 15 - 14 + 13 - 12$?

(a) 124 (b) 48

(c) 4 (d) 1

40. Which of the following figure has six faces ?

(a) 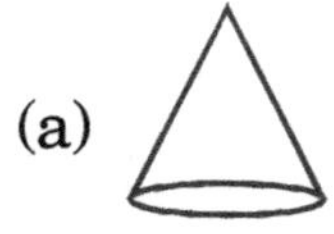 (b) 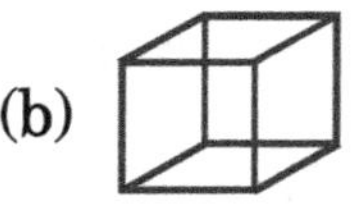

(c) 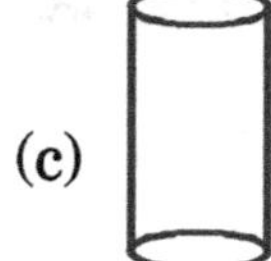 (d) 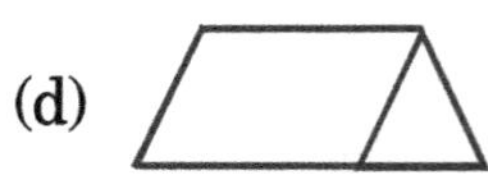

Space for Rough Work

OLYMPIAD

Mock Test

Name : ________

Max. Marks : 35

Number of Questions : 35

Time : 2 Hours

There is no negative marking in the test.

1. The number represented by given abacus is

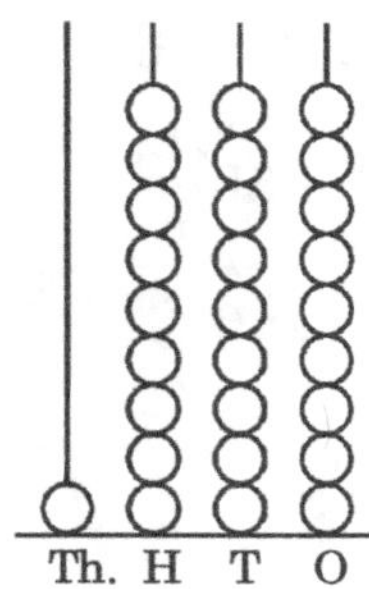

(a) 1999 (b) 1987

(c) 9991 (d) 9998

2. The number 5843 has __________ thousands.

(a) 15 (b) 12

(c) 5 (d) 6

3. The greatest 3-digit number among the following is

(a) 987 (b) 123

(c) 999 (d) 111

4. What number replaces question mark to make the number sentence true ?

8540 – ? = 6324

(a) 2238 (b) 6422

(c) 2422 (d) 2216

5. Kashi has 4888 balloons. Vivek has 4777 balloons. How many balloons are there in all?

(a) 9665 (b) 4978

(c) 9666 (d) 9555

Space for Rough Work

6. The measurement of an angle is 65°. What is the measurement of its complement?

(a) 23° (b) 25°

(c) 35° (d) 26°

7. △ + □ = 10

□ − △ = 2

(The two number sentences shown above are true.)

Which of the following values for △ and □ make both number sentences true ?

(a) □ = 6, △ = 4

(b) □ = 8, △ = 2

(c) □ = 7, △ = 3

(d) □ = 8, △ = 6

8. Write a multiplication sentence for the following figure ?

(a) $7 \times 3 = 21$ (b) $7 + 3 = 10$

(c) $7 \times 10 = 70$ (d) $3 + 3 + 3 = 9$

9. If, $200 \div 4 = 50$

$300 \div 6 = 50$

$400 \div 8 = 50$

_ _ _ _ _ _ _ _ _ _

_ _ _ _ _ _ _ _ _ _

then, $1000 \div 20 =$ ________

(a) 100 (b) 50

(c) 30 (d) 20

Space for Rough Work

10. Which of the following is wrong ?
   (a) 165 ÷ 5 is less than 165 × 0
   (b) 534 ÷ 6 is greater than 40 × 2
   (c) 5 × 70 = 70 + 70 + 70 + 70 + 70
   (d) 9563 – 5369 = 4000 + 100 + 90 + 4

11. When 1978 is divided by 8, the quotient and the remainder are respectively ________
   (a) 122, 8 (b) 220, 10
   (c) 247, 2 (d) 122, 9

12. Which list of the fractions is arranged from the smallest to the largest ?
   (a) $\frac{1}{8}, \frac{1}{4}, \frac{1}{2}$ (b) $\frac{1}{2}, \frac{1}{4}, \frac{1}{8}$
   (c) $\frac{1}{4}, \frac{1}{2}, \frac{1}{8}$ (d) $\frac{1}{2}, \frac{1}{8}, \frac{1}{4}$

13. Complete the pattern.
   13, 20, 27, 34 ________
   (a) 7 (b) 41
   (c) 31 (d) 9

14. Which of the following fractions is least?
   (a) $\frac{1}{2}$ (b) $\frac{1}{5}$
   (c) $\frac{1}{7}$ (d) $\frac{1}{9}$

15. Saumya saves ₹ 225 every month. Find her total savings for the year.
   (a) ₹ 2200 (b) ₹ 2250
   (c) ₹ 1750 (d) ₹ 2700

16. In India, the unit of currency is
   (a) paise (b) dollar
   (c) rupee (d) None of these

17. If 5 pens cost ₹ 425, what is the cost of 1 pen ?
   (a) 65 rupees (b) 75 rupees
   (c) 80 rupees (d) 85 rupees

18. The football game began at 11:25 a.m. It finished after 3 hours. What time did the game finished?
   (a) 8 : 25 a.m (b) 2 : 00 a.m
   (c) 2 : 25 p.m (d) 1 : 25 p.m

Space for Rough Work

19. Consider the following statements.

    Statement - I: Tally marks for 29 is

    𝍸 𝍸 𝍸 𝍸 𝍸 ||||

    Statement - II: Tally marks is the representation of data with the help of a group of lines.

    Now, choose the correct option.

    (a) Statement I is true and II is false.

    (b) Statement I is false and II is true.

    (c) Both statements I and II are true.

    (d) Both statements I and II are false.

20. How many minutes are there in one day?

    (a) 1440 (b) 86400

    (c) 76000 (d) 2440

21. Match the columns.

Column - I	**Column - II**
Solid figure	**Number of edges**
(A) Cone	(1) 12
(B) Cube	(2) 0
(C) Cylinder	(3) 1
(D) Sphere	(4) 2

	A	B	C	D
(a)	1	3	2	4
(b)	3	1	4	2
(c)	4	2	3	1
(d)	3	4	1	2

22. The minutes hand takes _______ rotations to move hour hand from 3 to 9.

    (a) 6 (b) 10

    (c) 20 (d) 30

23. Each ☐ weighs 1kg. How much does the sum of following figures weigh ?

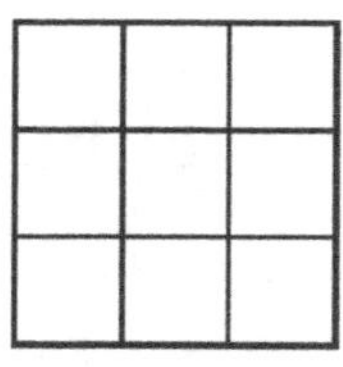 + 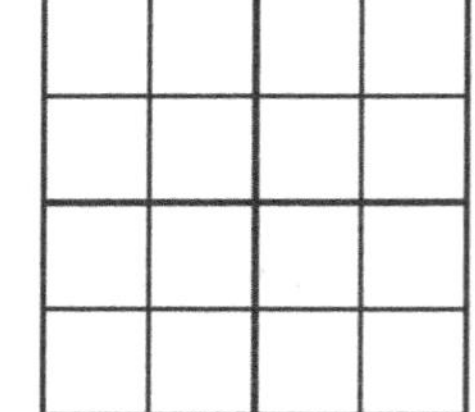

    (a) 16 kg (b) 12 kg

    (c) 9 kg (d) 25 kg

Space for Rough Work

24. 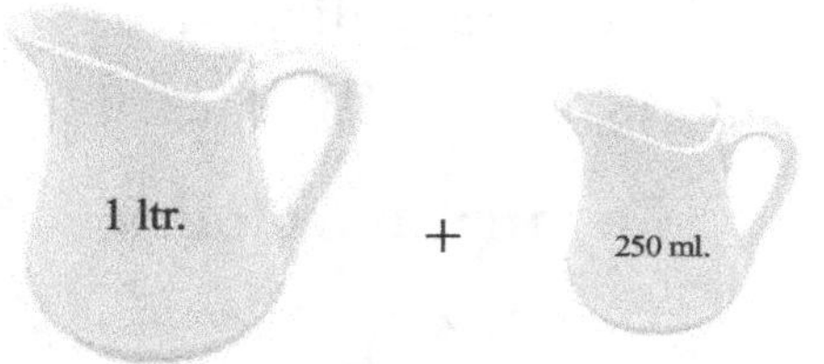

(a) 1250 ml (b) 10250 ml

(c) 1150 ml (d) 1550 ml

25. Which of the following statements is true about a cuboid?

(a) A cuboid has 6 faces

(b) A cuboid has 8 vertices

(c) A cuboid has 4 edges

(d) Both (a) and (b)

26. Observe the following diagrams and answer the question given below.

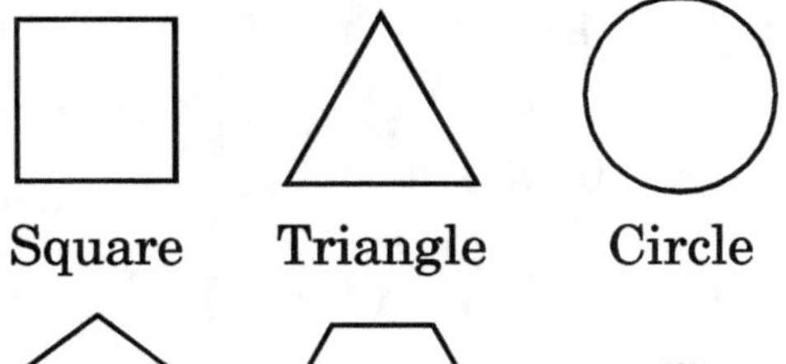

Square Triangle Circle

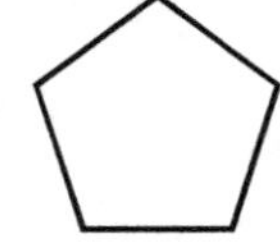

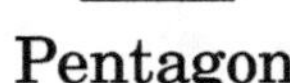

Pentagon Hexagon Semi circle

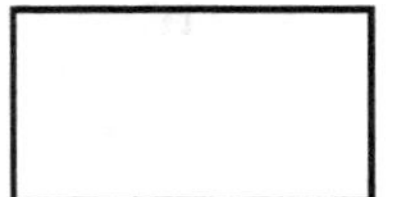

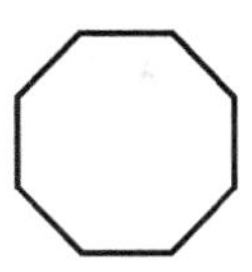

Rectangle Octagon

Which shape is made of curved line only ?

(a) Circle (b) Hexagon

(c) Pentagon (d) Octagon

27. This pictograph displays 3rd grade students' favourite sports

Sports played by 3rd Graders

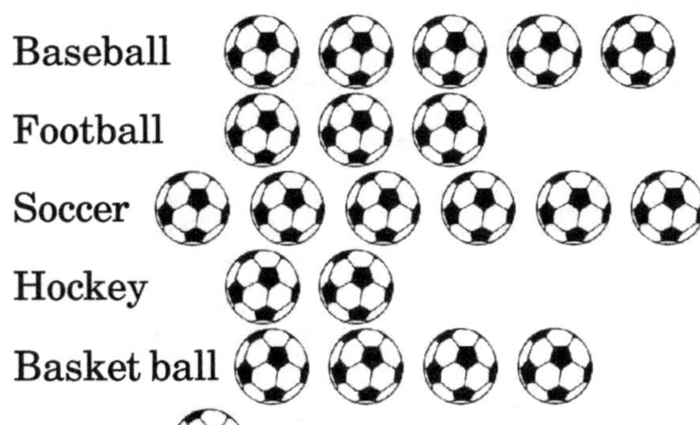

Key = 10 students

Which is the most popular sport ?

(a) Baseball (b) Football

(c) Soccer (d) Basketball

Space for Rough Work

28. The pictograph shows the number of fish in four houses.

Number of fish in neighbouring houses

House Number **Number of Fish**

House-1

House-2

House-3

House-4

How many more fish does house-2 have than house-3 ?

(a) 4 (b) 3

(c) 2 (d) 1

29. This pictograph displays favourite colours of class III students?

Favourite Colours

Red 

Blue 

Green

Purple

Which is the most favourite colour of students ?

(a) Red (b) Blue

(c) Green (d) Purple

30. Which of the following is equal to 104×50 ?

(a) $(100 \times 5) + (4 \times 5)$

(b) $(100 \times 5) + (4 \times 50)$

(c) $(100 \times 50) + (40 \times 50)$

(d) $(100 \times 50) + (4 \times 50)$

Space for Rough Work

31. Anupama divided 498 by 8 and obtained a quotient of 62 and remainder 2. For this problem, which of these checks will help Anupama to find out her mistakes?
    (a) Check if quotient × divisor + remainder = dividend
    (b) Check the calculation of 8 × 6 and 8 × 2
    (c) Check if remainder < quotient
    (d) Check if remainder < dividend

32. How many triangles can be seen in this drawing ?

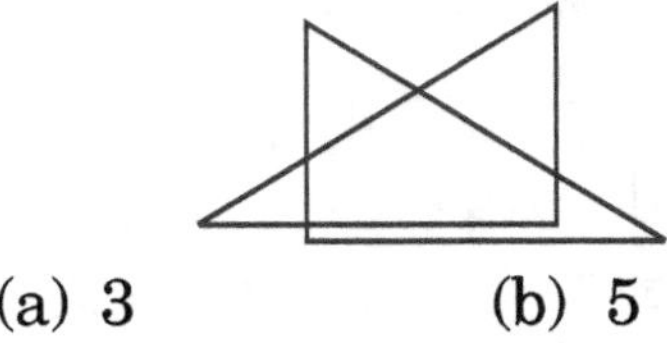

(a) 3 (b) 5
(c) 6 (d) 7

33. State whether the statements are True or False.
    (a) The standard unit of length is metre.
    (b) The standard unit of measuring weight is kilogram.
    (c) The standard unit of measuring volume of liquid is litre.
    (d) Millelitre is written as cm.

(a) TTFF (b) TFTF
(c) TFFT (d) FTTF

34. Convert 2050 m*l* to litre and m*l*.

(a) 20 *l* 50 m*l* (b) 200 *l* 5 m*l*
(c) 2 *l* 50 m*l* (d) 2 *l* 500 m*l*

35. Madhavi glued 4 white cubes together as shown below. Thus she painted the entire figure red.

How many faces of the 4 cubes were painted red ?

(a) 4 (b) 9
(c) 18 (d) 24

Space for Rough Work

OLYMPIAD

Mock Test

Name : ________ **Max. Marks : 35**

Number of Questions : 35 **Time : 2 Hours**

There is no negative marking in the test.

1. The greatest four-digit number that can be formed using 7, 0, 6, 5 without repeating the digits is ________

   (a) 6570 (b) 7560
   (c) 7650 (d) 7065

2. Ritu jogged 350 m on Monday. She jogged 170 m further on Tuesday than on Monday. How far did she jog altogether on the 2 day?

   (a) 520 m (b) 850 m
   (c) 690 m (d) 870 m

3. Which of the given abacus shows the number greater than 4321 ?

   (a) 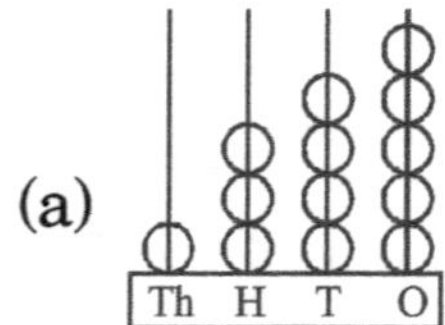

   (b) 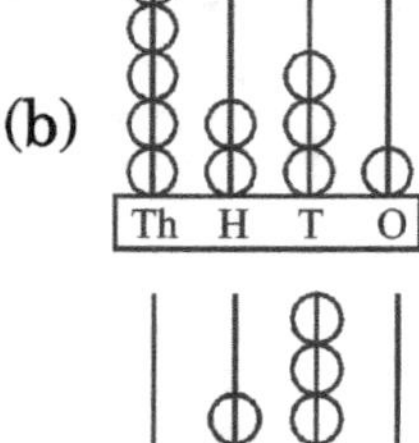

   (c) 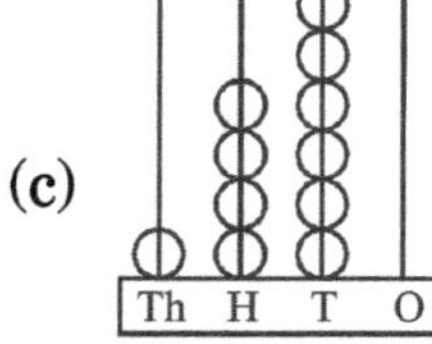

   (d) None of these

4. Madhuri wrote a number on the black board as shown below.

6		9

   If it is formed from three different digits, then which number could be placed in the gap to make it the biggest number ?

   (a) 0 (b) 5
   (c) 9 (d) 8

Space for Rough Work

5. Mr. Sharma wrote a 2-digit number on the blackboard. Three students Gopal, Raju and Prashant said the following about that number.

Gopal : "It is a 2-digit number but not the least".

Raju : "It is the predecessor of least 3-digit number".

Prashant: "It is having three different digits".

What is the number, if only two of the three students said the truth?

(a) 10 (b) 99

(c) 100 (d) 123

6. The chart shows the number of eggs produced on a farm in the first five months of the year.

Month	Numbers of Eggs
January	5,961
February	4,228
March	5,879
April	4,907
May	5,164

Which of the following statements is true or false?

(A) The number of eggs produced in April was less than in February.

(B) The number of eggs produced in May was less than in March.

(C) The number of eggs produced in January was less than in March.

(D) The number of eggs produced in March was less than in May.

(a) TFTF (b) FTFF

(c) TFFT (d) FFTF

7. Distance between two districts in Madhya Pradesh is 1000 km. If a bus travelled half of the distance in 10 hrs, how much distance is yet to be covered ?

(a) $\frac{1000}{2}$ km

(b) $\frac{1000+10}{2}$ km

(c) $\frac{10}{2}$ km

(d) $\left(1000-\frac{1}{2}\right)$ km

Space for Rough Work

8. Look at the number sentence below.

2467 + ☐ = 7121

Which number will make the number sentence true?

(a) 4654 (b) 4256

(c) 4664 (d) 4268

9. A ticket to the dolphin show costs ₹ 999 for 1 adult. Which estimate is closest to the total cost of tickets for 3 adults?

(a) ₹ 2000 (b) ₹ 4000

(c) ₹ 3000 (d) ₹ 1000

10. Roman numeral for 43 is

(a) XXXIII (b) XLIII

(c) IVIII (d) XXXIII

11. Meghna has 14 boxes of balls. She has 224 balls in all. Meghna used the number sentence below to find how many balls are in each box.

14 × ☐ = 224

What is the missing number that makes Meghna's number sentence true ?

(a) 14 (b) 16

(c) 17 (d) 18

12. Which of the following figure sets shows $\frac{1}{6} < \frac{4}{6}$?

(a) 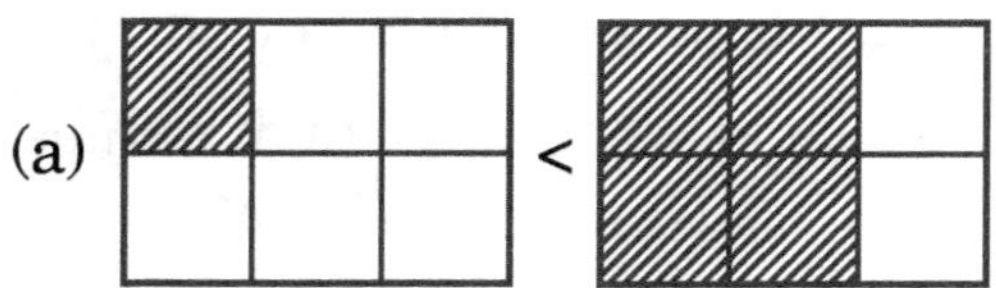

(b) 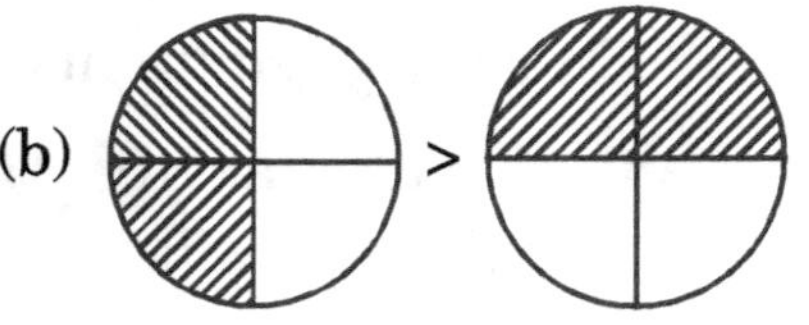

(c) 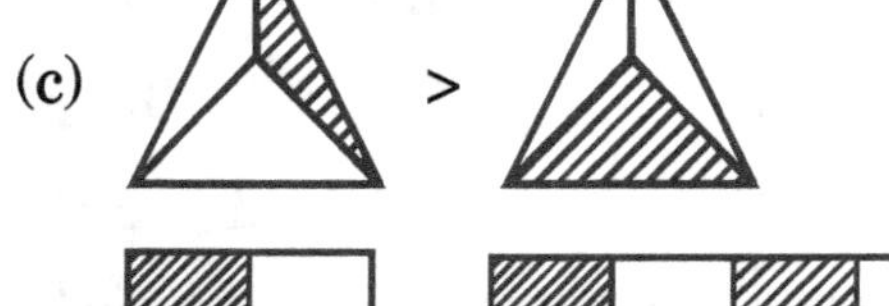

(d) 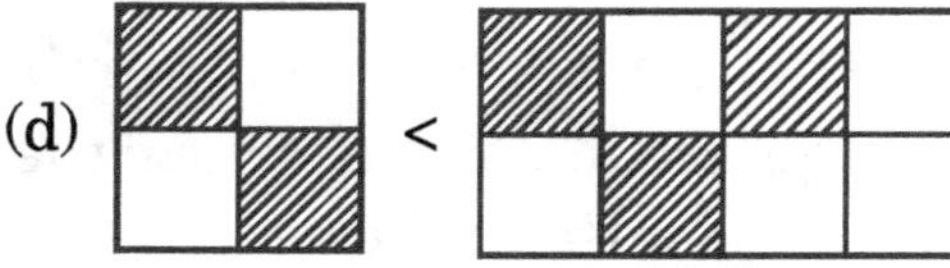

13. Sonu likes all numbers which have zeroes at the unit's place. What is the fraction of such numbers in the given box ?

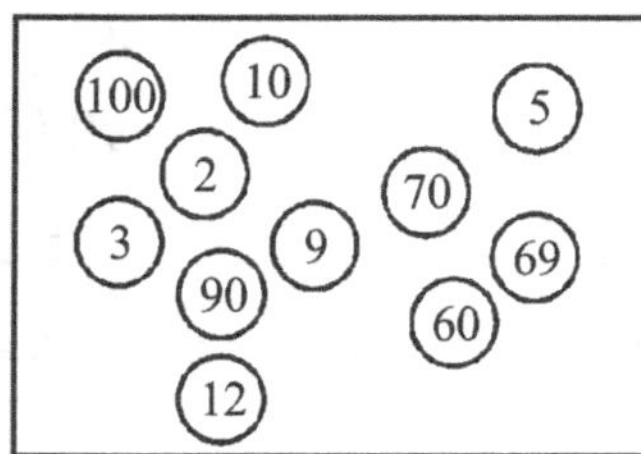

Space for Rough Work

(a) $\frac{15}{11}$ (b) $\frac{5}{11}$

(c) $\frac{12}{11}$ (d) $\frac{3}{11}$

14. Aditi's flight takes off at 3:30 p.m. The flight duration is 5 hours 30 minutes. At what time is the flight expected to reach its destination?

(a) 9 : 30 p.m. (b) 9 : 40 p.m.

(c) 9 : 00 p.m. (d) 8 : 30 p.m.

15. Jai and Nihal will paint a circle.

- First Jai will paint $\frac{2}{8}$ of the circle.
- Then Nihal will paint another $\frac{3}{8}$ of the circle.

Altogether, what fraction of the circle will they paint ?

(a) $\frac{5}{8}$ (b) $\frac{6}{8}$

(c) $\frac{5}{16}$ (d) $\frac{6}{16}$

16. Rahul has ₹ 1120.50. He wants to buy a Robot that costs ₹ 2080.75. How much more does he need to buy the Robot ?

(a) ₹ 850.75

(b) ₹ 950.75

(c) ₹ 960.25

(d) ₹ 890.25

17. Sanjay bought 16 packets of ice cream bricks for a party. The total cost for bricks was ₹ 6400. How he will calculate the cost of 1 ice cream brick ?

(a) $16 \div 6400$

(b) $(6400 \div 16)$

(c) $(6000 \div 16)$

(d) None of these

18. Hindu - Arabic numeral for XLIX is

(a) 71 (b) 69

(c) 49 (d) 61

19. You have ₹ 500. How much money will be left with you if you buy 2 ice creams, 2 milky bars, one pen and one burger ?

Space for Rough Work

(a) ₹ 150 (b) ₹ 185
(c) ₹ 175 (d) ₹ 155

20. Dia saves ₹ 51.50 everyday from her pocket money. How much does she save in 9 days ?

(a) ₹ 463.50 (b) ₹ 416.50
(c) ₹ 520.00 (d) ₹ 461.5

21. Simran has a rope of length 45 m. She cuts it into 5 equal pieces. How long is each piece of rope ?

(a) 19 m (b) 9 m
(c) 10 m (d) 11 m

22. The chart shows the number of pages Lalita read during four days.

Day	Monday	Tuesday	Wednesday	Thursday
Pages Read	24	17	31	26

How many more pages did she read on Wednesday than on Tuesday ?

(a) 15 (b) 14
(c) 12 (d) 26

23. Which of the following fractions are arranged in descending order?

(a) $\frac{11}{15}, \frac{11}{9}, \frac{11}{13}$ (b) $\frac{11}{9}, \frac{11}{13}, \frac{11}{15}$

(c) $\frac{11}{15}, \frac{11}{13}, \frac{11}{9}$ (d) $\frac{11}{9}, \frac{11}{15}, \frac{11}{13}$

24. This is a cuboid . How many of these cuboids are needed to make the figures shown below ?

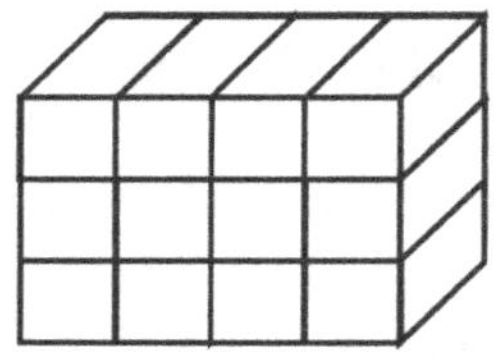

(a) 19 (b) 18
(c) 12 (d) 16

25. Which could be one of the faces of a cylinder ?

(a) 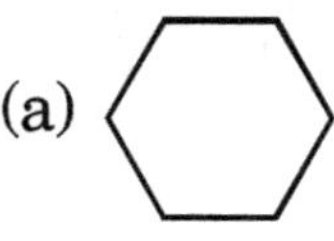 (b) 

(c)  (d) 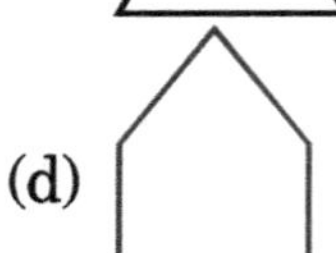

Space for Rough Work

26. Which of the following has 2 lines of symmetry?

(a) A (b) B

(c) I (d) F

27. The table shows the amount of time Komal spent on skating.

Day	Practice Time
Monday	30 minutes
Tuesday	45 minutes
Wednesday	60 minutes
Thursday	75 minutes
Friday	90 minutes
Saturday	?

If the pattern in the table continues, how many minutes will she spend practicing on Saturday ?

(a) 105 mins (b) 110 mins

(c) 100 mins (d) 95 mins

28. A leap year comes once every __________ years.

(a) 2 (b) 3

(c) 4 (d) 5

29. Look at this pattern of shapes.

Which of these shows the same kind of pattern?

(a) ↑ → ↑ → ↑ → ↑ →

(b) ↑ ↓ ↓ ↑ ↑ ↓ ↓ ↑

(c) ↑ → ↓ ← ↑ → ↓ ←

(d) ↑ → ↓ → ↑ → ↓ →

30. Match the following columns.

Column - I (Solid Shape)	**Column - II (Number of Faces)**
(A) Sphere	(1) 2
(B) Cuboid	(2) 3
(C) Cone	(3) 6
(D) Cylinder	(4) 1

	A	B	C	D
(a)	4	3	1	2
(b)	3	4	2	1
(c)	3	2	4	1
(d)	4	1	3	2

Space for Rough Work

31. The first five numbers in a pattern are shown below. A subtraction rule was used to find each new number in the pattern.

    125 105 85 65 45 ?

    If the subtraction pattern is continued in the same way, what be the next number in the pattern ?

    (a) 44 (b) 35
    (c) 25 (d) 46

32. Consider the following statements.

    Statement 1: The largest 4 - digit number formed by using the digits 6, 5 and 4 and using 6 twice is 6654.

    Statement 2: 999 is predecessor of smallest four digit number.

    Now, choose the correct option.

    (a) Statement - 1 is true and 2 is false.
    (b) Statement - 1 is false and 2 is true.
    (c) Both statements 1 and 2 are true.
    (d) Both statements 1 and 2 are false.

DIRECTIONS (Qs. 33 to 34): The following table shows number of buttons of different colour used in a school project by Amit.

Colour of button	Tally Marks	Total Number
Blue	𝍸 𝍸 ||||	14
Orange	𝍸 |||	8
Green	𝍸 𝍸 |||	13
Pink	𝍸 𝍸 |	11
Yellow	||||	4
	Total number of Buttons	50

33. How many more blue buttons were used than pink buttons?

    (a) 14 (b) 3
    (c) 11 (d) 4

34. How many less orange buttons were used than green buttons?

    (a) 4 (b) 3
    (c) 8 (d) 5

35. Ralph and Kim are talking about some large number they are studying in the Math class. Which is 1000 more than 5529. Which of the following is the number ?

    (a) 6539 (b) 6529
    (c) 6549 (d) 5539

Space for Rough Work

SCIENCE MOCK TEST 1–5

OLYMPIAD Mock Test

Name : ________ **Max. Marks : 35**

Number of Questions : 35 **Time : 2 Hours**

There is no negative marking in the test.

1. Matter is anything that occupies space and has mass. Which one of the following is correct about air?

   (a) Air is not a matter.

   (b) Air is a matter.

   (c) Air can partially be a matter.

   (d) All of these

2. Green plants make their own food. They are called?

   (a) heterotrophs

   (b) autotrophs

   (c) saprophytes

   (d) all of these

3. Which part of the body of the car do we get from plants?

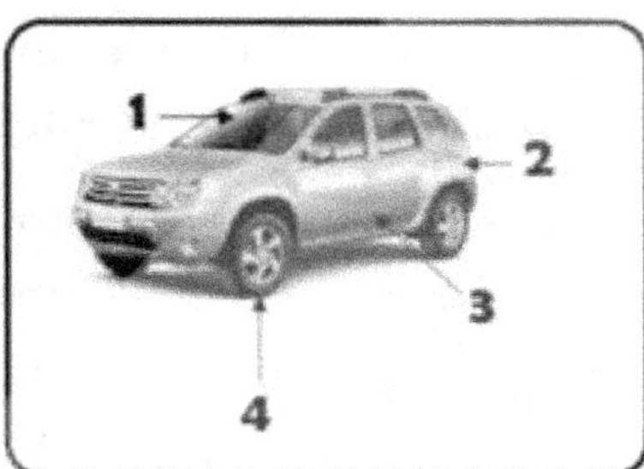

   (a) 1 (b) 2

   (c) 3 (d) 4

4. 1. Water flows from one place to another.

   2. Clouds moves from one place to another.

   3. The leaves of "Touch-Me-Not" plant closes after touching.

   4. Flowers of the sunflower plants move in the direction of sun.

Space for Rough Work

Which of the above mentioned activities show movement in living things?

(a) 1 and 2 (b) 2 and 3

(c) 1 and 3 (d) 3 and 4

5. Given below is the list of name of plants, categorized as per their roots. Which one of the given categories is correct?

(a) Tap root: Wheat, mustard Fibrous root: Onion, hibiscus

(b) Tap root: Onion, mustard Fibrous root: Wheat, hibiscus

(c) Tap root: Hibiscus, mustard Fibrous root: Onion, wheat

(d) All of these

6. Ice changes into water and water changes into water vapour. What do you conclude from this statement?

(a) Water is a solid.

(b) Water is a liquid.

(c) Water is a gas.

(d) Water is found in all the three states of matter.

7. Given below is the list of things that happen during different seasons:

1. You sweat a lot.
2. You need warm clothes.
3. Plants shed their leaves.
4. There are flowers everywhere.
5. It rains heavily.

Which one of the following options is correct?

(a) 1-summer, 2-winter, 3-spring, 4-autumn, 5-rain

(b) 1-summer, 2-winter, 3-spring, 4-rain, 5-autumn

(c) 1-summer, 2-winter, 3-autumn, 4-spring, 5-rain

(d) 1-summer, 2-spring, 3-winter, 4-autumn, 5-rain

8. Which statement is true?

Statement A : Sense organs help in obtaining information about the surroundings.

Statement B : Sense organs do not help in obtaining information about the surroundings.

Space for Rough Work

(a) Statement A is true.

(b) Statement B is true.

(c) Both statements A and B are true.

(d) Both statements A and B are false.

9. We eat the root of some plants that store food in them. Which one of the following plant's roots do we eat?

(a) Tomato

(b) Sugarcane

(c) Turnip

(d) Brinjal

10. What impact does the exhaled air make on lungs?

(a) Makes the lung expand.

(b) Makes the lung contract.

(c) Does not make any impact.

(d) All of these

11. Which one of the following processes is responsible for the changing of water into water vapour?

(a) Condensation

(b) Freezing

(c) Evaporation

(d) All of these

12. When water boils in a pot, we can see _ as mist.

(a) steam

(b) oxygen

(c) water vapour

(d) water droplets

13. A car travels 30 km in first hour, 31 km in second hour and again 30 km in third hour. What kind of motion does the car have?

(a) Uniform motion

(b) Non-uniform motion

(c) Circular motion

(d) All of these

Space for Rough Work

14. Which one of the following birds has chisel-shaped beak?
    (a) Woodpecker (b) Parrot
    (c) Crow (d) Eagle
15. The rocks are changed into soil by which one of the following processes?
    (a) Fusion
    (b) Soil erosion
    (c) Chemical reaction
    (d) Weathering
16. Males have more diet than __________.
    (a) females
    (b) children
    (c) animals
    (d) none of the above
17. How can we prevent the depletion of ozone layer?
    (a) By industrialization
    (b) By deforestation
    (c) By preventing pollution
    (d) All of these
18. We are able to see the moon because it ....
    (a) gives out light.
    (b) is a glowing star.
    (c) reflects light from the Sun.
    (d) reflects light from the Earth.
19. Which statement is true?
    Statement A : Population is a boon
    Statement B : Over population is a bane.
    (a) Statement A is true.
    (b) Statement B is true.
    (c) Both statements A and B are true.
    (d) Both statements A and B are false.
20. Which of the following birds can fly?
    (a) Parrot (b) Ostrich
    (c) Kiwi (d) All of these

Space for Rough Work

21. Which of the following statements is correct?
    (a) Plants require air, water and sunlight to make food.
    (b) Man requires food, air and water to live.
    (c) Man requires only air to live.
    (d) Both (a) and (b)
22. The seed needs ________, ________ and ________ to grow.
    (a) air, warmth and sunshine
    (b) water, warmth and good soil
    (c) water, air and warmth
    (d) water, air and sunshine
23. Which of the following statements are true about birds?
    (a) They have hollow bones.
    (b) They have solid bones.
    (c) They have strong chest muscles.
    (d) Both (a) and (c)
24. Which of the following organs helps us to make decisions?
    (a) Eyes (b) Ears
    (c) Brain (d) Nerves
25. Which muscles are the busiest in the human body?
    (a) Cheek muscles
    (b) Eye muscles
    (c) Hand muscles
    (d) Leg muscles
26. Which part of the Earth is the coolest?
    (a) Crust
    (b) Core
    (c) Mantle
    (d) All of these
27. Which of the following is the hardest substance?
    (a) Coal
    (b) Chalk
    (c) Slate
    (d) Diamond

Space for Rough Work

28. In which of the following forms fresh water is available?

(a) In the form of ice in glaciers

(b) As groundwater

(c) As water vapour in atmosphere

(d) All of these

29. Which of the following animals live on the land?

(a) 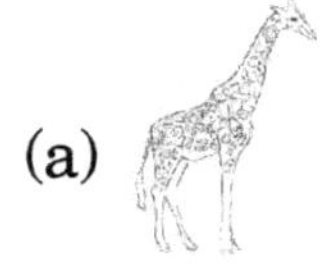

(b) 

(c) 

(d) All of these

30. Which of the following is a correct food chain?

(a) Plants → Deer → Tiger

(b) Plants → Eagle → Tiger

(c) Wheat → Eagle → Tiger

(d) Plants → Tiger → Deer

31. Which of the following statements is true?

Statement A : Seeds grow into plants.

Statement B : Buds grow into flowers.

(a) Statement A is correct.

(b) Statement B is correct.

(c) Statement A and B both are correct.

(d) Neither statement A nor statement B is correct.

32. Which of the following statements is true?

Statement A : The food made by the leaves travels through the stem to all parts of the plant.

Statement B : The food made by the leaves is always stored in stem.

(a) Statement A is correct.

(b) Statement B is correct.

(c) Statement A and B is both are correct.

(d) Neither statement A nor statement B is correct.

Space for Rough Work

33. Identify our body system by which the waste material is removed from the body.

(a) Circulatory system

(b) Nervous system

(c) Muscular system

(d) Excretory system

34. Match the following.

1.	Vulture	(A)	has red coloured beak
2.	Woodpecker	(B)	has long and sharp beak
3.	Kingfishers	(C)	has strong and sharp beak
4.	Parrot	(D)	has long and scissor-like beak

(a) 1-C, 2-B, 3-D, 4-A

(b) 1-A, 2-C, 3-D, 4-B

(c) 1-D, 2-B, 3-A, 4-C

(d) 1-D, 2-C, 3-A, 4-B

35. Four students have made statements about the skeletal system.

Who are the correct?

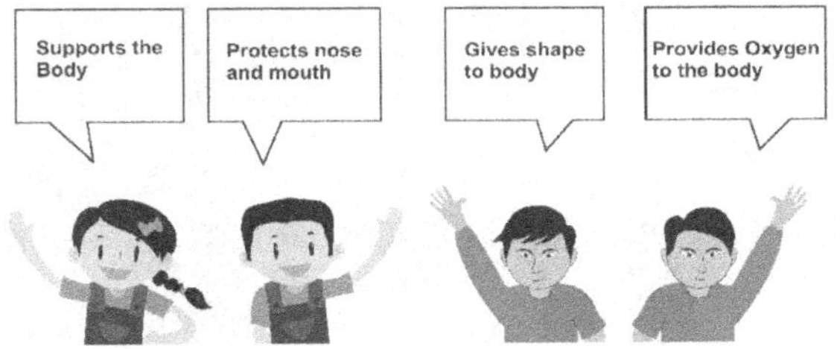

(a) Jill and Jane

(b) Jack and Jill

(c) Jane and Jack

(d) Larry and Jill

Space for Rough Work

OLYMPIAD

Mock Test

Name : ________

Number of Questions : 35

Max. Marks : 35

Time : 2 Hours

There is no negative marking in the test.

1. How many sets of teeth does a person get in their lifetime?
   (a) 3 (b) 2
   (c) 4 (d) 1
2. Where do cabbage and mint store food ?
   (a) In their roots
   (b) In their flowers
   (c) In their fruits
   (d) In their leaves
3. Photosynthesis is the process of making food in plants. Which one of the following gases is used in the process of photosynthesis?
   (a) Nitrogen (b) Oxygen
   (c) Carbon dioxide (d) Hydrogen
4. What causes a person to become sick from an infection?
   (a) Germs
   (b) Not practicing good hygiene
   (c) Both (a) and (b)
   (d) None of these
5. What do you mean by public transport?
   (a) The transport system that is used by few people.
   (b) The transport system that is used by large number of people.
   (c) The transport system that is used by an individual.
   (d) Both (a) and (b)

Space for Rough Work

6. Which kind of soil is found at the beaches?
   (a) Chalky soil (b) Sandy soil
   (c) Clayey soil (d) Loamy soil
7. Which one of the following soils is best for growing plants?
   (a) Clayey soil (b) Sandy soil
   (c) Loamy soil (d) All of these
8. What % of the Earth is covered by the oceans?
   (a) About 30% (b) About 71%
   (c) About 97% (d) About 76%
9. Match the following.

1. Glass	A. Cloth
2. Plastics	B. Window panes
3. Fibre	C. Tubes
4. Rubber	D. Televisions

   (a) 1-D, 2-B, 3-A, 4-C
   (b) 1-A, 2-D, 3-B, 4-C
   (c) 1-B, 2-A, 3-D, 4-C
   (d) 1-B, 2-D, 3-A, 4-C
10. **Statement A :** All elements and plants breathe in oxygen.
    Statement B : Plants make their food by using carbon dioxide gas.
    (a) Statement A is correct.
    (b) Statement B is correct.
    (c) Statement A and B both are correct.
    (d) Neither statement A nor statement B is correct.
11. The soft green stem can be found in the ________.
    (a) pine tree (b) coconut tree
    (c) banana tree (d) neem tree
12. Which of the following constitutes our breathing system?
    (a) Mouth, nose and windpipe
    (b) Mouth and lungs
    (c) Stomach, mouth and windpipe
    (d) Nose, windpipe and lungs
13. Identify the name of the organs of digestive system.
    (a) Stomach (b) Mouth
    (c) Small intestine (d) All of these

Space for Rough Work

14. Which three planets are in correct order?
    (a) Mercury, Venus, Earth
    (b) Earth, Mercury, Venus
    (c) Venus, Mercury, Earth
    (d) Mercury, Mars, Earth

15. Identify the celestial body nearest to the Earth.
    (a) Sun (b) Moon
    (c) Mars (d) Venus

16. Identify the colour of the humus.
    (a) Dark green
    (b) Light yellow
    (c) Light brown
    (d) Dark brown

17. Which of the following statements is correct?

    Statement A : The animals can feel changes around them because they have sense organs.

    Statement B : The plants do not feel changes around them because they do not have sense organs.

    (a) Statement A is correct.
    (b) Statement B is correct.
    (c) Statement A and B both are correct.
    (d) Neither statement A nor statement B is correct.

18. Which one of the given options based on the following statements is correct?

    Statement A : Birds have teeth to eat.

    Statement B : Birds use their claws to `catch food and protect themselves.

    (a) Statement A is correct.
    (b) Statement B is correct.
    (c) Statement A and B both are correct.
    (d) Neither statement A nor statement B is correct.

19. Which one of the given options based on the following statements is correct?

    Statement A : Surface of the Moon has mountains and huge ditches called craters.

    Statement B : The Moon revolves round the Sun.

Space for Rough Work

(a) Statement A is correct.

(b) Statement B is correct.

(c) Statement A and B both are correct.

(d) Neither statement A nor statement B is correct.

20. Other celestial bodies whose sizes are smaller in comparison to the planets but they also revolve around the Sun are called

(a) asteroids (b) satellites

(c) comets (d) all of these

21. The characteristic feature of a satellite is that it revolves around the Earth. What is the Moon called?

(a) Artificial satellite

(b) Natural satellite

(c) Both (a) and (b)

(d) Planet

22. The given picture shows movement of air from the sea towards the land.

What is it called?

(a) Sea breeze

(b) Land breeze

(c) Warm air

(d) All of these

23. Why does the government advice to discard the use of polythene bags?

(a) Polythenes are biodegradable.

(b) Polythenes are expensive.

(c) Polythenes are non-biodegradable.

(d) All of these

Space for Rough Work

24. Which of the following should come in the empty box in the flow chart given below?

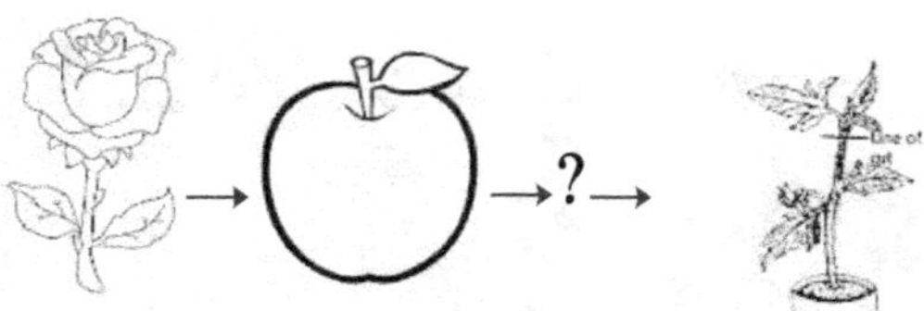

(a) Seed (b) Bird
(c) Fruit (d) Stem

25. We breathe fast after running. Why does it happen?
(a) We require more oxygen after running.
(b) We require less oxygen after running.
(c) We require lots of energy after running.
(d) All of these

26. Consider the following statements :
Statement 1 : Omnivore eats both plants and animal products.
Statement 2 : Herbivore eats both plants and animal products.
Which one of the following is correct about the above statements?
(a) Statement 1 is true and 2 is false.
(b) Statement 1 is false and 2 is true.
(c) Both statements are false.
(d) Both statements are true.

27. A type of plants which require support for their growth is called :
(a) pitcher
(b) herbs
(c) climbers
(d) all of these

28. Which of the following is NOT a function of the root?
(a) Support
(b) Production of food
(c) Storage of food
(d) Absorption of water and mineral

Space for Rough Work

29. Look at the following figure.

Which one of the following types of animal is this?

(a) Arboreal

(b) Amphibian

(c) Terrestrial

(d) All of these

30. Match the following.

	A		B
1.	Carnivore	A.	Frog
2.	Herbivore	B.	Snake
3.	Amphibian	C.	Goat
4.	Reptile	D.	Lion

(a) 1-B, 2-C, 3-A, 4-D

(b) 1-D, 2-A, 3-C, 4-B

(c) 1-C, 2-D, 3-A, 4-B

(d) 1-D, 2-C, 3-A, 4-B

31. Look at the following picture.

Which one of the following types of root does the given figure have?

(a) Fibrous

(b) Tap

(c) Aerial

(d) All of these

32. Consider the following statements :

Statement 1 : Silk is synthetic fibre which is used to make dress.

Statement 2 : Cotton is synthetic fibre which is used to make dress.

Which one of the following is correct about the above statements?

(a) Statement 1 is true and 2 is false.

(b) Statement 1 is false and 2 is true.

(c) Both statements 1 and 2 are false.

(d) Both statements 1 and 2 are true.

Space for Rough Work

33. Which one of the following best describes a plant of mushroom?
    (a) Desert plant
    (b) Non-green plant
    (c) Underwater plant
    (d) All of these

34. Which one of the following animals has a very good sense of smelling?

    (a) 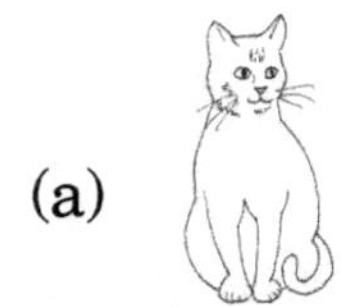
    (b) 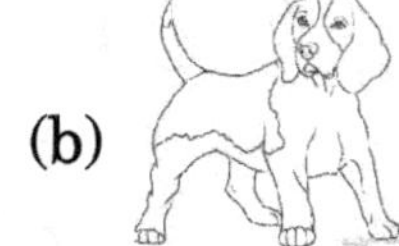
    (c) 
    (d) 

35. What is the name of the red-hot substance that comes from volcanoes?
    (a) Fire
    (b) Magma
    (c) Sand
    (d) Lava

Space for Rough Work

OLYMPIAD

Mock Test

Name : ________ **Max. Marks : 35**

Number of Questions : 35 **Time : 2 Hours**

There is no negative marking in the test.

1. Which one of the following is the locomotory organ of a bird?
   (a) Wings (b) Feather
   (c) Beak (d) All of these
2. Which one of the following is called parasite?
   (a) Lion (b) Protozoa
   (c) Calf (d) All of these
3. Namit was asked to pair one outdoor and one indoor activity. He made four pairs, but he made one incorrect pair. Select the INCORRECT pair.
   (a) Ludo and Carrom
   (b) Badminton and Table tennis
   (c) Football and Chess
   (d) Both (a) and (b)
4. Consider the following statements :
   Statement A : Some bacteria are harmful whereas some are useful for the human beings.
   Statement B : All bacteria are harmful for human beings.
   Which one of the following is correct about the above statements?
   (a) Both statements are false.
   (b) Statement 1 is false and 2 is true.
   (c) Both statements are true.
   (d) Statement 1 is true and 2 is false.
5. Which one of the following is responsible for the curd formation?
   (a) Virus (b) Bacteria
   (c) Protozoa (d) All of these

Space for Rough Work

6. Which one of the following medicines kills bacteria in our body?
   (a) Vitamins oral suspension
   (b) Digestive liquid
   (c) Acidity remover
   (d) Antibacterial medicine
7. Which one of the following processes involves the exchange of carbon dioxide and oxygen in the cells?
   (a) Digestion
   (b) Respiration
   (c) Excretion
   (d) All of these
8. Which one of the following area is most suitable for the human being to live?
   (a) Plain (b) Desert
   (c) Hills (d) All of these
9. Which one of the following is correct about the desert area?
   (a) Less rainfall
   (b) Favourable area for the growth of the trees
   (c) Fertile soil (d) All of these
10. The area near the mountain is called
   (a) desert area (b) hilly area
   (c) plains (d) all of these
11. How does the rabbit eat plants and plant part?
   (a) Swallowing
   (b) Chewing the cud
   (c) Gnawing
   (d) All of these
12. A plant is an example of a producer. Producers are living organisms that
   (a) make their own food.
   (b) break down dead organisms for food.
   (c) eat other organisms for food.
   (d) do not make their own food.
13. Look at the following picture of molecular structure of a solid. Which one of the following is correct about the solid?

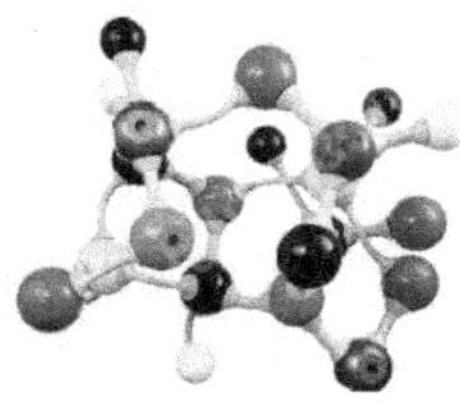

   (a) Molecules in solid are tightly packed.
   (b) Molecules in solid are loosely packed.
   (c) Molecules in solid move freely.
   (d) All of these

Space for Rough Work

14. What is measured in liquid form of a substance?
    (a) Length (b) Width
    (c) Volume (d) Height
15. Two substances, sodium and chlorine are mixed to form sodium chloride. This is an example of
    (a) physical change
    (b) both physical and chemical change
    (c) chemical reaction
    (d) partially physical and chemical change
16. Oxygen and digested food in our body react to form which one of the following?
    (a) Energy (b) Vitamins
    (c) Minerals (d) All of these
17. A man applies force for the displacement of the solid. If solid does not move from one place to another, what will be the conclusion?
    (a) Work has been done.
    (b) No work has been done.
    (c) No force on the solid.
    (d) All of these
18. A force which is naturally applied to everything on the earth is called
    (a) force of gravity
    (b) frictional force
    (c) applied Force
    (d) all of these
19. Which one of the following will fall fast on the ground if they are dropped from an equal height?

    A plastic ball  An iron ball 

    (a) Plastic ball
    (b) Iron ball
    (c) Both will take equal time
    (d) All of these
20. Which one of the following types of force will work between a magnet and a piece of iron?
    (a) Frictional force
    (b) Gravitational force
    (c) Magnetic force
    (d) All of these
21. Grass appears green because
    (a) it absorbs green light.
    (b) it reflects green light back to your eyes.
    (c) it reflects red light back to your eyes.
    (d) it reflects white light.
22. Which of the following completes one revolution around the Sun in 365¼ days?

    A. Moon B. Earth

    (a) A only (b) A and B
    (c) B only (d) Neither A nor B

Space for Rough Work

23. Experiment : Light a torch on a wall and put a ball between the torch and the wall. What will you observe?
    (a) A shadow of ball on the wall.
    (b) A shadow of torch on the wall.
    (c) A shadow of wall on the ball.
    (d) All of these

24. Arrange the following in increasing order according to their capacity :
    Bottle, Glass, Tub, Tank
    (a) Tank, Tub, Bottle, Glass
    (b) Glass, Bottle, Tub, Tank
    (c) Tub, Tank, Bottle, Glass
    (d) Bottle, Tank, Glass, Tub

25. Consider the following statements :
    Statement 1 : Circulatory system consists of the heart and blood vessels.
    Statement 2 : The blood vessels carry blood from the heart to different parts of the body.
    Which one of the following is correct about the above statements?
    (a) Statement 1 is true and 2 is false.
    (b) Statement 1 is false and 2 is true.
    (c) Both statements are false.
    (d) Both statements are true.

26. Recycling refers to
    (a) burning trash completely.
    (b) burying trash in a landfill.
    (c) reducing the amount of waste left over from using a product.
    (d) reusing a resource to make something new.

27. What is the name of the process by which a seed grows into a baby plant?
    (a) Germination (b) Gardening
    (c) Harvesting (d) All of these

28. A few substances change directly from solid into gas on heating. Which one of the following process involves for the same?
    (a) Sublimation
    (b) Freezing
    (c) Evaporation
    (d) All of these

29. Moon has gravity because ____________.
    (a) it borrows gravity from the Sun
    (b) it is made up of matter
    (c) it borrows gravity from the Earth
    (d) none of the above

Space for Rough Work

30. What is matter?
    (a) Anything that has mass
    (b) Anything that occupies space
    (c) Anything that has mass and occupies space
    (d) None of these
31. Individual cells in our body combine to form a tissue. What is formed by the combination of individual bones?
    (a) Skeletal system
    (b) Organs
    (c) Muscular system
    (d) All of these
32. Which one of the following lays eggs instead of giving birth to young one?
    (a)  (b) 
    (c)  (d) All of these
33. A mineral is a natural crystalline solid formed from geological processes. Which is not an example of a mineral?
    (a) Diamond
    (b) Wood
    (c) Gold
    (d) Salt
34. Which one of the following can control the possibility of heart attack?
    (a) Hard exercise
    (b) Low fat diet
    (c) High fat diet
    (d) All of these
35. Which one of the following is not a pet animal?
    (a) Cat (b) Dog
    (c) Rabbit (d) Tiger

Space for Rough Work

OLYMPIAD

Mock Test

Name : _________ **Max. Marks : 40**

Number of Questions : 40 **Time : 2 Hours**

There is no negative marking in the test.

1. Water droplets that are too heavy to float make
   (a) fog (b) clouds
   (c) rain (d) smoke
2. Which of the following does not take the shape of the container in which it is kept ?
   (a) Pencil (b) Oil
   (c) Water (d) Milk
3. Which of the following will not dissolve in water?
   (a) Salt (b) Sugar
   (c) Sand (d) Baking soda
4. I protect the brain. I consist of bones which are fused firmly together to form a shell-like structure. What am I?
   (a) Skull (b) Ribcage
   (c) Spine (d) Sternum
5. The bird that lays its eggs in the nest of a crow is
   (a) cuckoo (b) parrot
   (c) woodpecker (d) pigeon
6. Soil helps trees because soil
   (a) makes food for the trees.
   (b) moves the tree seeds to new places.
   (c) gives nutrients to the trees.
   (d) turns the roots into new trees.
7. The upper part of an umbrella is made of a special type of cloth. Which of the following BEST describes an umbrella cloth?
   (a) It must be very heavy.
   (b) It must be able to soak water.
   (c) It must be able to sink in water.
   (d) It must not allow liquids to pass through.

Space for Rough Work

8. ______are known as food factories of a plant.
   (a) Green leaves (b) Roots
   (c) Stem (d) Flower

9. Weather is caused by the
   (a) Sun (b) night air
   (c) temperature (d) clouds

10. The thick layer of________ under the bear's skin keeps them warm and allows them to go for weeks without eating, if necessary.
   (a) fat (b) blood
   (c) hair (d) pressure

11. What would you have to add to solid ice to make it turn into a liquid?
   (a) Liquid
   (b) Heat
   (c) pressure
   (d) More solid

12. In which layer of the soil do most grasses grow?
   (a) Solid rock (b) Subsoil
   (c) Topsoil (d) Bedrock

13. Which of these, people build to stop flooding?
   (a) Sidewalks (b) Dams
   (c) Bridges (d) Ponds

14. You decide to help your family cook breakfast one weekend. Which of the following actions would be considered a chemical change?
   (a) Cutting up the vegetables.
   (b) Slicing an orange.
   (c) Making scrambled eggs.
   (d) Folding the napkins.

15. Which is the longest bone of the human body?
   (a) Stapes (b) Skull
   (c) Ribs (d) Femur

16. Which of the following plants will not be able to survive?

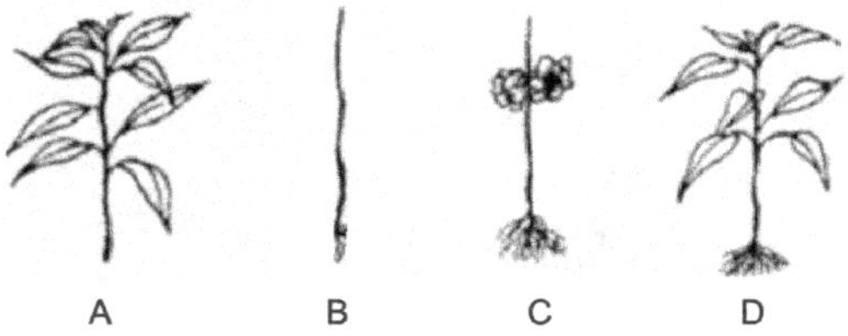

A B C D

Space for Rough Work

(a) (A) & (B) (b) (B) & (C)

(c) (C) & (D) (d) (A), (B) & (C)

17. Trunk is the main stem of the tree. It divides into many branches higher up in tree. The _______ of the tree protects the trunk.

(a) stem (b) bark

(c) leaves (d) roots

18. In desert plants, leaves modify into thorns. How do thorns help a plant?

(a) They catch food.

(b) They store water.

(c) They protect the plant from being eaten by animals.

(d) They make the plant attract bees.

19. Which of the following animals can change body colouring to protect themselves from their enemies?

(a)  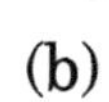 (b) 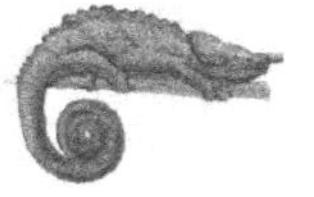

(c)  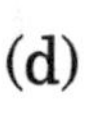 (d) 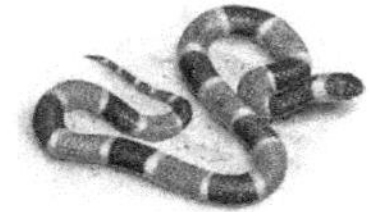

20. Look at the poster below.

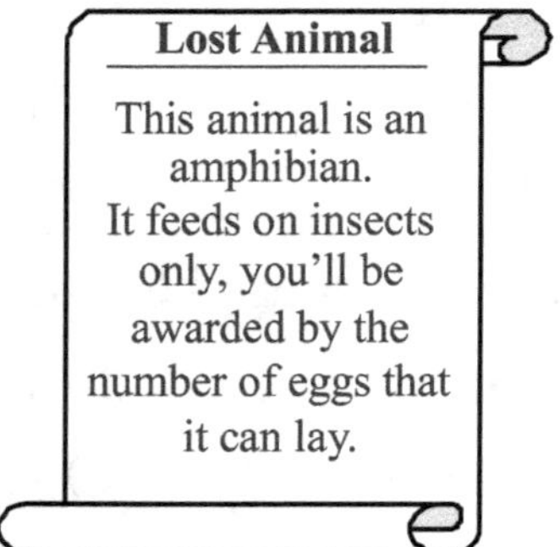

Based on the given information which of the following statements is true about the lost animal?

(a) It is a carnivore.

(b) It gives birth to young ones.

(c) It lives only on land.

(d) It lays one egg at a time.

21. Water boils at _______ and freezes at _______.

(a) 10°C, 100°C (b) 100°C, 0°C

(c) 36.7°C, 0°C (d) 100°C, 26°C

22. Mr. Verma reuses water which was used to wash vegetables, to water his plants. He is practicing _____. of water

(a) pollution

(b) conservation

(c) evaporation

(d) desalination

Space for Rough Work

23. Which part of the given figure, are you supposed to consume?

(a) Root (b) Leaf

(c) Stem (d) Fruit

24. Food with lots of sugar and starch are rich in
(a) fats
(b) proteins
(c) carbohydrates
(d) vitamins

25. Which of the following activities should be done in a house?
(a) We should keep our house clean.
(b) We should sweep the floor of all the rooms.
(c) Floor should be mopped with phenyl everyday.
(d) All of the above.

26. You will find me selling medicines in a medicine shop.
I am a ________.
(a) chemist
(b) doctor
(c) nurse
(d) surgeon

27. In a type of script, rows of raised dots are made on a thick paper, which can be read by running the fingers on them. This type of script is known as ________.
(a) Louis script
(b) Marconi script
(c) Braille script
(d) Wright script

28. Which of the following telephone services can be used within the country?
(a) PCO
(b) STD
(c) ISD
(d) Both (a) & (b)

29. Select the odd one out from the following

(a) (b)

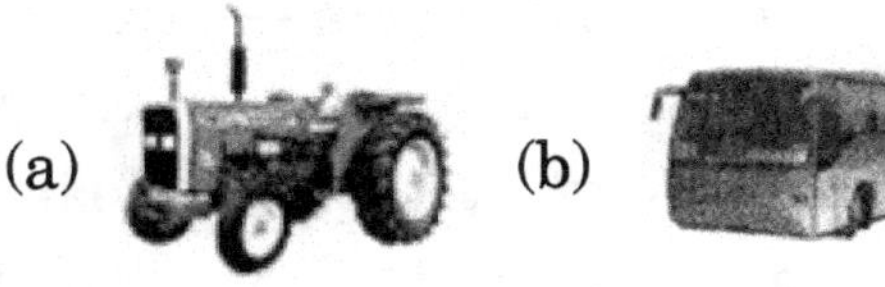

(c)  (d) 

Space for Rough Work

30. Your baby sister is sleeping in your room. You are reading a book at your study table. Your baby sister wakes up and cries. Which of your senses help you to know that your baby sister is crying?
    (a) Sense of touch and sight
    (b) Sense of smell and touch
    (c) Sense of hearing and touch
    (d) Sense of sight and hearing
31. Which of the following is WRONGLY classified?
    (a) Digestive system -- Stomach
    Skeletal system --- Skull
    (b) Digestive system --- Mouth
    Skeletal system ---- Ribcage
    (c) Digestive system --- Large intestine
    Skeletal system ---- Spine
    (d) Digestive system ---- Nostril
    Skeletal system ------Heart
32. Digestion starts here and food begins its journey through the digestive system.Here food is chopped and chewed into smaller pieces. Which part of the digestive system is being described above?
    (a) Teeth
    (b) Intestine
    (c) Stomach
    (d) Mouth
33. Why is the Sun important to the Earth?
    (i) It provides light and energy to green plants to make food.
    (ii) It provides heat to enable living things to survive on the Earth.
    (iii) It rotates around the Earth to give us seasons.
    (a) (i) & (ii)
    (b) (i) & (iii)
    (c) (ii) & (iii)
    (d) (i), (ii) & (iii)
34. You are making a model of the Earth and the Moon to show their relative sizes and massiveness. If you take cricket ball as an Earth, then _________ can be taken as a Moon
    (a) lawn tennis ball
    (b) table tennis ball
    (c) basketball
    (d) volleyball

Space for Rough Work

35. 

The best material to make the ball is

(a) cotton (b) plastic
(c) rubber (d) metal

36. Which of the following is made of one material only?

(a) (A) & (B) (b) (A), (B) & (D)
(c) (B) & (C) (d) (C) & (D)

37. Which of the following revolves around the Sun ?

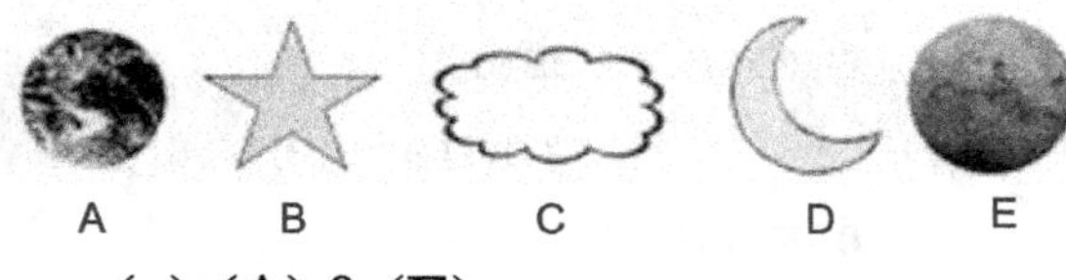

(a) (A) & (E)
(b) (A), (B) & (C)
(c) (A), (B), (D) & (E)
(d) (A), (B), (C) & (E)

38. I revolve around the Sun. I am the first member of the solar system. I am the hottest of all other members. What am I?

(a) Earth (b) Mercury
(c) Mars (d) Jupiter

39. In which of the following situations given below is the sense of smell, taste, touch and sight used at the same time?

(a) A blind person moving around.
(b) A girl using the telephone.
(c) A man doing repair works for his bicycle.
(d) A woman making and baking cookies.

40. Look at the animals below and select one that don't belong to the group.

(a)  (b) 

(c)  (d) 

Space for Rough Work

OLYMPIAD

Mock Test

Name : ________ **Max. Marks : 40**

Number of Questions : 40 **Time : 2 Hours**

There is no negative marking in the test.

1. Which of the following senses work for a tiger in the night?
   (a) Sense of touch
   (b) Sense of smell
   (c) Sense of sight
   (d) All of these

2. Which of the following is NOT correct regarding mushrooms and vultures?

Mushroom

Vulture

   (a) Both of them cannot prepare food on their own.
   (b) Both of them feed on dead matter.
   (c) Both of them are animals.
   (d) Both of them breathe air.

3. Duck, mouse and fish can be grouped together because

   (a) they eat both plants and animals.
   (b) they lay eggs.
   (c) of their similar outer body covering.
   (d) they live in water.

4. Match the following and select the correct answer.

A.	Dogs	i.	Burrows
B.	Fish	ii.	Kennels

Space for Rough Work

C. Hens iii. Aquarium
D. Rabbit iv. Coops
(a) A-ii, B-iii, C-iv, D-i
(b) A-i, B-iii, C-ii, D-iv
(c) A-ii, B-iii, C-i, D-iv
(d) A-i, B-ii, C-iii, D-iv

5. Which system is in charge of the senses?
(a) Skeletal system
(b) Circulatory system
(c) Digestive system
(d) Nervous system

6. Which of the following statements is true?
(a) Birds have teeth.
(b) All birds can fly.
(c) The peacock can fly over long distances.
(d) The duck is an aquatic bird.

7. Which of the following birds uses its beak to climb branches?

(a)  (b) 

(c)  (d) 

8. What did people use to tell time before clocks and watches?
(a) Stars (b) Cell phones
(c) Clouds (d) Shadows

9. Which of the following bird's nest is very attractive?
(a) Woodpecker (b) Patridge
(c) Bulbul (d) Weaver bird

10. The figure given below shows an experiment, where a leaf is covered with a plastic bag. After an hour, it was observed that droplets of water were formed inside the bag. These droplets come out from which of the following parts of the leaf?

(a) Leaf blade (b) Leaf vein
(c) Stomata (d) Leaf stalk

11. Which of the following should come in the empty box given below?
Water from roots → □ → Water in the leaves
(a) Flowers (b) Stem
(c) Fruit (d) Bark

Space for Rough Work

12. Which of the following is used to observe the cells of a leaf?
    (a) Camera
    (b) Magnifying glass
    (c) Telescope
    (d) Microscope
13. When you are eating sugarcane, you are actually eating the _____.
    (a) fruits of sugarcane.
    (b) roots of sugarcane.
    (c) stem of sugarcane.
    (d) grains of sugarcane.
14. In the experiment shown below, water was poured into a container which has some soil. Air bubbles were seen rising. What does this mean?

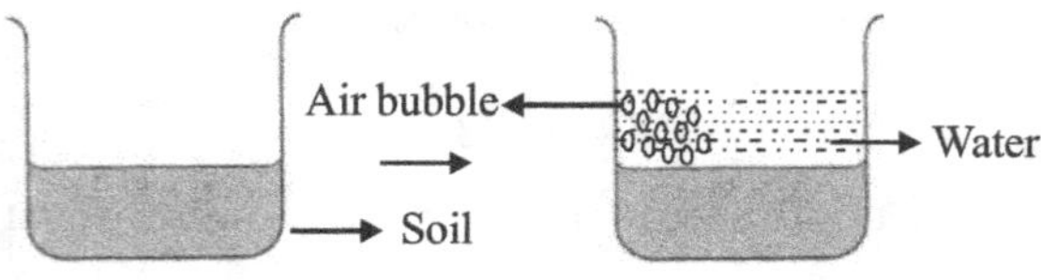

    (a) Soil contains moisture.
    (b) Soil contains water.
    (c) Soil contains air.
    (d) None of these
15. Which soil can hold both water and air in adequate amounts?
    (a) Sandy soil
    (b) Gravel
    (c) Clayey soil
    (d) Loamy soil
16. What provides information to your brain about external conditions?
    (a) Heart
    (b) Blood vessels
    (c) Nerve receptors
    (d) Bones
17. A puddle of water on a marble floor is left untouched for some hours. How will it change?
    (a) It becomes smaller.
    (b) It becomes larger.
    (c) It changes into ice.
    (d) It changes into marble.
18. The days are longer in ________.
    (a) summer season
    (b) rainy season
    (c) winter season
    (d) spring season
19. What small particles make up matter?
    (a) Molecules (b) Atoms
    (c) Gas (d) Elements

Space for Rough Work

20. Which part of the Earth will receive almost the same amount of sunlight throughout the year?
    (a) North Pole
    (b) South Pole
    (c) Equator
    (d) Any part of the Earth
21. Match the following and select the correct answer :

	System	Function
A.	Circulatory system	i. Helps in production of offspring
B.	Skeletal system	ii. Helps the body to move
C.	Reproductive system	iii. Helps in the movement of blood
D.	Respiratory system	iv. Helps in exchange of air

    (a) A-iii, B-iv, C-i, D-ii
    (b) A-iii, B-ii, C-i, D-iv
    (c) A-iv, B-iii, C-ii, D-i
    (d) A-iii, B-i, C-iv, D-ii
22. Which organ of our body belongs to both the respiratory and the excretory system?
    (a) Lungs (b) Skin
    (c) Kidneys (d) Intestine
23. What does the following figure represent?

    (a) Pedestrian crossing
    (b) Place where U-turns can be made
    (c) Speed limit zone
    (d) No speed limit
24. Which of the following kinds of houses is most effective in a place that is very hot and dry?
    (a) A house made of bricks and mortar.
    (b) A house made up of ice.
    (c) A house made up of clay and thatch or coconut branches.
    (d) All of these
25. Pick the odd one out.
    (a) Coal
    (b) Petroleum
    (c) Air
    (d) Natural gas

Space for Rough Work

26. Cotton clothes are preferred during summer because these clothes
    (a) are light.
    (b) do not absorb heat.
    (c) allow the body heat to escape.
    (d) All of these
27. Which of the following statements is NOT true?
    (a) Fire protected early man from wild animals.
    (b) Fire protected early man from cold.
    (c) Fire helped the early man to eat roasted food.
    (d) Early man produced fire with the help of a match box.
28. Which of these catch fire quickly?
    (a) Stone (b) Sand
    (c) Wood (d) Iron
29. ______________ is very useful in communication for the people working in police and army.
    (a) Newspaper
    (b) Wireless communication
    (c) Television
    (d) Telegram
30. The diagrams show a plant in a cup on a Sunday and again next Tuesday. In the beginning, the cup was filled to the top with water. By Tuesday, the level of the water has decreased. What is the reason?

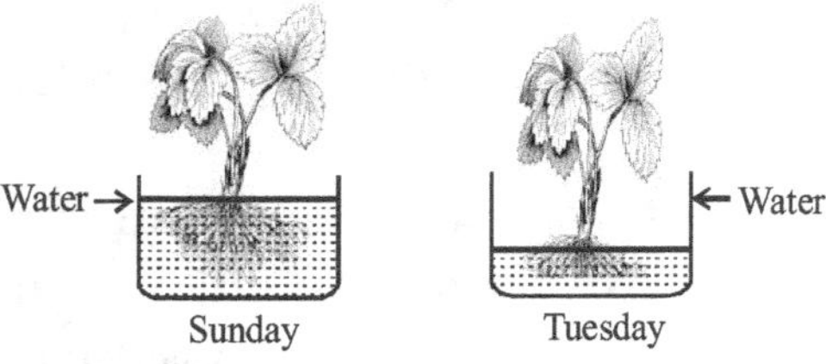

    (a) Water in the cup has frozen.
    (b) Water in the cup has condensed.
    (c) Water has been absorbed by the roots.
    (d) Water has disappeared from the cup.
31. Which of the following diagrams does NOT represent the growth of an organism?

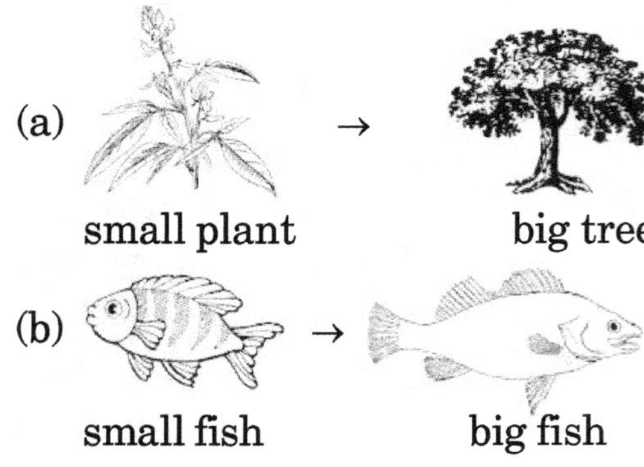

Space for Rough Work

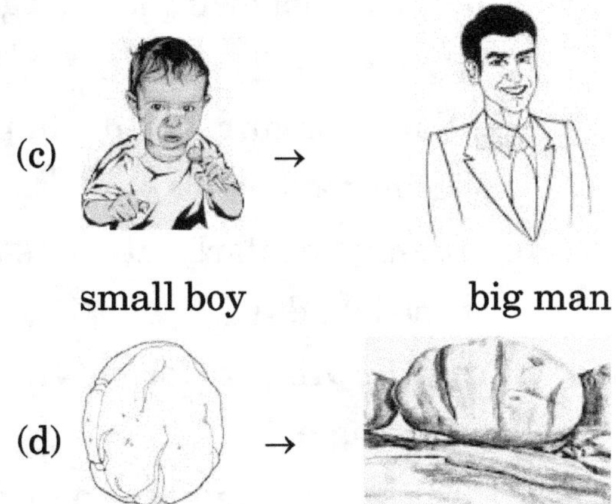

32. Which of the following plant has the sense of touch?
    (a) Touch-me-not
    (b) Sunflower
    (c) Carrot
    (d) Jasmine
33. Some animals first swallow the food without chewing it. After sometime, when they relax they bring this food back into their mouth from stomach. Then they chew it well very slowly. Such animals are called ________.
    (a) gnawing animals
    (b) cud-chewing animals
    (c) blood sucking animals
    (d) flesh eating animals
34. Snake is a.
    (a) parasite (b) producer
    (c) herbivore (d) carnivore
35. Which of the following parts of a bird is most important to help the bird fly in the air?
    (a) Down feathers
    (b) Flight feathers
    (c) Beak and legs
    (d) Colour of the bird
36. Veins
    (a) absorb water and minerals from the soil.
    (b) absorb carbon dioxide from the atmosphere.
    (c) transport water, food and minerals in a leaf.
    (d) release oxygen and carbon dioxide into the atmosphere.

Space for Rough Work

37. Which of the following present in the soil is most helpful for the growth of plants?
(a) Humus
(b) Sand
(c) Clay
(d) Small porous rocks

38. Which of the following shows the correct arrangement of layers of the soil?

(a)

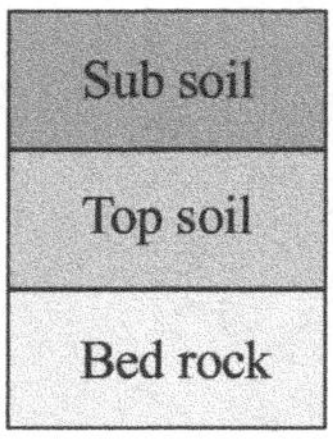

Sub soil
Top soil
Bed rock

(b)

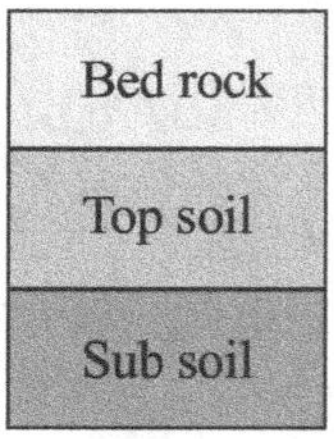

Bed rock
Top soil
Sub soil

(c)

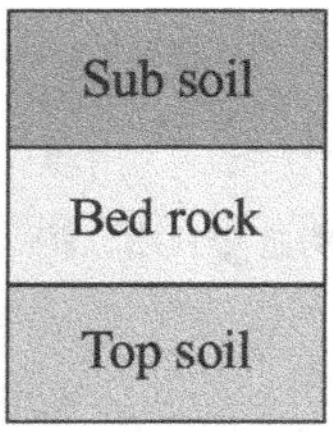

Sub soil
Bed rock
Top soil

(d)

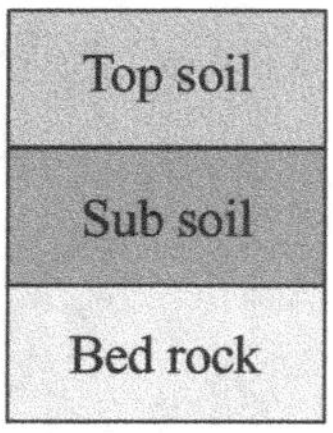

Top soil
Sub soil
Bed rock

39. Which of the following is not a good habit?
(a) Washing our hands before eating food.
(b) Eating regularly at the same time in a day.
(c) Swallowing the food without chewing it.
(d) Eating fresh and warm food.

40. Study the flow chart given below :

Plants $\rightarrow$ X $\rightarrow$ Lion

The arrow sign means "is eaten by". Which of the following animals can X be?
(a) Snake
(b) Eagle
(c) Goat
(d) Frog

Space for Rough Work

GENERAL KNOWLEDGE MOCK TEST 1–5

OLYMPIAD

Mock Test

Name : ________

Number of Questions : 25

Max. Marks : 25

Time : 1 Hour

There is no negative marking in the test.

1. I am a scientist and study universe and the objects within it. Who am I?
   (a) Astronomer
   (b) Chemist
   (c) Ophthalmologist
   (d) Biologist

2. One who specializes in the treatment of diseases of the skin is called __________ .
   (a) dermatologist
   (b) cardiologist
   (c) neurologist
   (d) pathologist

3. Why do animals cannot produce their own food?
   (a) Because they do not have chlorophyll.
   (b) Because they do not have haemoglobin.
   (c) Because they do not have roots.
   (d) Because they do not receive sunlight.

4. Who celebrate the festival Hanukkah, also known as the Festival of Lights?
   (a) Christians (b) Muslims
   (c) Jews (d) Parsis

Space for Rough Work

5. I am a flightless bird native to New Zealand, having the size of a domestic chicken. I lay the largest egg related to my body size. I have a strong, musty smell and predators can smell me from far away. Who am I?

(a) Penguin (b) Ostrich

(c) Kiwi (d) Duck

6. This bird can be easily recognized by its white head, brown body, and hooked yellow beak. It has been the national emblem of the United States of America since 1782. It is living near a source of water and eats fish, ducks, snakes and turtles. Identify the bird.

(a) Bald Eagle

(b) Vulture

(c) Sea Eagle

(d) Golden Eagle

7. This plant needs the support of another plant or sticks to stand. This is also called a climber and is known by a special name in Nepal, India and Bangladesh. Which plant is this?

(a) Mint

(b) Pea

(c) Money Plant

(d) Tulsi

8. 'World Literacy Day' is on

(a) 8th August

(b) 18th August

(c) 8th September

(d) 18th September

Space for Rough Work

9. Which one of the following is an insectivorous plant?

   (a) Tomato

   (b) Rose

   (c) Pitcher Plant

   (d) Tulip

10. Which of the following is correctly matched?

    (a) Crocodile—Herbivore

    (b) Deer—Omnivore

    (c) Mango—Herb

    (d) Blood—Hemoglobin

11. The photograph of which of the following persons is shown on a hundred dollar note of the United States?

    (a) Benjamin Franklin

    (b) Abraham Lincoln

    (c) Andrew Jackson

    (d) George Washington

12. The Olympic games were held in ancient Greece in the honour of which Greek God?

    (a) Apollo (b) Zeus

    (c) Jupiter (d) Uranus.

13. This is the residence of the first citizen of India. It has 340 rooms and is known for having huge gardens called Mughal Gardens. Identify the building.

    (a) Sansad Bhavan, New Delhi

    (b) Rashtrapati Bhavan, New Delhi

    (c) Red Fort, Delhi

    (d) Supreme Court, New Delhi

Space for Rough Work

14. Renewable energy uses energy sources that are not used up. Non-renewable energy uses energy resources that are lost forever after use. Overuse of non-renewable energy resources will cause energy crisis for us. Which of the following is a renewable energy source?
    (a) Coal
    (b) Sun
    (c) Petrol
    (d) Natural Gas

15. We feel air pressure when wind blows. We can measure atmospheric pressure with a__________.
    (a) thermometer
    (b) anemometer
    (c) barometer
    (d) calorimeter

16. In which field Shri Karimul Hak given Padam Shri 2017 award?
    (a) Public Affair
    (b) Social Work
    (c) Medicine
    (d) Arts

17. United Nations World Youth Skills Day is observed on which of the following dates?
    (a) 15th July (b) 16th July
    (c) 17th July (d) 18th July

18. Makdee is an Indian comedy horror. The film tells the story of a young girl from north India and a witch living in a mansion. It also explains the belief in witches and witchcraft in India. Who played the role of 'Makdee' in the film?
    (a) Shabana Azmi
    (b) Shweta Prasad
    (c) Makrand Deshpande
    (d) Vineet Kumar

19. He is a Hollywood actor who was featured in the hit film 'Titanic'. His other films include 'The Aviator' and 'The Revenant'. He received the Best Actor award at the 2016 Oscars. Who is he?

Space for Rough Work

(a)  (b) 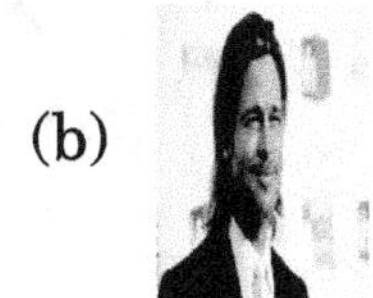

(c)  (d) 

20. Signs are often used at common public places. What does this sign mean?

(a) Do not smoke
(b) Do not litter
(c) Do not eat
(d) Do not sing

21. Which of the modes of the transportation uses compass?

(a) Air
(b) Water
(c) Land
(d) Both (a) and (b)

22. Which of the following statements is true about cricket player Sachin Tendulkar?

(a) He is the second highest run scorer in one day international cricket.
(b) His full name is Sachin Pawar Tendulkar.
(c) Sachin is the first Indian cricketer to have a waxwork at Madame Tussaud's wax museum.
(d) Ramakant Sahai coached Sachin at Shivaji Park in Dadar, Mumbai.

23. Which Indian personality has been crowned the Miss Asia (Deaf) 2018 ?

(a) Deshna Jain
(b) Pratista Sharma
(c) Sonali Bhargav
(d) Chandra Prabha Kumari

Space for Rough Work

24. The Official mascot of FIFA World Cup 2018?
    (a) Zabivaka
    (b) Ishikova
    (c) Mituako
    (d) Xiamio

25. Which company has become the official sponsor of the FIFA World Cup 2018 and 2022?
    (a) 

    (b) 

    (c) 

    (d) 

Space for Rough Work

OLYMPIAD

Mock Test

Name : __________

Number of Questions : 25

Max. Marks : 25

Time : 1 Hour

There is no negative marking in the test.

1. Select the odd one out in this group.

   Heart, Lungs, Kidneys, Stomata

   (a) Heart

   (b) Kidneys

   (c) Lungs

   (d) Stomata

2. Which of the following planets of our solar System does not have a natural satellite?

   (a) Venus (b) Jupiter

   (c) Uranus (d) Mars

3. First nuclear plant in India was

   (a) Tarapur, Maharashtra

   (b) Narora, Uttar Pradesh

   (c) Kaiga, Karnataka

   (d) Rawabhata, Rajasthan

4. Which of the following is a good source of protein?

   (a) Apple

   (b) Fish

   (c) Noodle

   (d) Mushroom

5. Heart is an important organ found in most of the animals. Which of the following functions is carried out by the heart?

Space for Rough Work

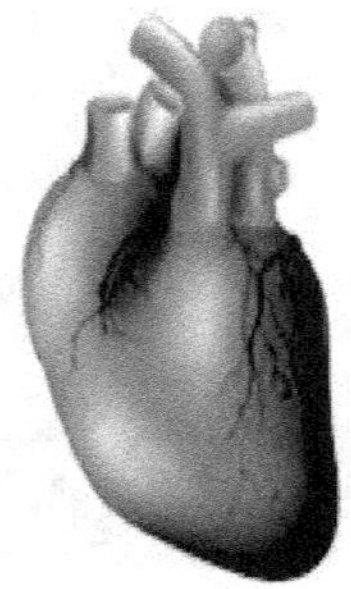

(a) Helps in the circulation of blood.

(b) Helps in the formation of urine.

(c) Helps in the digestion of food.

(d) Helps in animal reproduction.

6. This is a kind of herb the leaves of which droop once touched by hand but reopens after sometime. Which plant is this?

(a) Pitcher plant

(b) Rose

(c) Touch-me-not

(d) Wheat

7. I am a flying animal and come out of my house only at night for hunting. I produce sound to locate insects I eat. Who am I?

(a) Eagle

(b) Owl

(c) Flying snake

(d) Bat

Space for Rough Work

8. Which of the following is correctly matched?
   (a) Neem—Herbs
   (b) Elephant—Omnivores
   (c) Mangroves—Costal area
   (d) Dinsaurs—Birds

9. Which of the following is not true about elephant bird?

   (a) It is a flightless bird.
   (b) It lives on the island of Madagascar.
   (c) Its closest living relatives are ostrich.
   (d) None of these

10. Which of the following is not utilized by plants?
   (a) Water
   (b) Oxygen
   (c) Carbon dioxide
   (d) None of these

11. Who appoints the chief of Army, Navy, and Air Force?
   (a) Prime Minister
   (b) Defense Minister
   (c) Foreign Minister
   (d) President

12. This dance form from Tamil Nadu expresses Hindu religious themes and spiritual ideas. It is the oldest classical dance tradition of India. Which dance form is it?

Space for Rough Work

(a) Bharatanatyam
(b) Kuchipudi
(c) Kathak
(d) Odissi

13. Sun is a _________.

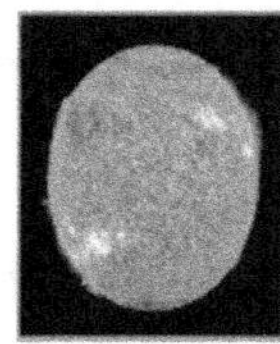

(a) star
(b) planet
(c) galaxy
(d) solar system

14. What is the Great Red Spot on Jupiter?

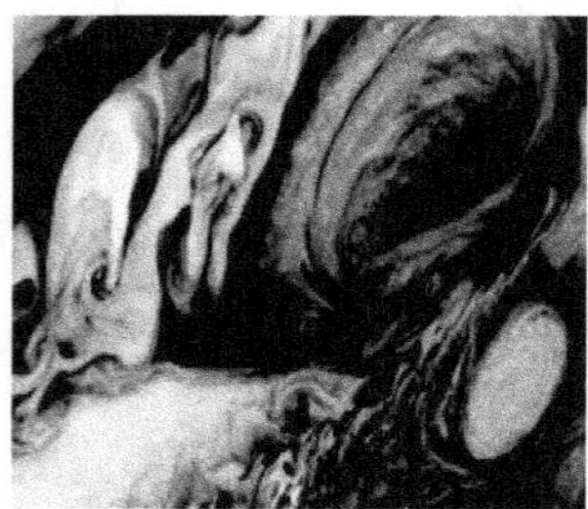

(a) Lake
(b) Massive storm
(c) Craters
(d) Volcanoes

15. The honey you eat is
(a) flower nectar
(b) syrup produced by bees
(c) fruit juice
(d) dissolved sugar

16. The place where earthquake originates is called _________.
(a) focus (b) centre
(c) epicentre (d) epix

17. The Gandhi Sagar Dam is built on which river in Madhya Pradesh?
(a) Narmada (b) Chambal
(c) Son (d) Tapti

18. 'Koi... Mil Gaya', an Indian film shows an alien who gets separated from his friends while they landed on the earth from the other planet. What is the name of the alien in the film?

Space for Rough Work

(a) Xian (b) Jaadoo

(c) Miracle (d) Tom

19. Volleyball is the national game of which country?

(a) France (b) Nepal

(c) India (d) China

20. Who among the following was the first test captain of India?
    (a) Kapil Dev
    (b) Vinod Mankand
    (c) Bishen Singh Bedi
    (d) C.K. Nayudu
21. Who among the following was first to receive Rajiv Gandhi Khel Ratna?
    (a) Viswanathan Anand
    (b) Geet Sethi
    (c) Karnam Malleswari
    (d) Nameirakpam Kunjarani
22. Which country's President has been invited as chief guest in the 2019 Republic Day of India?
    (a) Japan (b) United States
    (c) Maldivies (d) Portugal
23. Who won the Nobel Prize in Literature in 2016?
    (a) Bob Dylan
    (b) Svetlana Alexievich
    (c) Patrick Modiano
    (d) Alice Munro

Space for Rough Work

24. Which Indian wrestler clinched gold in 74 kg freestyle category in junior Asian wrestling Championships 2018?
    (a) Deepak Punia
    (b) Mohit Sharma
    (c) Suraj Rajkumar Kokate
    (d) Sachin Rathi

25. Which Indian state was the first to launch cyber police stations in each district in November 2016?
    (a) Maharashtra
    (b) Uttar Pradesh
    (c) Manipur
    (d) Rajasthan

Space for Rough Work

OLYMPIAD

Mock Test

Name : __________ **Max. Marks : 25**

Number of Questions : 25 **Time : 1 Hour**

There is no negative marking in the test.

1. The branch of medicine that deals with medical care of children is called
   (a) pediatrics
   (b) psychiatry
   (c) geriatrics
   (d) ophthalmology

2. These are cells of nervous system which are specialized in sending and receiving brain information. These cells have branch-like structure differentiated into a tail and a tail. What are these cells called?

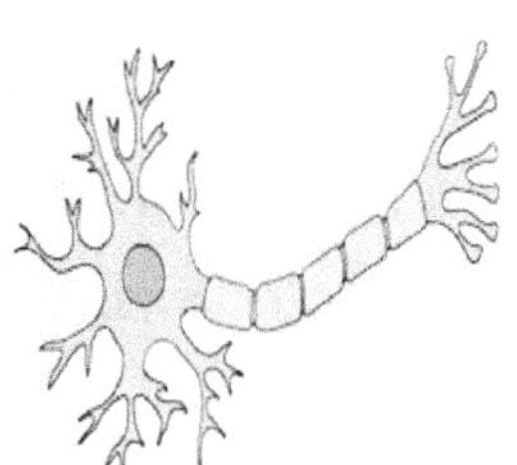

   (a) Dendron (b) Neuron
   (c) Leukocyte (d) Basophils

3. Which one of the following correctly describes AGNI?
   (a) A long range gun
   (b) A long range missile
   (c) A fighter plane
   (d) A versatile tank

Space for Rough Work

4. Tear is a clear liquid which keeps your eyes moist and protect them from infection. Where are tear-producing glands located?

(a) Skin (b) Eyes
(c) Neck (d) Bone

5. Which of the following is correctly matched?
(a) Bat—Diurnal
(b) Cassowary—Flightless
(c) Crocodile—Gills
(d) Sharks—Herbivore

6. Which of the following is a communicable disease?
(a) Diabities
(b) Diptheria
(c) Hypertension
(d) None of these

7. Banyans are considered sacred trees in India. You might have often seen a banyan tree with hanging thread-like structures. Can you guess what these hanging structures are?

(a) Roots
(b) Stems
(c) Modified leaves
(d) Bark

8. We are always told to plant trees and avoid cutting them. Have you ever thought what will happen if all the trees on the Earth are cut?

Space for Rough Work

(a) We will die due to lack of food and oxygen.

(b) There will be no rainfall.

(c) We will experience climate change.

(d) All of these

9. He invented dynamite. He did not want to be remembered as a propagator of violence after his death. He donated his entire wealth to the institute of Nobel Prize. Who was he?

(a) Albert Einstein

(b) George Washington

(c) Alfred Nobel

(d) Alexandar Graham Bell

10. Which of the following gives red colour to blood?

(a) Haemoglobin

(b) Chlorophyll

(c) Vitamin

(d) Protein

11. This is one of the famous towers in the world and a major tourist attraction. It is located in Paris, France and has been named after an engineer whose company designed and built the tower. What is the name of the tower?

(a) Notre Dam

(b) Eiffel Tower

(c) Canton Tower

(d) Macau Tower

Space for Rough Work

12. The Red Fort is a historical fort in the city of Delhi in India. It was the main residence of the emperors of the Mughal dynasty until 1857. Which architect designed the map of the Red Fort?

(a) Ashna Chauhan
(b) Raj Rewal
(c) Prem Nath
(d) Charles Correa

13. What is the correct alignment during a solar eclipse?

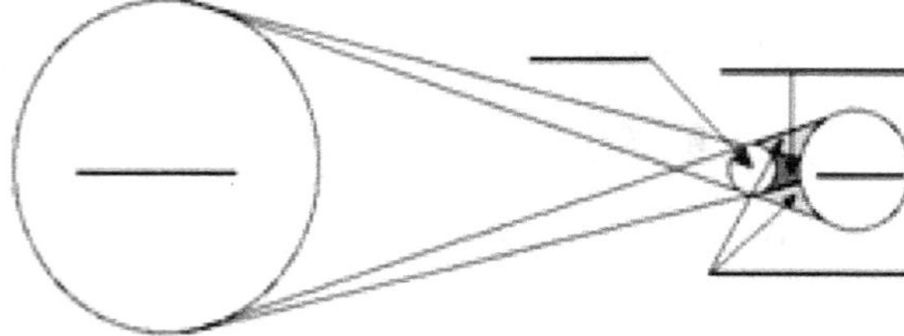

(a) Sun, Moon, Earth
(b) Sun, Earth, Moon
(c) Moon, Sun, Earth
(d) Earth, Sun, Moon

14. He was an Indian physicist born in Tamil Nadu, who is known for his work in the field of light scattering. He received the Nobel Prize for Physics in 1930. In 1954, he was honored with highest civilian award Bharat Ratna. Who is he?

(a) Homi J. Bhabha
(b) C.V. Raman
(c) Vikram Sarabhai
(d) Meghnad Saha

Space for Rough Work

15. The study of animals is called

(a) astronomy (b) botany

(c) zoology (d) physics

16. 'Mahabharata' is one of the two major Sanskrit epics of ancient India. In 'Mahabharata', who is the father of Abhimanyu?

(a) Duryodhan (b) Arjun

(c) Yudhisthir (d) Bhim

17. Where was the 12th International film festival on Art and Artist 2018 organised?

(a) Odisha (b) Karnataka

(c) Tamil Nadu (d) Kerala

18. What is the capital of Thailand?

(a) Yangon

(b) Bangkok

(c) Kaula Lumpur

(d) Naypyidaw

19. Which film won the best film award at the 63rd Jio Filmfare Award 2018?

(a) Tumhari Sulu

(b) Hindi Medium

(c) Newton

(d) Dangal

20. She is an Indian female boxer from Manipur. She is a five-time World Amateur Boxing champion, and the only woman boxer to have won a medal in each one of the six world championships. She is the only Indian woman boxer to have qualified for the 2012 Summer Olympics. Who is she?

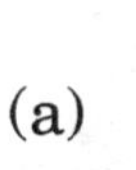
(a) 

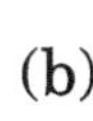
(b) 

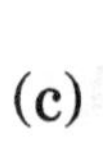
(c) 

(d) 

Space for Rough Work

21. Who is the current President of Nepal?
    (a) Bidhya Devi Bhabdari
    (b) Dr. Ram Baran Yadav
    (c) Girija Prasad Koirala
    (d) Nanda Kishor Pun

22. On which day is the Army Day celebrated?
    (a) 22nd January
    (b) 15nd January
    (c) 15nd February
    (d) 22nd December

23. Which one of the following cities will host the 2018 Asian Games?
    (a) Colombo (b) Beijing
    (c) Jakarta (d) Bangkok

24. Who among the following has/have won the Bharat Ratna award?
    (a) Madan Mohan Malaviya
    (b) Atal Bihari Vajpayee
    (c) A.P.J. Abdul Kalam
    (d) All the above

25. Which of the following banks is not owned by the government of India?

(a) 

(b) 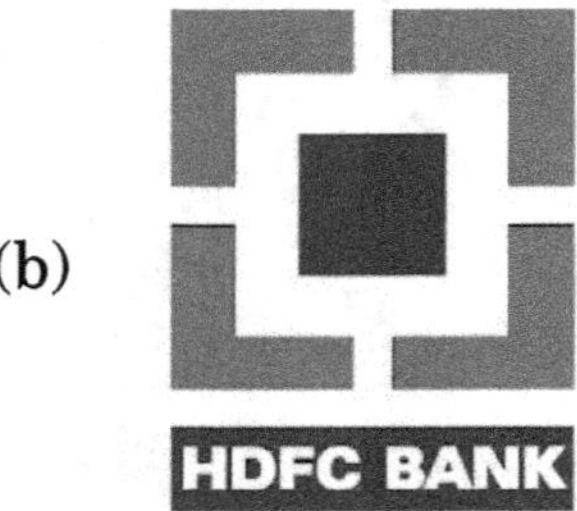

(c) 

(d) 

Space for Rough Work

OLYMPIAD

Mock Test 4

Name : ________ **Max. Marks : 40**

Number of Questions : 40 **Time : 2 Hours**

There is no negative marking in the test.

1. Omnivores are animals that eat both plants and animals. Which of these animals is an omnivore?

   (a) Deer (b) Cow

   (c) Lion (d) Bear

2. Which of the following is correctly matched?

   (a) Canines—Food biting

   (b) Stomata—Plant Breathing

   (c) Ophthalmologist—Checking teeth

   (d) Milk—Carbohydrate

3. Which of the following organs produces urine?

   (a) 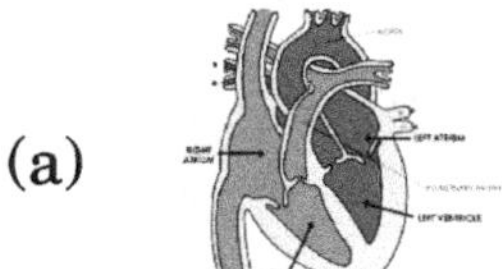

   (b) 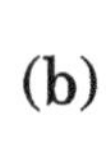 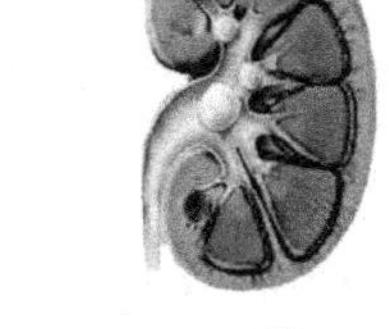

   (c) 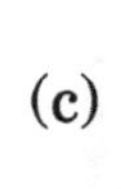 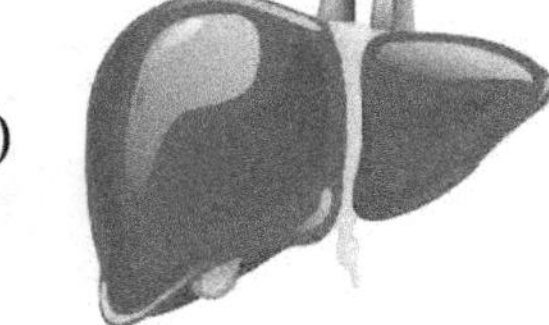

   (d)  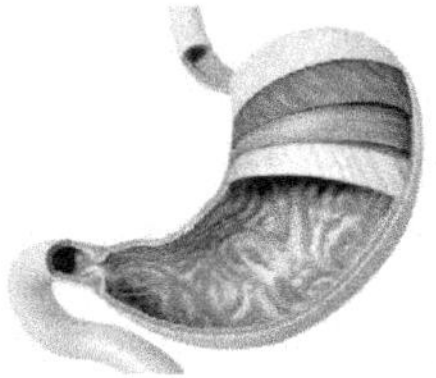

Space for Rough Work

4. In April 2015, several people were killed and many buildings were destroyed due to earthquake in Nepal. Which district of Nepal was the epicenter of the earthquake?
   (a) Gorkha
   (b) Dolpa
   (c) Humla
   (d) Surkhet

5. Which of these organs can be transported from a healthy person to a patient?
   (a) Kidney (b) Heart
   (c) Liver (d) All of these

6. Which of the following statements is true?
   (a) Fried foods are good for health because they kill all the germs.
   (b) Butter is a milk product.
   (c) Food can be stored by freezing them.
   (d) Both B and C

7. Which of the following statements is correct about aardvark?

   (a) An aunt-eater
   (b) A South American wild pig
   (c) A creature that eats termites
   (d) A small horse with a long tail

8. What do ostriches, rheas and emus have in common?
   (a) They are birds.
   (b) They lay eggs.
   (c) They cannot fly.
   (d) All of these

9. What part of a plant is used to absorb water and minerals from outside?

Space for Rough Work

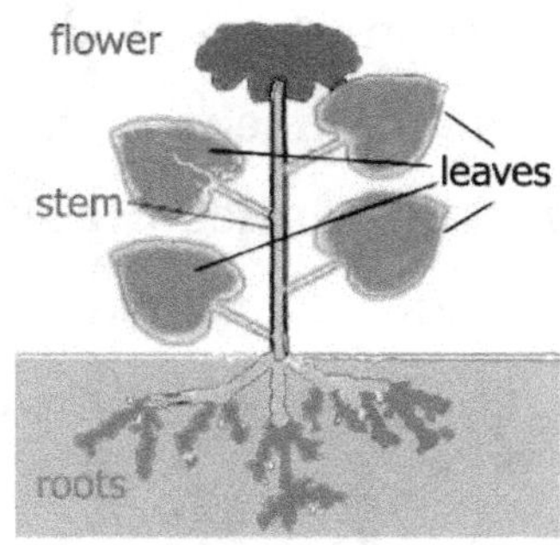

(a) Stem (b) Root

(c) Leaf (d) Flower

10. We can find them growing on ground in deserts, on sides of dry rock, hanging from branches of trees. It is

(a) crabq (b) amoeba

(c) lichens (d) snail

11. Microwave oven was invented by

(a) Percy Spencer

(b) Victor Vacquier

(c) George Inman

(d) Raytheon

12. I am the largest animal in the world, and I weigh more than thirty elephants. I live in the oceans and I love sea food. One of my friends, Willy, acted in an English film recently. Who am I?

(a) Blue Whale

(b) Shark

(c) Dolphin

(d) Crocodile

13. I have a round body which is covered with a number of thorn-like things called spines. When I want to protect myself I roll up into a tight ball. Anyone who touches me gets hurt and feels sorry for her or him. What is my name?

(a) Porcupine (b) Squirrel
(c) Hedgehog (d) Lizard

14. This statue is an under construction monument dedicated to Indian independence movement leader Vallabhbhai Patel. It is located in

Space for Rough Work

the Indian state of Gujarat. What this statue is called?

(a) Statue of Unity
(b) Statue of Liberty
(c) Statue of Wisdom
(d) Statue of Freedom

15. Which of the following is not a neighbouring county of India?

(a) Bhutan (b) Sri Lanka
(c) Maldives (d) Singapore

16. He was an American politician and lawyer who served as the 16th President of the United States from March 1861 to April 1865. He became more famous for leading the United States during the American Civil War?

(a) George Washington
(b) Abraham Lincoln
(c) Franklin Roosevelt
(d) Benjamin Franklin

17. The Mona Lisa is a half-length portrait painting which has been described as the best work of art in the world. It holds the Guinness World Record for the highest known insurance valuation in history. Who is the painter of Mona Lisa?

Space for Rough Work

(a) Pablo Picasso

(b) Claude Monte

(c) Marc Chagall

(d) Leonardo Vinci

18. Which Indian music composer has won two Oscar awards for his first western music score and has received Padma Shree as well as two Grammy awards?

(a) 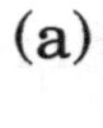

(b) 

(c) 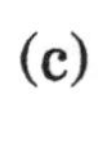

(d) 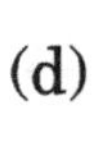

19. Which continent has the largest desert?

(a) Africa

(b) Antarctica

(c) South America

(d) Asia

Space for Rough Work

20. Carrot is a good source of ______.

(a) vitamin
(b) protein
(c) fat
(d) carbohydrate

21. Distances in space are measured in light-years. What is a light-year?

(a) A light-year is a year that has more sunlight due to good weather.
(b) A light-year is the distance light can travel through space in a year.
(c) A light-year is the distance from the earth to the moon.
(d) A light-year is the distance from the sun to the earth.

22. What is a satellite?

(a) An object that revolves around the Sun.
(b) Any piece of equipment that has fallen back to Earth from space.
(c) A special kind of light that is emitted by the Sun.
(d) Anything that orbits around a bigger object.

23. Who was the Indian-American biochemist who shared the 1968 Nobel Prize for Physiology or Medicine with Marshall

Space for Rough Work

W. Nirenberg and Robert W. Holley in the field of genetics?

(a) Har Gobind Khorana

(b) Birbal Sahni

(c) Vikram Sarabhai

(d) Meghnad Saha

24. Which of the following gases is filled in balloon to make it fly in the sky?

(a) Nitrogen (b) Hydrogen

(c) Oxygen (d) Carbon dioxide

25. The world's second highest peak is

(a) Mt. Everest

(b) K2

(c) Mt. Annapurna

(d) Mt. Kanchanjunga

26. Swami Vivekananda attended the Parliament of World Religious in 1893- 94 at

(a) New York

(b) London

(c) Tokyo

(d) Chicago

27. Give one word for the following.

The study of diagnosis, treatment, and prevention of disease is

(a) medicology

(b) medicine

(c) medical care

(d) none of the above

28. Who was the brand ambassador of 2018 ODI Blind Cricket World Cup?

(a) Virender Sehwag

(b) Sachin Tendulkar

(c) Sahid Afridi

(d) Anil Kumble

Space for Rough Work

29. Which dog is Mickey Mouse's dog?

(a) Pluto (b) Motimer
(c) Odie (d) Scooby Doo

30. 'Peter Pan' is an American-British-Australian fantasy adventure film. In the film, who is Captain Hook's pirate-buddy?

(a) Big Chief (b) Smee
(c) Peter (d) Tink

31. Ram's school is on the other side of a road. One day, as he was about to cross the road, the traffic signal turns green. What should he do?

(a) He should cross the road, when no vehicle is nearby.
(b) He should wait until the traffic light turns red.
(c) He should stop the running vehicles, and cross the road.
(d) None of the above

32. Which of the following vehicles does not have visual warning lights?

(a) Ambulance (b) Fire brigade
(c) Police van (d) School bus

33. What type of race is the Tour de France?

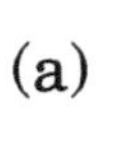  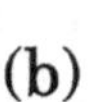 

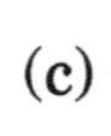   

Space for Rough Work

34. This yoga posture has been named after the shape it takes. It involves lying on one's back with the feet together and arms beside the body. Which yoga asana has been described here?

(a) Naukasana
(b) Uttanasana
(c) Dhanurasana
(d) Kapalbharti

35. 'Me-Dam-Me-Phi' festival is a festival of which the communities in North Eastern India?

(a) Tai-Ahom
(b) Deori Tribe
(c) Garo
(d) Khasi

36. The 2018 Nelson Mandela International Day (NMID) is observed on which date?

(a) 17th July (b) 19th July
(c) 18th July (d) 16th July

37. Which day is observed as World Malaria Day?

(a) 25th April
(b) 25th May
(c) 24th June
(d) 2nd December

38. Which of the following became India's first World Heritage City?

(a) Ahmedabad
(b) Vadodra
(c) Thiruvananthapuram
(d) Hyderabad

39. Gopal Das Neeraj, who passed away recently, was associated with which field?

(a) Journalism (b) Cartoon
(c) Poetry (d) Sports

Space for Rough Work

40. The water park 'Worlds of the Wonder' is located at

(a) Gurugram
(b) Noida
(c) Delhi
(d) Faridabad

Space for Rough Work

OLYMPIAD

Mock Test

Name : ________

Number of Questions : 40

Max. Marks : 40

Time : 2 Hours

There is no negative marking in the test.

1. Which of the following animals is associated with the Easter?
   - (a) Rabbits
   - (b) Lambs
   - (c) Sheep
   - (d) Both A and B

2. The deficiency of which of the following causes goiter disease?

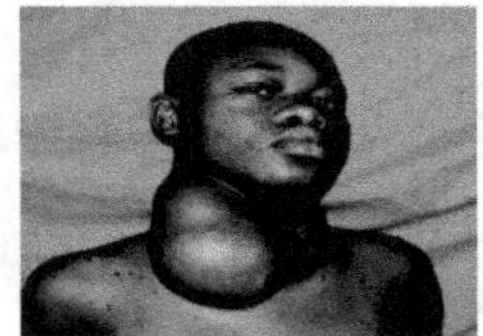

   - (a) Iodine
   - (b) Sodium
   - (c) Vitamin
   - (d) Carbohydrate

3. Besides brain, which of the following organs helps in maintaining body balance?
   - (a) 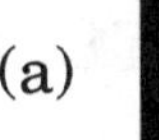 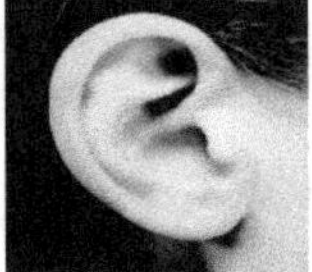
   - (b) 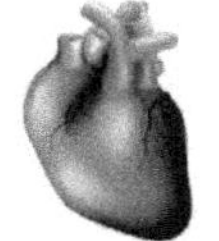
   - (c) 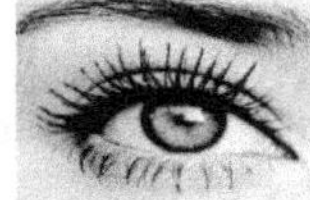
   - (d) 

Space for Rough Work

4. One of the chief characteristics of this group of animals is that they have three pairs of legs. They also have wings. Which group of animals are we talking about?
   (a) Amphibians
   (b) Birds
   (c) Insects
   (d) Reptiles

5. Rahul is having irritation in his eyes. Which of the following persons he should consult to?
   (a) Cardiologist
   (b) Ophthalmologist
   (c) Dentist
   (d) Zoologist

6. What is a clone?
   (a) An alien from outer space.
   (b) An exact copy with all the same genes.
   (c) Something that you eat with ice cream.
   (d) Something that looks similar from outside but has different genes.

7. Which of the following is an endangered plant species?
   (a) Baobab
   (b) Mango
   (c) Neem
   (d) Pine

8. The bottom of the ocean is totally dark and very cold. Are there any animals that can survive there?

   (a) No animals would want to be there. There's nothing to do!
   (b) No. Animals need light to survive.
   (c) Only a few old penguins.
   (d) Yes, lots of animals can survive there.

9. Plants can be used as herbal medicines. Which part of plants can be used as herbal medicine?

Space for Rough Work

(a) Root (b) Leaves

(c) Stem (d) All of these

10. Which of the following is correctly matched?

(a) Dodo—Flying bird

(b) Whale—Egg laying

(c) Dolly—Cloned sheep

(d) Rat— Camouflage

11. Which of the following is not grown on the slope of hills?

(a) Tea

(b) Cocoa

(c) Rice

(d) None of these

12. Which of the followers blooms only at night?

(a) Moon flowers

(b) Lily

(c) Rose

(d) Tulip

13. What is a baby bear called?

(a) Calf (b) Cub

(c) Pup (d) Fawn

14. This is the statue of Jesus Christ in Rio de Janeiro, Brazil. The statue is 30 meters tall and 28 meters wide, and is listed as one of the New Seven Wonders of the World. Name the statue.

(a) Statue of Liberty

(b) Christ the Redeemer

(c) Statue of Unity

(d) Statue of Freedom

15. What is the world's largest man-made lake?

Space for Rough Work

(a) Lake Kariba
(b) Caspian Sea
(c) Lake Superior
(d) Lake Michigan

16. What is the currency of Belgium?
(a) Krone (b) Dollar
(c) Euro (d) Pound

17. Who gave Gandhi the title of 'Mahatma'?

(a) Pandit Jawaharlal Nehru
(b) Rabindranath Tagore
(c) Sardar Vallabhbhai Patel
(d) Maulana Azad

18. What is the Parsi New Year known as?
(a) Hina Matsuri
(b) Passover
(c) Navroz
(d) Rosh Hashana

19. Which was the first superfast train in India?
(a) Rajdhani Express
(b) Shatabdi Express
(c) Duronto Express
(d) Sampark Kranti Express

20. He is a former American NASA astronaut who made history by becoming the second man to walk on the moon during the Apollo 11 lunar landing mission in 1969. He began his career as a fighter pilot for the United States Air Force. Who is he?

(a) Roger Chaffee
(b) Buzz Aldrin

Space for Rough Work

(c) James Lowell
(d) Neil Armstrong

21. What happens when the temperature of water reaches zero degree Celsius?

(a) It evaporates.
(b) It boils.
(c) It turns into ice.
(d) None of these

22. Which of the following substance is made up of carbon?

(a) Diamond (b) Lead pencil
(c) Coal (d) All of these

23. What causes day and night?

(a) Revolution of the Earth around the Sun.
(b) Rotation of the Earth around its axis.
(c) Revolution of the Sun around the Earth.
(d) Rotation of the Moon around the Sun.

24. Which of the following is true?

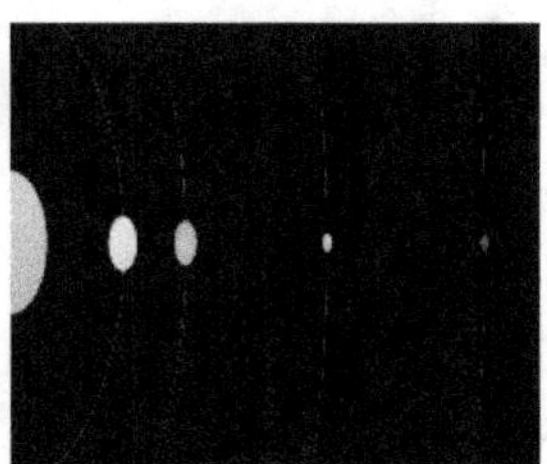

(a) Neptune is the farthest planet from the Sun.
(b) The third largest planet is Saturn
(c) Both A and B
(d) None of these

25. Which of the following devices is used to hear your heartbeat?

(a) Stethoscope
(b) Sphygmomanometer
(c) Sonometer
(d) Magnetic resonance imaging

Space for Rough Work

26. Which of the following singers is called 'Nightingale of India'?

(a) 

(b) 

(c) 

(d) 

27. 'The Angry Birds Movie' is a 3D computer-animated comedy film, which is about flightless birds living on Bird Island. In the film, what is the name of the bird, which is sent for an anger management class?

(a) Red (b) Chuck

(c) Bomb (d) Matilda

28. This is a watercraft which can operate underwater. Militaries and scientists use this type of vessels to travel deep under the ocean. What are these vessels called?

(a) Catapult (b) Sled

(c) Boat (d) Submarine

29. With a length over 1 km, which platform in India holds the record for being the world's longest

Space for Rough Work

railway platform?

(a) Howrah
(b) Mughalsarai
(c) Delhi
(d) Kharagpur

30. Which of the following stadiums was used for the opening ceremony of the 2010 Commonwealth Games?
(a) Jawaharlal Nehru Stadium
(b) Indira Gandhi Sports Complex
(c) Talkatora Indoor Stadium
(d) Tyagaraj Sports Complex

31. In the given picture, what is the cricket umpire signaling?

(a) Not out (b) No ball
(c) Wide ball (d) Leg bye

32. Archery is the national sport of which country?

(a) Japan
(b) India
(c) Bhutan
(d) Afghanistan

33. Who among these is the writer of the famous children's book 'Green Egg and Ham'?
(a) Eric Carle
(b) Dr Seuss
(c) Nina Laden
(d) Dorothy Kunhardt

34. What does this traffic sign mean?

Space for Rough Work

(a) No parking
(b) No turning back
(c) No U-turn
(d) No entry

35. Which of the following films won the National Film Award for Best Children's Film in 2016?
(a) Duronto
(b) Chillar Party
(c) Dhanak
(d) Duronto

36. When is national sports day of India celebrated?
(a) 6th April
(b) 29th August
(c) 14th September
(d) 11th October

37. Which of the following was the first to get nominated as smart city?
(a) Puducherry
(b) Bangalore
(c) Ahmedabad
(d) Hyderabad

38. Who has been sworn-in as the new President of Costa Rica?
(a) Fabricio Alvarado Munoz
(b) Carlos Alvarado
(c) Epsy Campbell Barr
(d) Luis Guillermo Solis

39. Which state is to host the International Children's Theatre Festival 2018?
(a) Uttar Pradesh
(b) West Bengal
(c) Madhya Pradesh
(d) Kerala

40. What is the theme of the 2018 World Water Day (WWD)?
(a) Why Waste Water?
(b) Nature for Water
(c) Water is Life
(d) Better Water, Better Jobs

Space for Rough Work

LOGICAL REASONING MOCK TEST 1–5

OLYMPIAD

Mock Test 1

Name : ________ **Max. Marks : 25**

Number of Questions : 25 **Time : 1 Hour**

There is no negative marking in the test.

1. Find the odd one out.

(a)  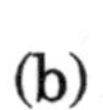 (b) 

(c)  (d) 

2. Find the missing figure which completes the series below.

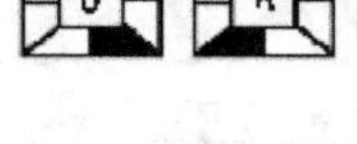 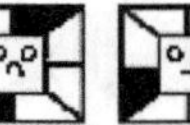   ? 

(a)  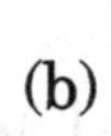 (b) 

(c) 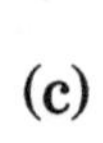   (d) 

3. Form the word using given letters and find the category in which they belong?

U D E S A T Y

(a) Name of Month
(b) Name of Bird
(c) Name of an Animal
(d) Name of Day

4. If in a code language, PAINT is written as 74128 and EXCEL as 93596, then how ACCEPT will be written in that language?

(a) 455978 (b) 544978
(c) 455378 (d) 733961

5. If 'bat' is 'racket' , 'racket' is 'football', 'football' is 'shuttle' , 'shuttle' is 'ludo'and 'ludo' is 'carrom' , what is cricket played with?

(a) Bat (b) Football
(c) Racket (d) Carrom

Space for Rough Work

6. Arrange the following words in the question in a logical sequence.

1. Evening   2. Night
3. Morning   4. Afternoon

(a) 2,1,4,3   (b) 3,4,1,2
(c) 1,2,3,4   (d) 1,3,2,4

7. If today is 3rd day from Tuesday, then what day is today?

(a) Monday   (b) Wednesday
(c) Thursday   (d) Friday

8. In how many different ways a tiger can return to his home?

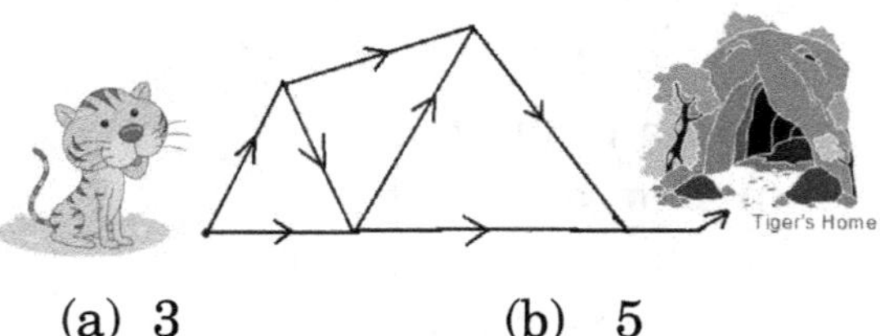

(a) 3   (b) 5
(c) 6   (d) 4

9. Identify the relation between the given pair on either side of : : and find the missing figure.

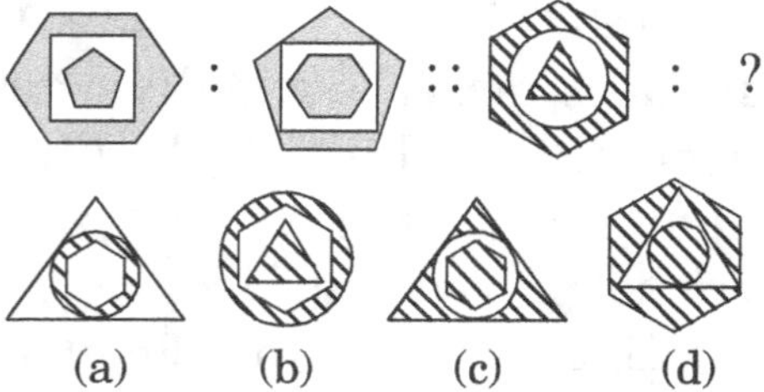

10. Find the mirror image of the figure given below.

(a)    (b) 

(c)    (d) 

11. How many corners does the figure have?

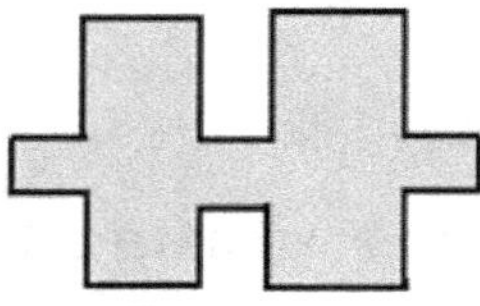

(a) 20   (b) 25
(c) 30   (d) 35

DIRECTIONS (Qs. 12 & 13): Observe the given figure carefully and answer the questions based on it.

Space for Rough Work

12. If one more butterfly is added on the left of butterfly 1, then how many butterflies are on the left of butterfly 7?

(a) 5 (b) 6
(c) 7 (d) 4

13. If two butterflies 2 and 3 are removed, then which butterfly is 3rd from the right end?

(a) 7 (b) 5
(c) 8 (d) 9

14. In which of the following figures, shape is exactly embedded as one of its part?

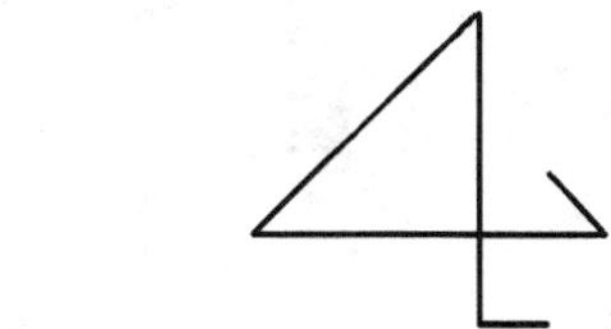

(a) 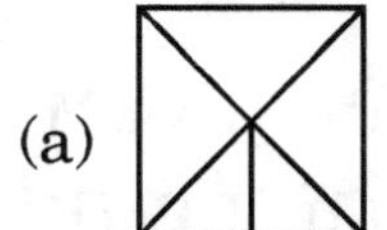 (b) 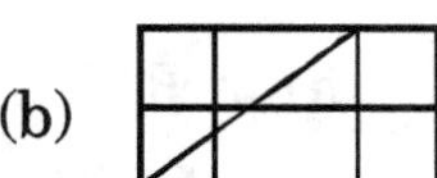

(c) 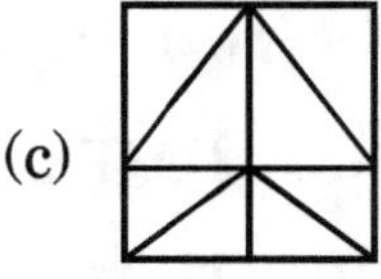 (d) 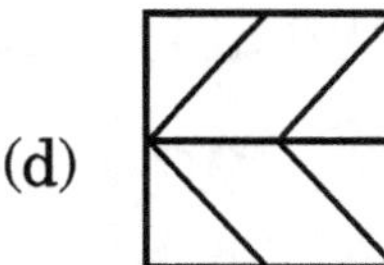

15. Find the word that CANNOT be formed from the letters of the given word.

INFORMATION

(a) NATION (b) INFORM
(c) MOTION (d) ACTION

16. Maya runs faster than Gautam.
Lily runs faster than Maya.
Gautam runs faster than Lily.
If the first two statements are true, the third statement is

(a) True
(b) False
(c) Uncertain
(d) None of these

17. Which is heavier 1 kg feather or 1 kg soap? Which one of the following statement is correct?

(a) 1 kg soap is heavier than 1 kg feather.
(b) 1 kg feather is heavier than 1 kg soap.
(c) Both are equal
(d) Cannot be determined

DIRECTIONS (Qs. 18 to 20): Study the given information to answer the questions.

Five friends are sitting on a bench facing north. Shekhar is to left of Rina and right of Bunny. Megha is to right of Rina sitting on the right end. Saumya is between Rina and Megha.

Space for Rough Work

18. Who is sitting immediate right to Shekhar?
(a) Megha (b) Saumya
(c) Bunny (d) Rina

19. Who is second from the left?
(a) Shekhar (b) Bunny
(c) Megha (d) Saumya

20. Who is sitting in the middle of a bench?
(a) Megha (b) Shekhar
(c) Rina (d) Bunny

21. How many oranges will be there in Pattern 5?

Pattern 1 Pattern 2 Pattern 3

(a) 16 (b) 18
(c) 20 (d) 22

22. Arrange the given picture in a logical sequence by ordering them in numbers.

1

2

3

4

(a) 1,2,3,4 (b) 3,2,1,4
(c) 2,3,4,1 (d) 4,3,2,1

23. In a class test, Tushar scored more than Anusha only. Nandy scored more than Purvi. Who scored highest marks among these four?
(a) Nandy (b) Tushar
(c) Purvi (d) Anusha

DIRECTIONS (Qs. 24 & 25): Study the table and answer the following questions.

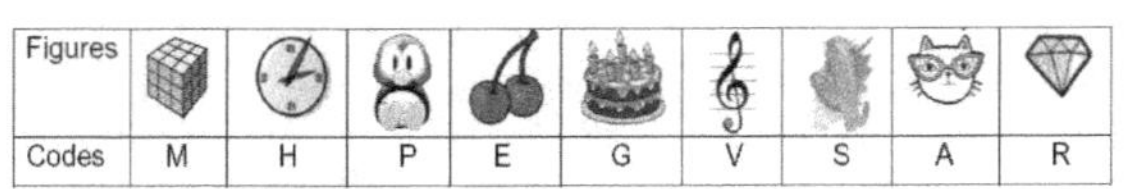

Figures									
Codes	M	H	P	E	G	V	S	A	R

24. What is the code of ?
(a) MRVE (b) RVEM
(c) EVRM (d) EPMR

25. What is the code of ?
(a) HGAP (b) PAGH
(c) GHPA (d) HPGA

Space for Rough Work

OLYMPIAD

Mock Test

Name : _________ **Max. Marks : 25**

Number of Questions : 25 **Time : 1 Hour**

There is no negative marking in the test.

1. Select the correct mirror image of fig.(X).

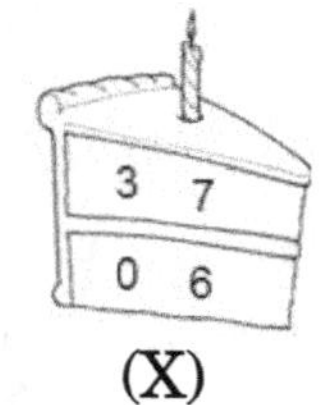
(X)

(a)  (b) 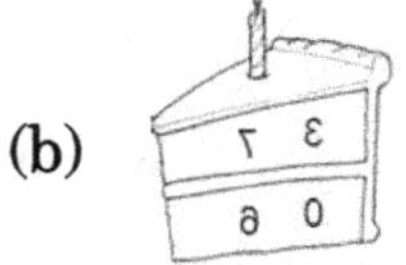

(c) 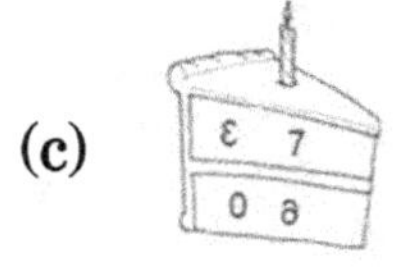 (d) 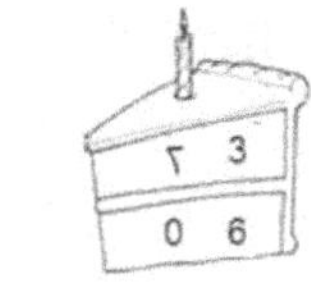

2. Hindi, English and Maths books are kept in the manner explained below.

(i) Maths book is not the last book.

(ii) Hindi book is above the Maths book.

(iii) English book is not at the second place.

Which book is the last book?

(a) English

(b) Maths

(c) Hindi

(d) Can't be determined

3. Find the word that cannot be made from the letters of the given word.

CELEBRATE

(a) R A T E (b) L A T E

(c) C A R E (d) B O R E

Space for Rough Work

4. Find the missing number in the given number pattern below.

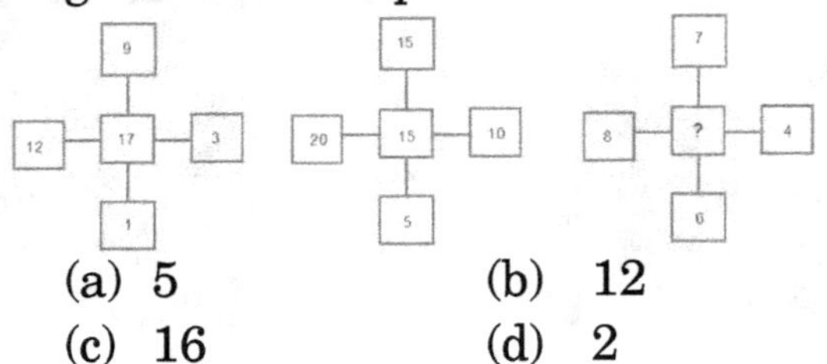

(a) 5 (b) 12
(c) 16 (d) 2

5. Find the odd one out.

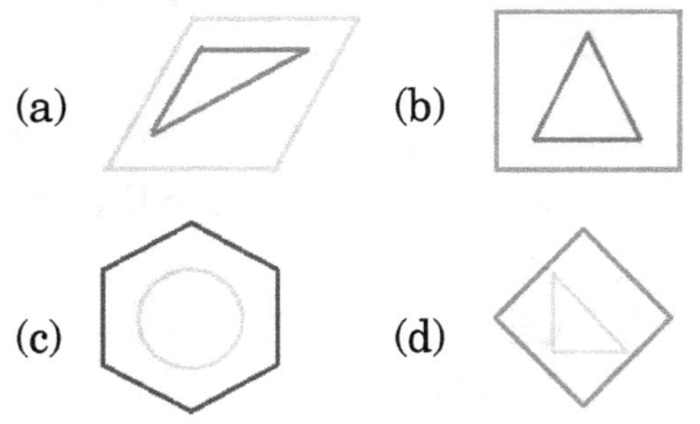

6. Which of the following belongs to group (X)?

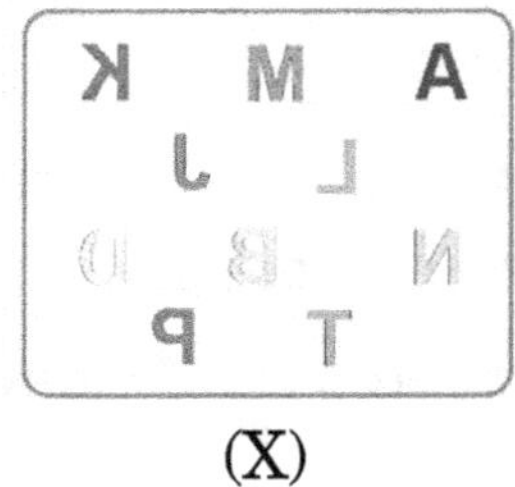

(X)

(a) (b)
(c) C (d)

DIRECTIONS (Qs. 7 & 8): Study the information carefully and answer the questions.

7. Number of rectangles in the above figure is__________

(a) 10 (b) 12
(c) 14 (d) 16

8. Number of circles is ________ more than number of triangles.

(a) 10 (b) 11
(c) 13 (d) 9

9. Identify the relation between the given pair on either side of : : and find the missing figure

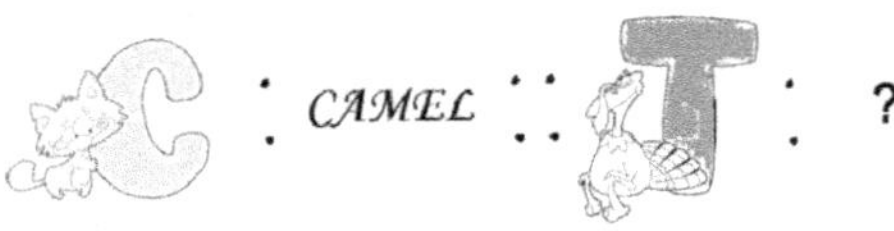

(a) TEN (b) TENNIS
(c) TIGER (d) TUBE

Space for Rough Work

10. If yesterday was 2nd day after Wednesday, then what is today?

(a) Monday (b) Saturday

(c) Friday (d) Sunday

11. What will be the number on barbie doll 12?

(a) 1 (b) 7

(c) 6 (d) 2

12. If 'December' is called 'March', 'March' is called 'July', 'July' is called 'February' and 'February' is called 'August', then which of the following months has 29 days?

(a) March (b) July

(c) February (d) August

DIRECTIONS (Qs. 13 & 14): Observe the given figure carefully and answer the questions based on it.

A B C D E F G H

13. Train_____ is the third train to the left of fifth train from left end.

(a) A (b) B

(c) G (d) H

14. If train D is removed from the row, then which train is in the middle of the row?

(a) E (b) F

(c) C (d) G

15. Find the word that cannot be made from the letters of the given word.

DISTURBANCE

(a) TURBAN

(b) BANKS

(c) BAND

(d) DISTANCE

16. If the code of RENT is TNER and code of MAN is NAM, then what will be the code of PAPER?

(a) PAPRE (b) PPAER

(c) REPAP (d) REPPA

17. In which group does number 49 belongs?

(a) 3,6,9,12,....

(b) 5,10,15,.....

(c) 6,12,18,24,.....

(d) 7,14,21,32,....

Space for Rough Work

18. Which solid is used to draw the shape (X)?

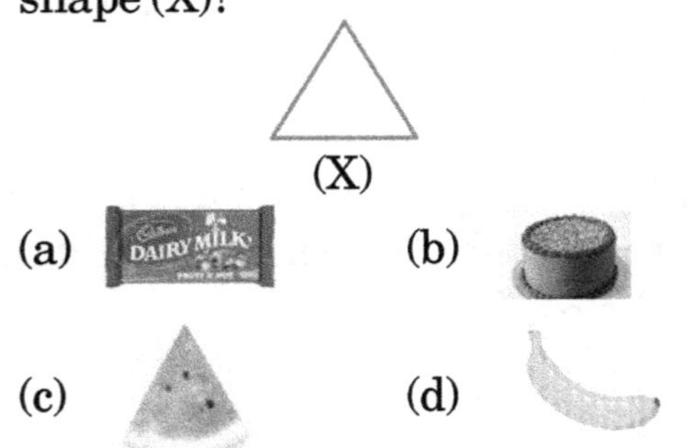

19. If numbers given below are arranged in the ascending order, then which number will be the fourth from the left?

321 467 283 952 438 641 158 764

(a) 321 (b) 438
(c) 467 (d) 641

20.

Raghav brought

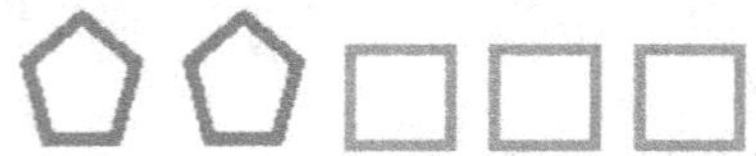

How many more strawberries than guavas did he buy?

(a) 3 (b) 4
(c) 1 (d) 0

21. Robin remembers that her sister Ritika's birthday was after 16th but before 21st October, while her father remembers that Ritika's birthday was after 18th but before 20th October. On which date of October was Ritika's birthday?

(a) 19th (b) 18th
(c) 17th (d) 20th

22. Find the odd one out.

(a) 6×6 (b) 9×4
(c) 12×3 (d) 15×2

23. If there are 60 seconds in one minute, then how many seconds are there in 12 minutes?

(a) 720 seconds (b) 620 seconds
(c) 520 seconds (d) 420 seconds

24. Kavya and her sister Nia baked 583 muffins. Which number is closet to 583?

(a) 480 (b) 500
(c) 580 (d) 575

25. Find the number of triangles in the given figure.

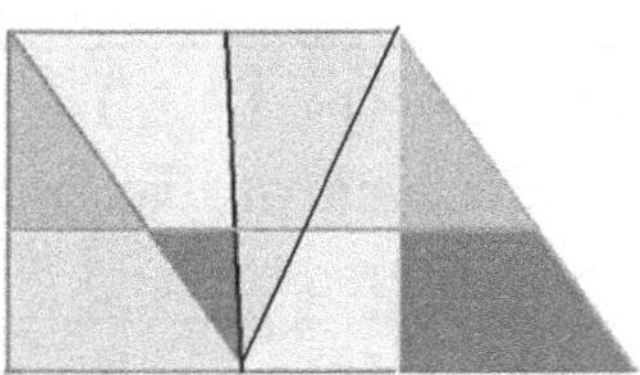

(a) 12 (b) 14
(c) 15 (d) 10

Space for Rough Work

OLYMPIAD

Mock Test

Name : _________

Number of Questions : 25

Max. Marks : 25

Time : 1 Hour

There is no negative marking in the test.

1. Choose the star fish that does not belong to the group.

(a) 

(b) 

(c) 

(d) 

2. Identify the relation between the given pair of either side of : : and find the missing term.

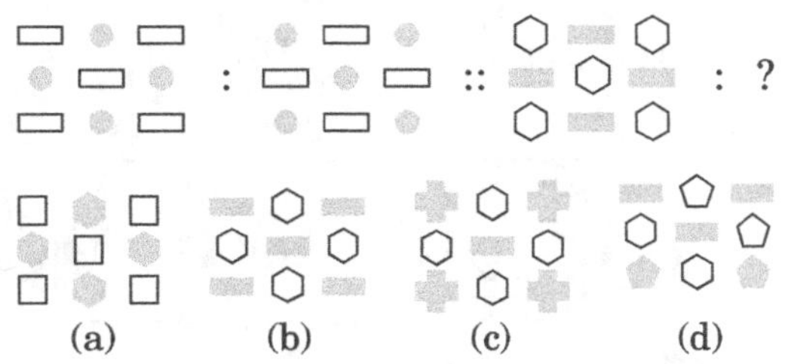

3. Which number will replace the (?), if the same rule is followed in the figure?

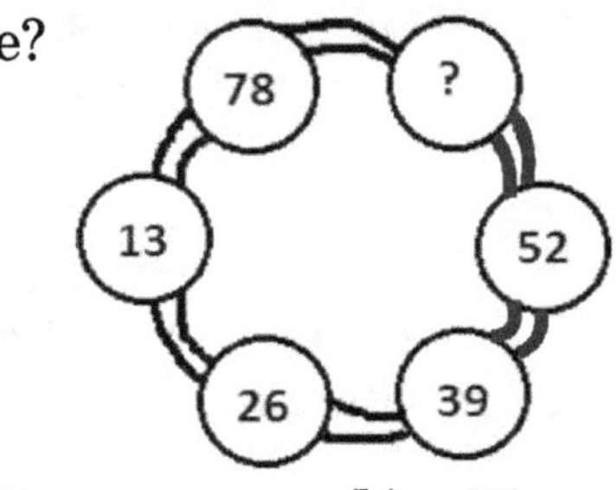

(a) 60 (b) 65

(c) 62 (d) 75

4. Arrange the given pictures in logical sequence by ordering them in alphabets?

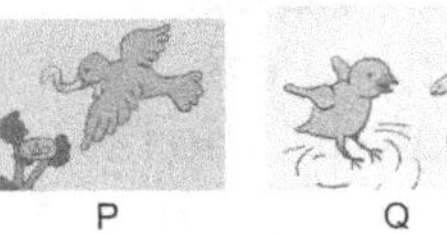  

P Q R S

(a) SPRQ (b) QRPS

(c) PQSR (d) SPQR

Space for Rough Work

5. Form the word using given letters and find the category to which they belong?

S L I P

(a) Flower (b) Animal
(c) Vegetable (d) Body Part

DIRECTIONS (Qs. 6 & 7): Observe the given figure carefully and answer the questions based on it.

1 2 3 4 5 6 7 8 9 10

6. If one more seahorse is added on right of seahorse 10, then how many seahorses are on the right of seahorse 6?
(a) 4 (b) 5
(c) 6 (d) 7

7. If three seahorses 2,4 and 6 are removed, then which seahorse is 5th from the left end?
(a) 5 (b) 9
(c) 1 (d) 8

8. If 'Book' is called 'Watch', 'Watch' is called 'Bag', 'Bag' is called 'Pen' and 'Pen' is called 'Pencil', then which is used to read time?
(a) Book (b) Bag
(c) Watch (d) Pen

9. Saumya will arrive at the Rio resort in Goa on 10th November and will stay six nights. What date will Saumya check out the resort?
(a) 15th November
(b) 16th November
(c) 14th November
(d) 17th November

10. How many triangles are there in the dotted line?

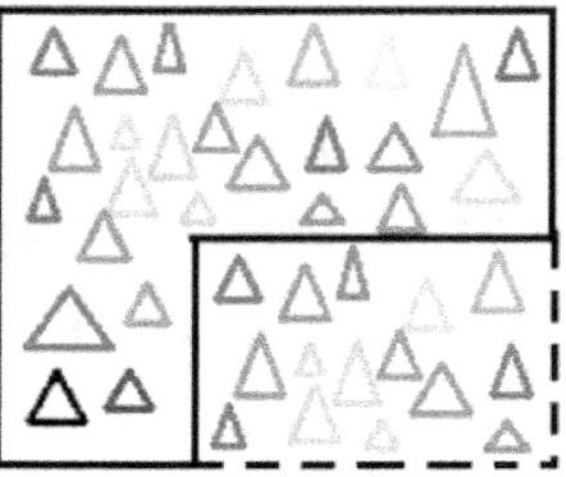

(a) 18 (b) 20
(c) 15 (d) 25

11. Select the option figure which is embedded in the given figure (X).

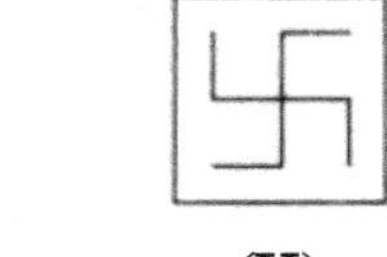

(X)

(a) 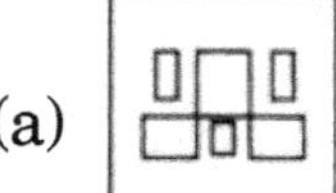 (b) 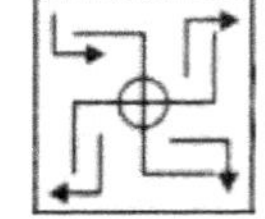

(c) 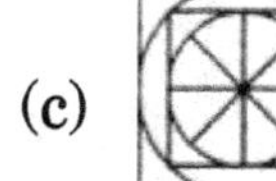 (d) 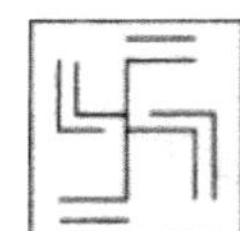

Space for Rough Work

12. What will be the mirror image of the given figure (X)?

(a) 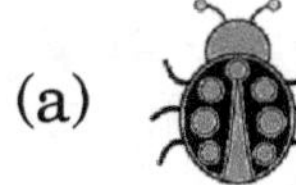 (b) 

(c)  (d) 

DIRECTIONS (Qs. 13 to 15): Look at the picture of pizza carefully and answer the questions based on it.

13. Number of sectors in the picture of pizza is__________.

(a) 10 (b) 4
(c) 18 (d) 20

14. Number of black circles in the picture of pizza is___________.

(a) 26 (b) 16
(c) 24 (d) 27

15. How many white circles are there in the picture of pizza?

(a) 2 (b) 3
(c) 4 (d) 5

16. Look at the figure carefully and check what is missing in the second picture.

PICTURE-A

PICTURE-B

(a) Shoes of a boy, Shirt of a boy and Top of a girl.

(b) Slippers of a boy, Hair band of a girl and Top of a girl.

(c) Shirt of a boy, Slippers of a boy and Shoes of a boy.

(d) None of the above

Space for Rough Work

17. Ekta has five more bananas than Jenny. Jenny has 12 bananas. How many bananas does Ekta have?

(a) 5 (b) 12
(c) 17 (d) 7

18. If CD = 7 then DGA = ?

(a) 10 (b) 12
(c) 15 (d) 5

19. Find the odd one out.

(a) Sparrow (b) Cuckoo
(c) Eagle (d) Duckling

20. What are the next two numbers in the pattern below?

7, 10, 15, 18,?, ?

(a) 23, 26 (b) 20,26
(c) 23,20 (d) 25,26

21. Identify the relation between the given pair of either side of : : and find the missing term.

72 : 9 : : 64 : ?

(a) 2 (b) 24
(c) 10 (d) 12

22. Choose the correct order of letters which are required to form a meaningful word.

C L Y E C
1 2 3 4 5

(a) 5,1,2,3,4 (b) 1,3,5,2,4
(c) 4,2,1,3,5 (d) 1,4,2,3,5

23. Which word can be formed from the given combination of letters?

STATEMENT

(a) TEMP (b) MAGNET
(c) ESTATE (d) MENTAL

24. Select the mirror image of given figure (X).

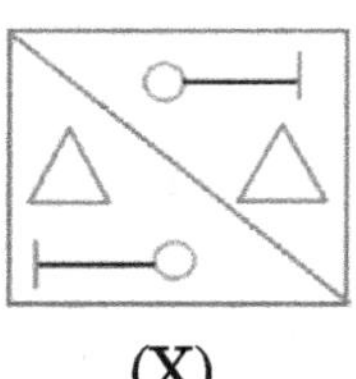

(X)

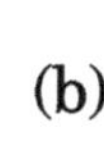
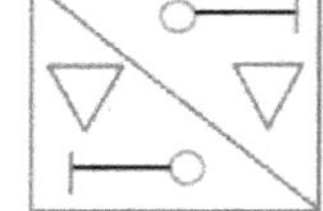

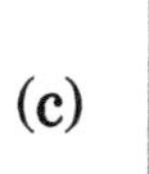
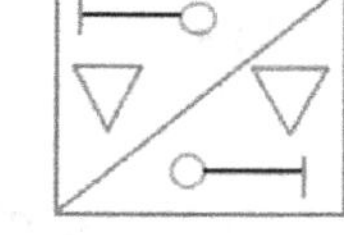
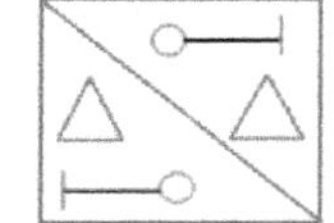

25. If yesterday was Friday, then day after tomorrow will be________.

(a) Tuesday
(b) Monday
(c) Saturday
(d) Wednesday

Space for Rough Work

OLYMPIAD

Mock Test 4

Name : ________ **Max. Marks : 25**

Number of Questions : 25 **Time : 1 Hour**

There is no negative marking in the test.

1. Find the odd one out.

   (a) 26 (b) 34

   (c) 62 (d) 54

2. Select the correct mirror image of fig.(X).

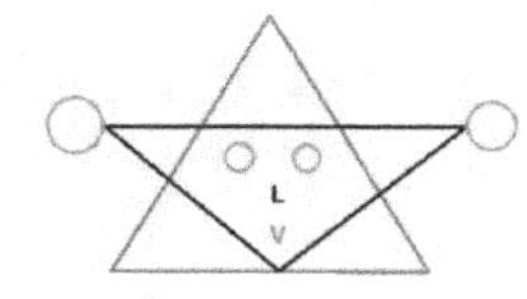

(a) 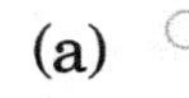

(b) 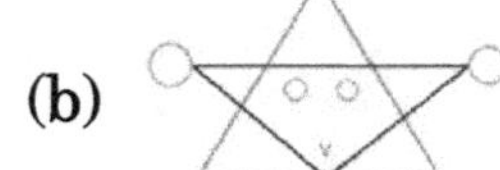

(c) 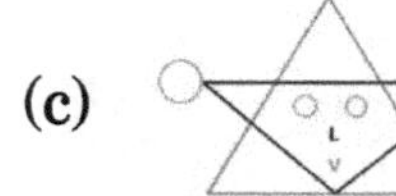

(d) 

3. Form the word using given letters and find the category in which they belong.

   L A I P R

   (a) Name of Bird

   (b) Name of Month

   (c) Name of an Animal

   (d) Name of Day

4. Find the word that cannot be made from the letters of the given word.

   DEMAND

   (a) MAN (b) DAM

   (c) DONE (d) MAD

5. If in a code language, RENT is written as 4628 and LEAST as 16598, then how EAST will be written in that language?

   (a) 8956 (b) 6598

   (c) 6859 (d) 8569

Space for Rough Work

6. Find the missing number in the given number pattern below.

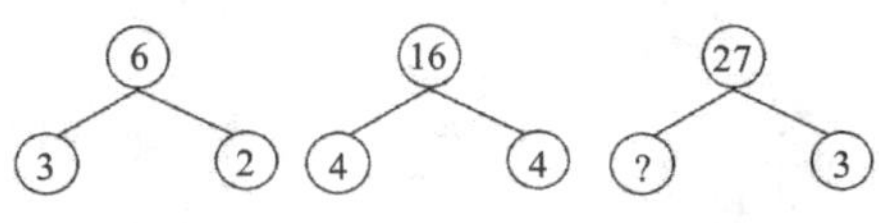

(a) 6 (b) 8
(c) 9 (d) 10

7. Identify the relation between the given pair on either side of : : and find the missing term.

AD : BE : : PS : ?

(a) QR (b) RS
(c) ST (d) QT

8. If Rohit takes a leave of 2nd Friday and 4th Friday in November 20XX, then how many days are working? (Assumed that every Sunday is a holiday)

(a) 24 (b) 25
(c) 26 (d) 23

9. How many tigers will be there in Pattern 5?

Pattern 1 Pattern 2 Pattern 3

(a)

(b)

(c)

(d)

10. Which is the lightest vegetable?

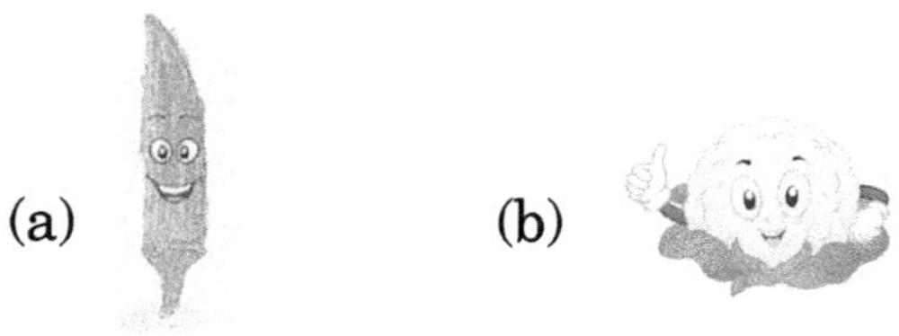

(a) (b)

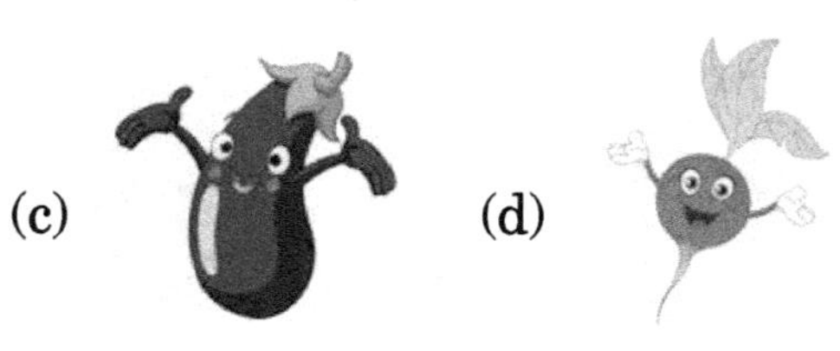

(c) (d)

Space for Rough Work

11. Keshav saw 2 cows and 2 horses outside. How many legs did he see?

(a) 12 (b) 14
(c) 16 (d) 20

DIRECTIONS (Qs. 12 to 14): Observe the diagram and answer the following questions.

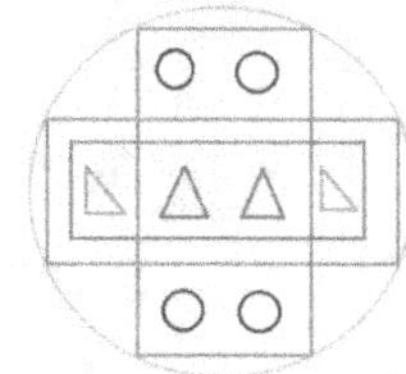

12. How many triangles are there in the given diagram?

(a) 4 (b) 3
(c) 2 (d) 0

13. How many circles are there in the given diagram?

(a) 6 (b) 5
(c) 8 (d) 10

14. How many shapes are there in the given diagram?

(a) 6 (b) 3
(c) 4 (d) 1

15. In how many different ways Shanaya can return to her home?

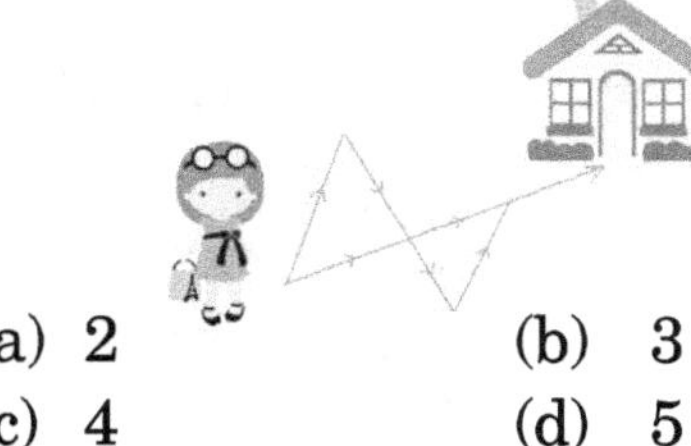

(a) 2 (b) 3
(c) 4 (d) 5

DIRECTIONS (Qs. 16 & 17): Observe the given figure carefully and answer the questions based on it.

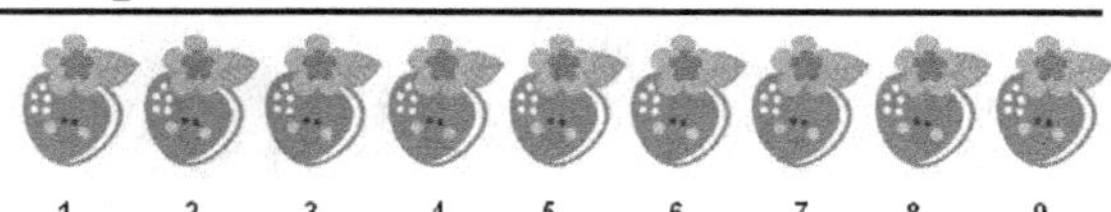

16. Strawberry_____ is the third strawberry to the right of eighth strawberry from right end.

(a) 5 (b) 6
(c) 7 (d) 4

17. Which of the following strawberries is in the middle of strawberry 3 and 7?

(a) 4
(b) 5
(c) 6
(d) None of these

18. If given below numbers are arranged in the descending order, then which number will be the sixth from the right?

406 329 103 119 986 732 768 685

(a) 732 (b) 329
(c) 406 (d) 768

Space for Rough Work

19. Select the option figure which is embedded in the given figure (X).

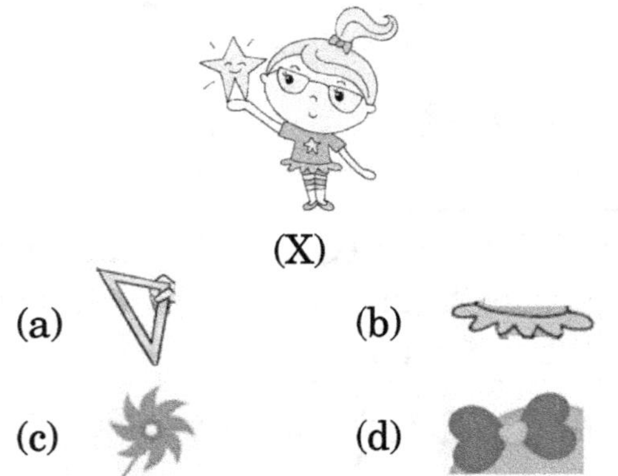

(X)

(a) (b)

(c) (d)

20. How many straight lines are there in the given figure?

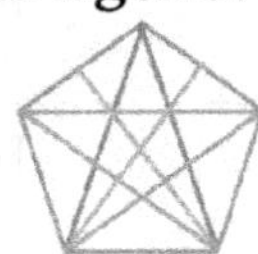

(a) 12 (b) 14

(c) 10 (d) 15

21. Arrange the given picture in a logical sequence by ordering them in numbers.

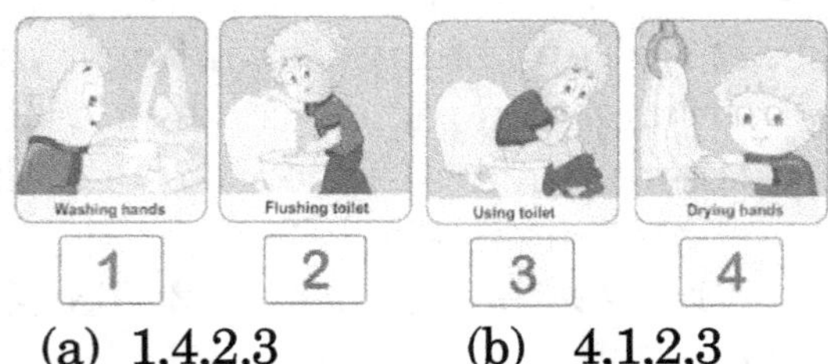

(a) 1,4,2,3 (b) 4,1,2,3

(c) 3,2,1,4 (d) 3,1,4,2

22. In a class test, Sapna scored more than only Kanak. Neha scored more than Gunjan. Who scored lowest marks among these four?

(a) Neha (b) Sapna

(c) Gunjan (d) Kanak

23. Select a suitable option that would complete the figure matrix.

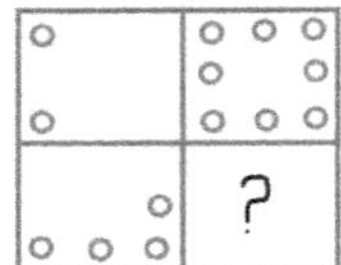

(a) (b)

(c) (d)

24. If 'Delhi' is called 'Agra', 'Agra' is called 'Mumbai', 'Mumbai' is called 'Chennai', then in which city is Red Fort situated?

(a) Delhi (b) Mumbai

(c) Chennai (d) Agra

25. Find the next term.

(a) 18 (b) 20

(c) 25 (d) 28

Space for Rough Work

OLYMPIAD Mock Test

Name : ________ **Max. Marks : 25**

Number of Questions : 25 **Time : 1 Hour**

There is no negative marking in the test.

1. Choose the elephant that does not belong to the group.

(a) 

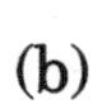
(b) 

(c) 

(d) 

2. Identify the relation between the given pair of either side of : : and find the missing figure.

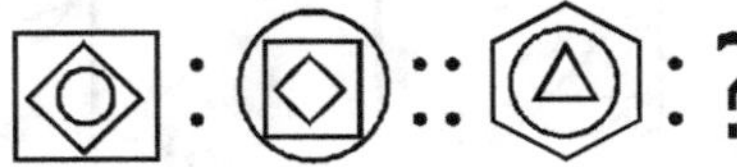

(a) 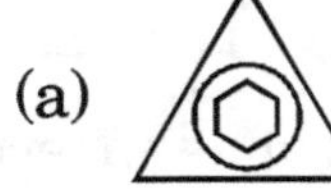
(b) 

(c) 
(d) 

3. Select the correct mirror image of fig.(X).

BASKET

(X)

(a) (b)

(c) (d)

4. Jenny loves flowers ! Can you put these pictures in the logical sequence by ordering them in numbers to create a logical story?

(a) 1,2,3,4 (b) 1,4,3,2

(c) 2,3,4,1 (d) 4,1,2,3

Space for Rough Work

5. Find the word that can be made from the letters of the given word.

DESTINATION

(a) INCITE (b) MOTION
(c) ACTION (d) TENTION

6. If in a certain code, NOSE is written as PQUG. What will be the code of SHOUT?

(a) UJQWV (b) VWQJU
(c) QWJUV (d) UHQUV

7. The following question is based on the following alphabet series.

Which letter will be in the middle of W and C

(a) I (b) J
(c) H (d) G

8. Isha spent 25 minutes on her homework last night? She started at 8:10 p.m. What time did she finish her work?

(a) 8:35 a.m. (b) 8:25 a.m.
(c) 8:45 p.m. (d) 8:35 p.m.

9. There are 25 boats. If each boat can hold 30 people. How many people in total do all the boats hold?

(a) 750 (b) 700
(c) 850 (d) 800

10. Find the x and y in the given number pattern below.

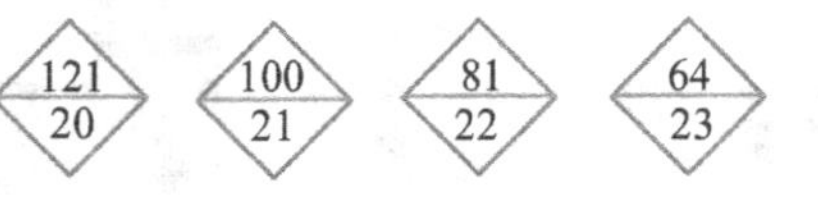

(a) 36,24 (b) 49,24
(c) 25,24 (d) 16,24

11. Which of the following options will complete the pattern in fig.(X)?

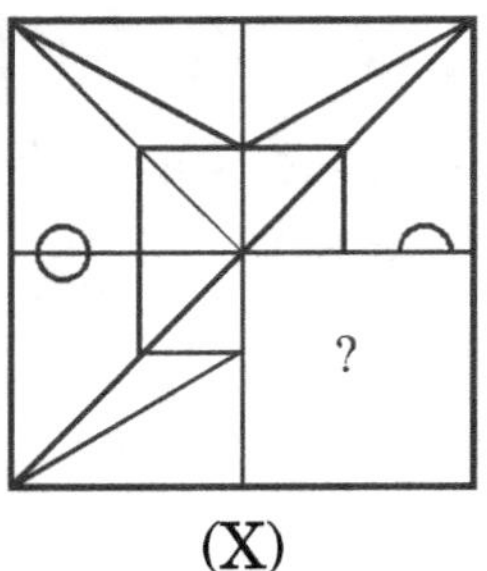

(X)

(a) 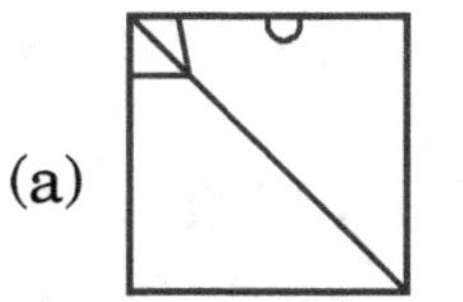 (b) 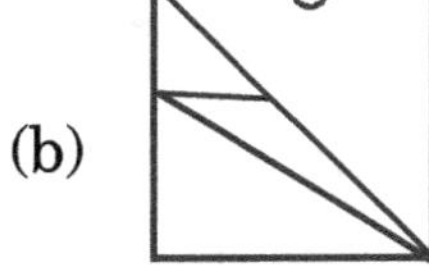

(c) 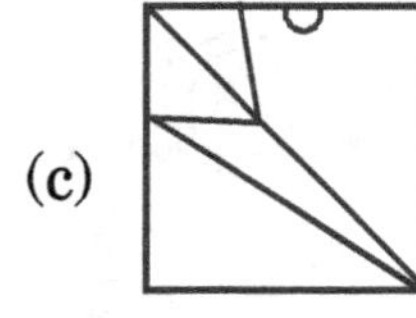 (d) 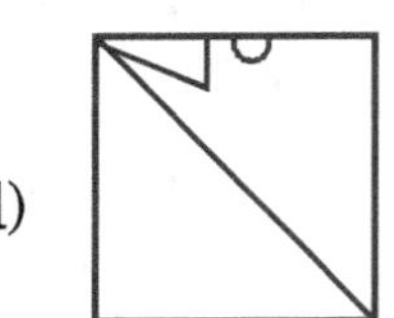

12. Estimate the weight of a butterfly.

(a) 30 g (b) 40 g
(c) 50 g (d) 10 g

Space for Rough Work

13. How many straight lines are there in the diagram given below.

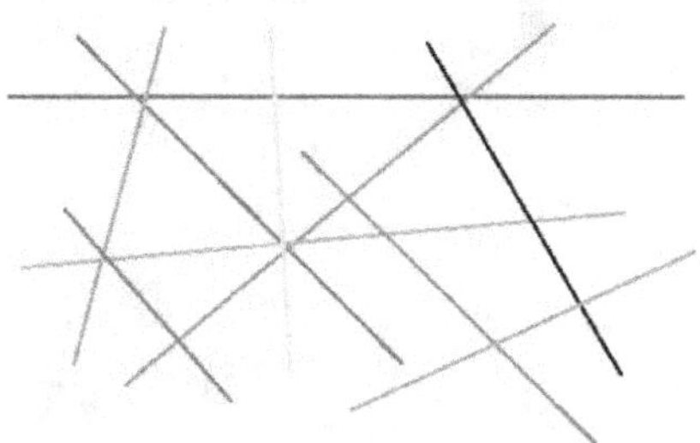

(a) 9 (b) 12
(c) 15 (d) 17

14. Ritesh was born on July 10th, Naman was born on September 10th of the same year. How many months older is Ritesh?

(a) 3 months (b) 5 months
(c) 4 months (d) 2 months

DIRECTIONS (Qs. 15 & 16): The number in each question below is to be codified in the following code.

Digit	9	6	3	2	1	4	5	7	8
Letter	K	L	A	Y	W	S	N	B	P

15. What is the code for 7916?

(a) BKWL (b) LWKB
(c) WKLB (d) KBLW

16. What is the code for 3825?

(a) KPNB (b) APYN
(c) NYPA (d) YPNA

17. Ritu arranged her pictures in a straight row. The prettiest one is in the middle. It is placed fourth from the left as well as from the right side. How many pictures does Ritu have altogether?

(a) 5 (b) 9
(c) 7 (d) 11

18. Look at the figure carefully and check what is missing in the second picture.

Picture -A

Picture -B

Space for Rough Work

(a) Boots, Guitar and Hat
(b) Boots, Belt and Rope
(c) Guitar, Belt and Hat
(d) Guitar, Rope and Boots

19. If 'Sunflower' is called 'Rose', 'Rose' is called 'Lotus', 'Lotus' is called 'Lily' and 'Lily' is called 'Popy', which is king of flowers?

(a) Popy (b) Rose
(c) Lily (d) Sunflower

20. Select the option figure which is embedded in the given figure (X).

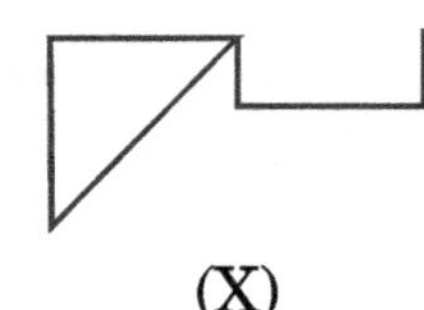

(X)

(a)  (b) 

(c) 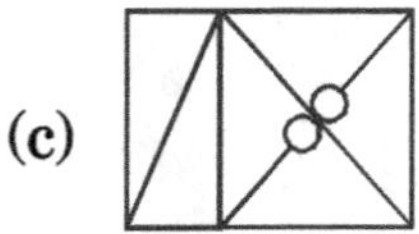 (d) 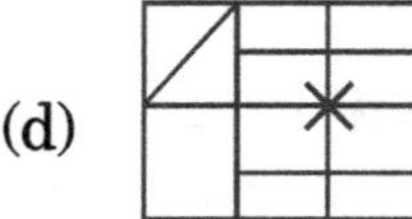

21. Find the missing term in the given series.

(a) 20 (b) 25
(c) 23 (d) 26

22. Find the odd one out.

23. Identify the relation between the given pair of either side of : : and find the missing term.

2 × 3 × 2 : 12 : : 3 × 4 × 3 : ?

(a) 13 (b) 9
(c) 12 (d) 36

24. Choose the correct order of letters which are required to form a meaningful word.

H I A C R

(a) ARCHI (b) CHAIR
(c) RIACH (d) RACIH

25. Mohita has eight more apples than Kritika. Kritika has 20 apples. How many apples does Mohita have?

(a) 12 (b) 15
(c) 28 (d) 8

Space for Rough Work

CYBER MOCK TEST 1–3

OLYMPIAD

Mock Test

Name : ________ **Max. Marks : 25**

Number of Questions : 25 **Time : 1 Hour**

There is no negative marking in the test.

1. Which of the following statements is/are incorrect about a computer?
   (a) You can watch movies on it.
   (b) You can solve your sums on it.
   (c) You can play games on it.
   (d) You can cook food with it.

2. The control unit of the computer controls the ________
   (a) working of the computer keyboard.
   (b) flow of electricity within the computer.
   (c) complete workflow of the CPU.
   (d) control unit can take inputs and give output.

3. Which of the following statements is incorrect?
   (a) Blu-ray disc is used as main memory in computers.
   (b) ROM is a permanent memory.
   (c) Auxiliary memory is also known as secondary storage device.
   (d) Scanner is an image/document scanning device.

Space for Rough Work

4. Designing is the process of deciding the look of something and nowaday's computers are used for designing, one can design ________ using computers.
   (a) metro train control system
   (b) blue print of Building
   (c) aircraft control system
   (d) all of these.

5. Which of the following is an input device?
   (a)  (b) 
   (c) 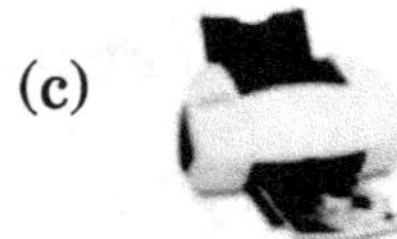 (d) Both (a) and (b)

6. Find the odd term out.
   (a) Keyboard (b) Mouse
   (c) Monitor (d) Joystick

7. Which among the following is a cursor control input device?
   (a) 
   (b) 
   (c) 
   (d) None of these.

8. What is the full form of GPS?
   (a) Global packet system
   (b) Geo positioning system
   (c) Geometrical position system
   (d) Global positioning system

Space for Rough Work

9. Select the INCORRECT match of brushes in MS-Paint of Windows 7 with their corresponding names.

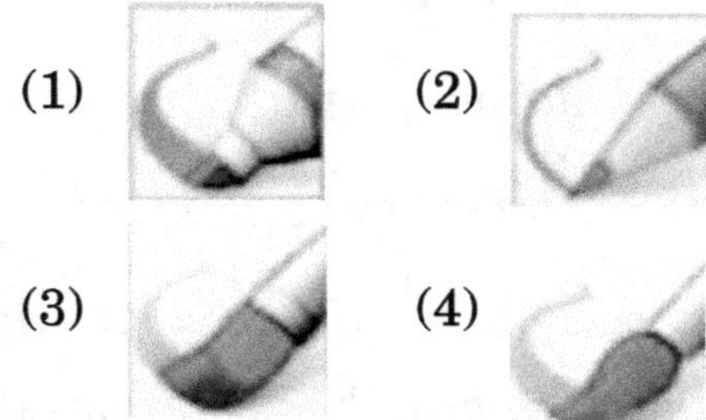

(a) 1 – Marker

(b) 2 – Natural pencil

(c) 3 – Oil brush

(d) 4 – Calligraphy brush 1

10. Which of the following brushes are present under brushes tool in MS-Paint of Windows 7?

(a) Natural pencil, marker, crayon, water colour, airbrush

(b) Liquid colour, marker, crayon, spray colour, natural pencil

(c) Doted colour, marker colour, crayon, spray colour, wind colour.

(d) Light colour, permanent marker, crayon, waterproof colour, oil-proof colour.

11. Which of the following icons is used to draw perfect circle in MS-Paint?

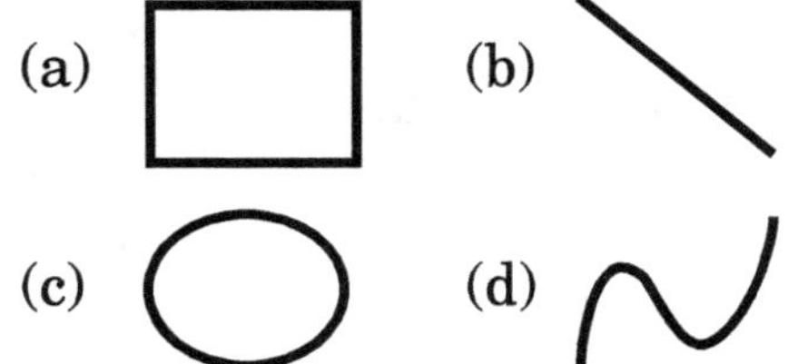

12. MS-Paint is a Windows program that is used for ________.

(a) calculations

(b) writing letters

(c) drawing purposes

(d) preparing presentations

Space for Rough Work

13. Which of the following is NOT an example of search engine?

(a) Google (b) facebook

(c) bing (d) YAHOO!

14. Which of the following is not a web browser?

(a) Mozilla

(b) Internet Explorer

(c) Windows Explorer

(d) Chrome

15. Internet is used

(a) to share information between connected computers.

(b) for searching the relevant information.

(c) for communication such as video conferencing.

(d) all of these

16. What is WWW (World Wide Web)?

(a) App

(b) Game

(c) Internet servers

(d) Another name of internet

17. Match the given MS-word shortcuts with the operations they perform.

Column-1	Column-2
(1) Undo the last operation	(I) Ctrl + X
(2) Save a file	(II) Ctrl + I
(3) Cut the selected text	(III) Ctrl + S
(4) Change selected text from normal to italic	(IV) Ctrl + Z

Space for Rough Work

(a) 1-IV, 2-III, 3-I, 4-II

(b) 1-II, 2-IV, 3-I, 4-III

(c) 1-III, 2-IV, 3-II, 4-I

(d) 1-IV, 2-I, 3-II, 4-III

18. What is the codename of latest version of android7.0?

    (a) Nougat

    (b) Jelly Bean

    (c) Lollipop

    (d) Ice Cream Sandwich

19. How you can change the font size in MS-word?

    (a) Selecting the font and using the resizing handles.

    (b) Font Size under font on the home tab of the ribbon.

    (c) Font size under the view tab of the ribbon

    (d) You cannot change the font size after you have used the font.

20. Predefined set of formatting options that have been named and saved are called__________.

    (a) font Styles

    (b) format

    (c) toolbar

    (d) view

21. Which of the following devices is connected to software and converts human speech into commands or text?

    (a)  (b) 

    (c)  (d) All of these

22. Which of the following is used as a storage medium in portable hand-held smartphone device?

    (a) 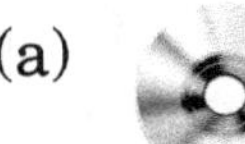  (b) 

    (c)  (d) All of these

Space for Rough Work

23. Pressing which key allows you to jump the cursor five spaces forward? Identify this device given below.
    (a) Tab
    (b) Space bar
    (c) Delete
    (d) Backspace

24. Which of the following is a mobile phone accessory that is not an integral part of a smartphone but provides some support to take selfie and enhance its look .
    (a) 
    (b) 
    (c)
    (d) All of these

25. An android mobile operating system was developed by________.
    (a) Microsoft (b) Google
    (c) Apple Inc (d) IBM

Space for Rough Work

OLYMPIAD

Mock Test

Name : ________

Number of Questions : 25

Max. Marks : 25

Time : 1 Hour

There is no negative marking in the test.

1. Which of the following statements is/are incorrect?

   (a) The output that is printed on the paper is called hardcopy.

   (b) The computer understands instructions in the form of mechanical signals.

   (c) Storing the data on the computer is called storage or memory.

   (d) The results displayed on the monitor screen are called softcopy.

2. Complete the given word and select the statement which is correct about it.

   P_I_T_R

   (a) It gives the hardcopy of the computer screen.

   (b) It gives the softcopy of the computer screen.

   (c) Worked when it connected to the computer.

   (d) Both (a) & (c)

Space for Rough Work

3. Computer helps scientists in......

   (a) Launching rockets

   (b) Scientific research

   (c) Launching Aircraft

   (d) All of these

4. Which of the following can be used in a microcomputer?

   (a) (b)

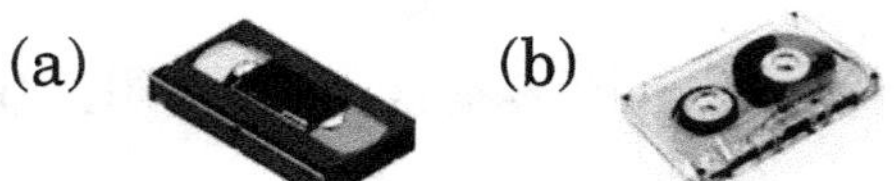

   (c) (d) All of these

5. Which of the following printers is more suitable where continuous paper stationery is used?

   (a) Laser printer

   (b) Inkjet printer

   (c) Dot matrix printer

   (d) Daisy wheel printer

6. Identify the given device.

   It reads pictures, words or numbers from a page directly and can change them into a form that a computer can understand.

   (a) (b) (c) (d)

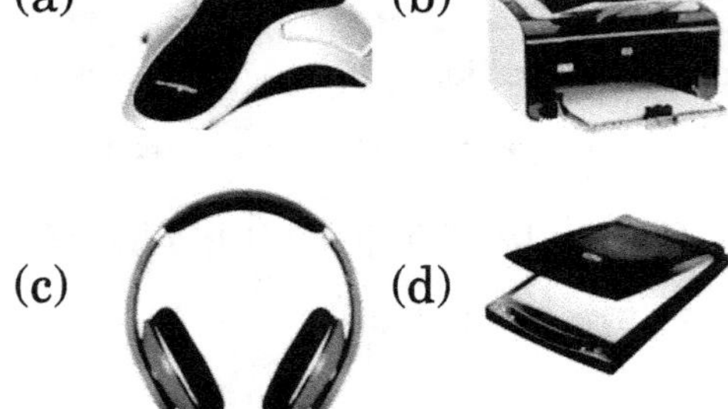

7. Which of the following device is connected to the computer through the data cable?

   (a) (b) (c) (d)

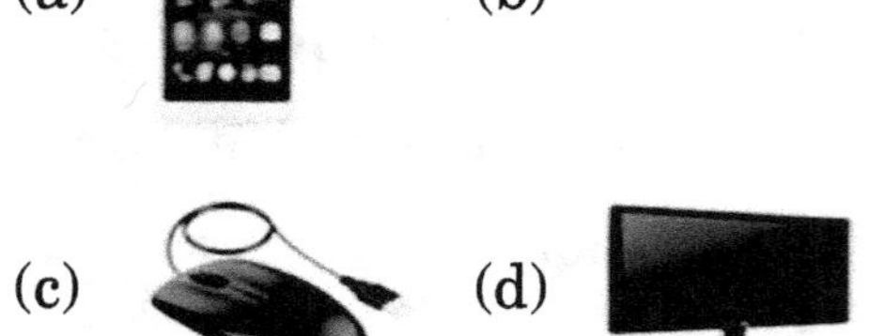

Space for Rough Work

8. Select the incorrect statement.
   (a) Webcam is a small video camera that is primarily used for recording videos and to take picture.
   (b) Optical mark reader is a special type of scanner used for scanning OMR evaluated sheets.
   (c) Plotter is a larger format printer used to print the big size of maps, blueprint of building maps, banners, etc.
   (d) Joystick and light pen are the output devices.

9. Which operation would change the image-I to image -II?

Image I

Image II

   (a) Flip vertical
   (b) Skew
   (c) Rotate 180 degree
   (d) Flip horizontal

10. Which of the following is not a part of shape tools in MS-Paint?
   (a) 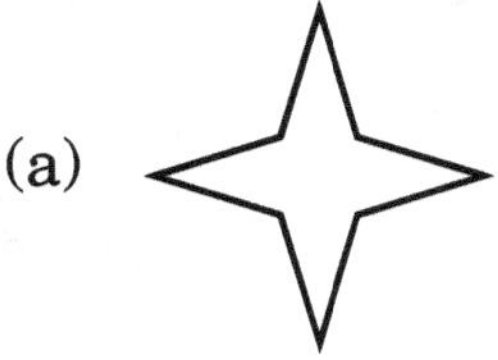
   (b) 
   (c) 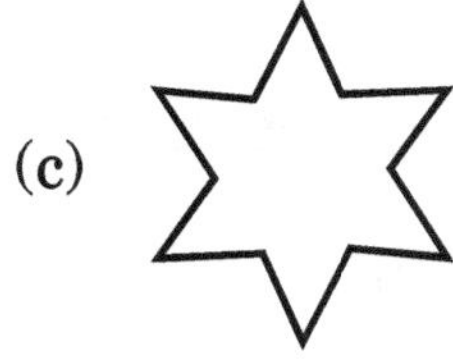
   (d) 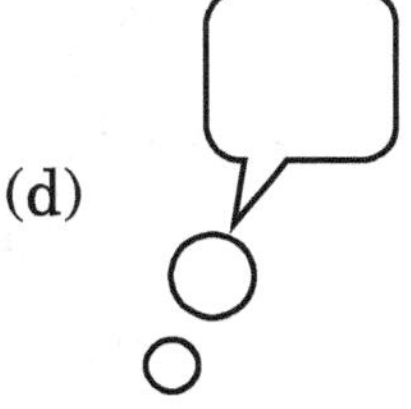

Space for Rough Work

11. What is the function of given image in MS-PAINT?

(a) It sets the image as desktop background.

(b) It shows a larger version of an image.

(c) It shows the frame on the image.

(d) None of these

12. Select the correct match.

Column-1	Column-2
(1)	(i) Allows you to change or skew the height or width of your picture.
(2)	(ii) Allows you to cut the picture so that is only contains a certain section.
(3)	(iii) Allows you to select the medium of your outline.
(4)	(iv) Allows you to flip the picture or selection.

(a) 1-ii, 2-i, 3-iv, 4-iii

(b) 1-ii, 2-iv, 3-i, 4-iii

(c) 1-iii, 2-iv, 3-ii, 4-i

(d) 1-iv, 2-i, 3-ii, 4-iii

13. Which of the following statements is INCORRECT about the internet?

(a) It is an interconnected system of networks that allows communication.

(b) It is a public network.

Space for Rough Work

(c) It is a vast network that connects millions of computers around the world

(d) It supports only wired communication.

14. Which of the following statements is/are correct about Uniform Resource Locator (URL)?

(a) It provides a way to locate a resource on the web.

(b) It is a computer application program.

(c) It is a computer language.

(d) It is a computer memory chip.

15. Select the correct match.

Column-1	Column-2
(1)	(i) Internet explorer
(2)	(ii) Opera
(3)	(iii) Google chrome
(4)	(iv) Mozilla

(a) 1-iii, 2-i, 3-iv, 4-ii

(b) 1-ii, 2-iv, 3-i, 4-iii

(c) 1-iii, 2-iv, 3-ii, 4-i

(d) 1-iv, 2-i, 3-ii, 4-iii

16. Which of the following statements is/are correct about the given figure?

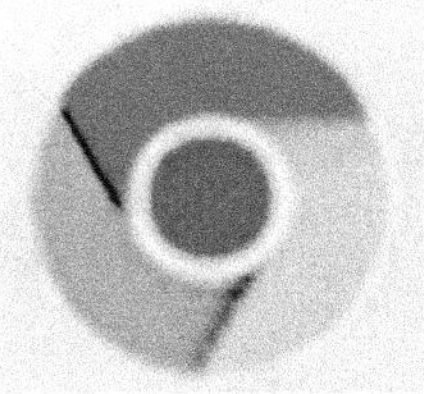

I. It has an address bar in which URL of the websites is typed.

Space for Rough Work

II. It can be used to open a search engine.

(a) Both (1) & (2)

(b) Only (1)

(c) Only (2)

(d) Neither (1) Nor (2)

17. Which of the following is the latest version of MS word?

(a) MS word 2010

(b) MS word 2007

(c) MS word 2018

(d) MS word 2016

18. The size of the area in which you want to type the text or align the text can be set by_________. ?

(a) Scrollbar

(b) Ruler

(c) Status bar

(d) None of these

19. Identify the given figure.

(a) MS-Word format painter

(b) MS-Paint brush

(c) MS-Paint oil brush

(d) MS-Word paint brush

20. Identify the given app.

Space for Rough Work

(a) Window play

(b) Apple play

(c) IBM play

(d) Google play

21. The first computer program was developed by________.

(a) Charles Babbage

(b) Dennis Ritchie

(c) James Gosling

(d) Lady Ada Lovelace

22 ______________ is a computer program that blanks the screen or fills it with moving images or patterns when the computer is not in use?

(a) Screen saver

(b) Wallpaper

(c) Screen Timer

(d) Screen mover

23. Which of the following is a microcomputer?

(a) 

(b) 

(c) 

(d) All of these

Space for Rough Work

24. Which of the following is a social networking game?
    - (a) Ping-Pong
    - (b) Ghost House
    - (c) Melissa
    - (d) Farmville

25. What is PlayStation 4?
    - (a) A keyboard especially designed for blind people.
    - (b) A home video game console.
    - (c) An online service to play video games with your added friends.
    - (d) A social networking site only for video game players.

Space for Rough Work

OLYMPIAD

Mock Test

Name : ___________ **Max. Marks : 25**

Number of Questions : 25 **Time : 1 Hour**

There is no negative marking in the test.

1. The working of Central Processing Unit (CPU) is compared with which of the following organs of human body?

   (a) (b) 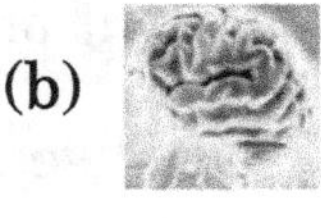

   (c) (d)

2. Which of the following is the image of Abacus?

   (a) 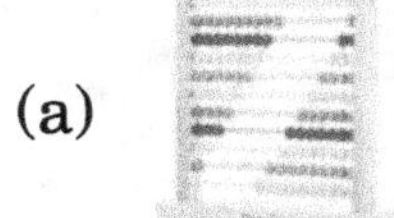 (b) 

   (c)  (d) None of these

3. Match the following columns.

	Column-1		Column-2
(1)	The device which provides power to a computer (if there is a power failure)	(i)	Hard drive
(2)	The scan image and printed text which gets converted into digital image is known as	(ii)	UPS
(3)	It helps us to point at and selects things on computer screen.	(iii)	Scanner

Space for Rough Work

(4)	It store the data permanently	(iv) Mouse

(a) 1-ii, 2-iii, 3-iv, 4-i

(b) 1-ii, 2-iv, 3-i, 4-iii

(c) 1-iii, 2-iv, 3-ii, 4-i

(d) 1-iv, 2-i, 3-ii, 4-iii

4 Which of the following is a multifunction device which consists of printer, scanner, fax and photocopier?

(a) 

(b) 

(c) 

(d) 

5. Match the column-1 and column-2 given in the following table. Choose the correct option.

Column-1	Column-2
(i) Key used to remove text to the right of the cursor.	(1) Spacebar
(ii) Key used to cancel the current operation.	(2) Enter
(iii) Key used to insert spaces	(3) Delete
(iv) Key used to go to the next line.	(4) Esc

(a) (i-3, ii-4, iii-1, iv-2)

(b) (i-2, ii-1, iii-4, iv-3)

(c) (i-4, ii-3, iii-2, iv-1)

(d) (i-1, ii-4, iii-2, iv-3)

Space for Rough Work

6. Which of the following is/are the toggle key?

(a) Caps Lock (b) Scroll Lock

(c) Num Lock (d) All of these

7. In colours group of the Home tab, when you click colour 1 and then a colour square in the colour palette, what is most likely to happen in MS-Paint?

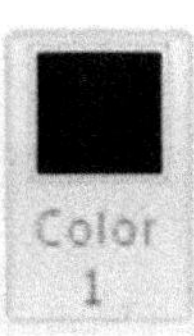

(a) It changes the background colour of the drawing.

(b) It changes the colour of recently closed file.

(c) It changes the background colour selection.

(d) It sets the new color as the foreground colour.

8. The site Wikipedia.org provides ___________.

(a) online encyclopedia.

(b) online news.

(c) online dictionary

(d) online game.

9. What do you mean by the term 'online' ?

(a) When you are connected to the internet through ISP or a network.

(b) When you yourself go on the internet.

(c) When you are connected to a telephone.

(d) None of these

Space for Rough Work

10. How to open two and more files simultaneously?
    (a) Press (ctrl + o) keys and then select two or more files which you want to open.
    (b) Type 2 or more digit number in Run Box and press enter key.
    (c) Press (ctrl + shift + o) keys and then select two files which you want to open.
    (d) Both (b) & (c)

11. Ram wants to create a shortcut for MS-Word, so that he can quickly access it. But he does not know the correct sequence of steps required to follow to create a desktop shortcut. Help him by rearranging the given steps in the CORRECT order.
    1. Select/click 'All Programs'.
    2. Click Microsoft Office folder.
    3. Click Desktop (create shortcut) option.
    4. Click on Start button.
    5. Right click.
    6. Go to Microsoft Word 2010.

    (a) 4 1 2 6 5 3
    (b) 1 2 4 3 6 5
    (c) 4 3 2 1 5 6
    (d) 6 1 5 2 4 3

12. To change the margins of the document, you should use the ___________
    (a) home tab of the ribbon and click margins.
    (b) page Layout tab on the ribbon and click margins.
    (c) design tab of the ribbon.
    (d) page setup tab of the ribbon.

Space for Rough Work

13. Which of the following statements is/are correct about the given device?

1. It is a general purpose personal computer.
2. It has monitor, keyboard, touch pad, CD/DVD drive, and hard drive.
3. It is a battery operated package.

(a) Only (1)

(b) Both (2) & (3)

(c) Both (1) & (2)

(d) All (1), (2) & (3)

14. Match the famous people names in column-1 with their developments in column-2.

Column-I	Column-II
(1) Lady Ada Lovelace	(i) Facebook
(2) John Napier	(ii) Microsoft
(3) Mark Zuckerberg	(iii) Napier's bones
(4) Bill Gates	(iv) First computer program

(a) 1-iv, 2-iii, 3-i, 4-ii

(b) 1-ii, 2-iv, 3-i, 4-iii

(c) 1-iii, 2-iv, 3-ii, 4-i

(d) 1-iv, 2-i, 3-ii, 4-iii

Space for Rough Work

15. Which of the following devices is found inside laptops and desktop computers?

(a)  (b) 

(c) 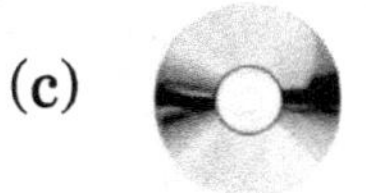 (d) 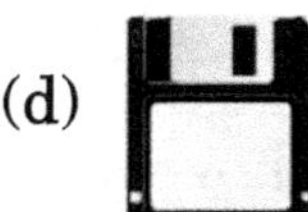

16. Which of the following statements is/are correct about the given device?

1. It controls all the functions of CPU.
2. It is known as processor and also the brain of computer.

(a) Only (1)
(b) Only (2)
(c) Both (1) & (2)
(d) Neither (1) Nor (2)

17 A computer should be protected from____________.

(a) dust
(b) water
(c) oil items
(d) all of these.

18. Which of the following is/are correct with respect to save as commands?

(i) Save as command allows you to save all the changes to the file using different name.

(ii) By default file is saving as word document.

(a) Both (I) & (II)
(b) Only (II)
(c) Only (I)
(d) Neither (I) nor (II)

Space for Rough Work

19. Identify the name of built-in app with respect to Windows 8.1.

(a) World (b) People

(c) Mail (d) Chat

20. What does the following display?

(a) The home screen of Windows 8.

(b) The home screen of Windows mobile

(c) The start screen of Windows 8.1.

(d) The charms menu on Windows 8.

21. Which of the following statements is/are correct for the main features of windows 10?

I. Being lazy just got a lot easier

II. Xbox & Universal App

III. Improved Multitasking

(a) Only (III)

(b) Both (II) & (III)

(c) (I), (II) & (III)

(d) None of these

22. One drive is an online file storage service given by__________.

(a) IBM

(b) Microsoft

(c) Google

(d) Apple

Space for Rough Work

23. What is the name of the component of MS-word 2010 that is indicated by arrow, shown in figure below.

(a) Quick access tool-bar

(b) Status-bar

(c) Ruler

(d) MS-office button

24 Select the odd one out.

(a) 

(b) BHIM

(c) PayPal

(d) paytm

25. What is the latest version of windows operating system?

(a) Windows 8.1

(b) Windows 10

(c) Windows 10.2

(d) Windows 8

Space for Rough Work

HINTS & EXPLANATIONS

ENGLISH

MOCK TEST 1

ANSWER KEY									
1	(c)	8	(a)	15	(d)	22	(b)	29	(b)
2	(b)	9	(c)	16	(c)	23	(a)	30	(c)
3	(b)	10	(b)	17	(b)	24	(c)	31	(b)
4	(c)	11	(b)	18	(d)	25	(b)	32	(b)
5	(b)	12	(c)	19	(c)	26	(d)	33	(c)
6	(d)	13	(c)	20	(b)	27	(b)	34	(c)
7	(d)	14	(c)	21	(b)	28	(a)	35	(a)

1. (c) Hammar

2. (b) Carpenter is a person who makes and repairs wooden objects and structures.

3. (b) Desire

4. (c) Foundation

5. (b) Wooden

6. (d) Except gloves all other things are related to feet.

7. (d) Except carpet all others are furniture items.

8. (a) Except mango all others are vegetables.

9. (c) Knife : Clean is the odd pair. A knife is not used to clean but to cut.

10. (b) Car : Mechanic is the odd pair. A car should be classified under automobile.

11. (b) We were stuck in the traffic jam.

12. (c) The show begins at 11 o'clock in the morning.

13. (c) We plan to see him between two and three in the afternoon tomorrow.

14. (c) The wings of the butterfly are very beautiful.

15. (d) The cat was sitting under the table.

16. (c) Aditya should improve his handwriting.

17. (b) Are you?

18. (d) Rain has stopped now. The match might resume shortly.

19. (c) How are you going to Mumbai?

20. (b) Statement I is incorrect because teacher is not related to garden in the same way as doctor is related to patient.

21. (b) Statement I is grammatically incorrect. It should be "Anita writes a letter".

22. (b) Because there was no food to eat

23. (a) Because there was no one left to eat

24. (c) There would be another lion.

25. (b) very long

26. (d) king of the jungle

27. (b) Jane: I was planning a trip to Germany during the summer vacation

Davis: What a coincidence! Even I was discussing the same trip yesterday.

28. (a) Do you have any hobby?

Yes, I like playing chess and reading.

29. (b) What do you do?

I am into property business.

30. (c) Sales Girl: Good morning, Sir. May I help you?.

Customer: Yes, do you have split A.C's?

31. (b) In which class do your children study?

My son is in 2nd standard and my daughter is in 4th standard.

32. (b) If good is to better, then cool is to cooler.

33. (c) If pen is to pens, then tooth is to teeth.

34. (c) Why are you so happy today?

35. (a) My children like white rabbits.

MOCK TEST 2

ANSWER KEY									
1	(b)	8	(c)	15	(a)	22	(c)	29	(c)
2	(a)	9	(a)	16	(c)	23	(b)	30	(b)
3	(c)	10	(a)	17	(d)	24	(a)	31	(d)
4	(a)	11	(a)	18	(a)	25	(b)	32	(b)
5	(d)	12	(c)	19	(a)	26	(b)	33	(d)
6	(a)	13	(a)	20	(a)	27	(a)	34	(d)
7	(d)	14	(c)	21	(c)	28	(a)	35	(c)

1. (b) Beetroot

2. (a) Fawn

3. (c) Marigold

4. (a) Achieve is the correct spelling.

5. (d) Across is the correct spelling.

6. (a) Calendar is the correct spelling.

7. (d) Except knife all others are crockery items.

8. (c) Except bananas all other are vegetables.

9. (a) Except an all others are used to refer to more than one.

10. (a) Except sandwich all others are in liquid form.

11. (a) Except grave all others are synonyms of one another.

12. (c) Both statements are correct.

13. (a) Only statement I is correct.

14. (c) If hexagon is to six, then octagon is to eight.

15. (a) If dog is to bitch, then bear is to sow.

16. (c) Yuvraj hit the ball into the stands for a six.

17. (d) We have been living in Delhi since 2010.

18. (a) Oh! that garage is on fire. Call for help.

19. (a) A herd of cattle is crossing the road.

20. (a) Those women are going for a party.

21. (c) Because his father was taking him out for picnic

22. (c) Deer park

23. (b) Five

24. (a) Outdoor games

25. (b) Small. Antonyms are opposite words.

26. (b) Hello, Karen. How are you feeling today?

Karen: Much better, thanks for your concern.

27. (a) Hello, Harry. It's my birthday today. I am throwing a party at my place. Will you come?

Harry: Thanks for inviting me. Many-many happy returns of the day. Yes I will come

28. (a) Do you know, what is the date today?

Of course, today is 30th march

29. (c) Tom: Ms. Jannet, is it your first trip to California?

Jannet: Yes, everything is new to me. California is lovely.

30. (b) The scenery out there is so beautiful.

Yes, the scenery is beautiful.

31. (d) Srinagar is extremely beautiful.

32. (b) Abhishek is as tall as his father.

33. (d) My examination result is better than yours.

34. (d) big step

35. (c) The sun rises in the east.

MOCK TEST 3

ANSWER KEY									
1	(d)	8	(b)	15	(d)	22	(c)	29	(c)
2	(b)	9	(a)	16	(b)	23	(b)	30	(b)
3	(d)	10	(a)	17	(b)	24	(a)	31	(b)
4	(b)	11	(d)	18	(c)	25	(d)	32	(c)
5	(a)	12	(a)	19	(c)	26	(a)	33	(c)
6	(c)	13	(c)	20	(d)	27	(d)	34	(c)
7	(a)	14	(b)	21	(d)	28	(a)	35	(b)

1. (d) I missed the train because I was late.

2. (b) Rima met Ruchi when she was in Mumbai.

3. (d) Abstract noun of child is childhood.

4. (b) He went to his friend's house.

5. (a) I am going to stay at home this weekend.

6. (c) The sun rises in the east.

7. (a) He works in a post office.

8. (b) Congratulations

9. (a) There is a garden in the backyard.

10. (a) I have kept my books on the table.

11. (d) Resolute

12. (a) Punishment

13. (c) Qualified is the correct spelling.

14. (b) Reciprocal is the correct spelling.

15. (d) All words are correctly spelled.

16. (b) This is Jack's car.

17. (b) Bull

18. (c) Duck

19. (c) Except fridge all others have blades that move.

20. (d) Except monkey all others are flesh eating animals.

21. (d) Except South Africa all others are neighbouring counties of India.

22. (c) Mahatma Gandhi believed in the policy of truth and non-violence.

23. (b) 2nd October is celebrated as International Day of Non-Violence worldwide.

24. (a) **25. (d)** **26. (a)**

27. (d) **28. (a)**

29. (c) Of course, it's my pleasure.

30. (b) A sentence whose meaning is unclear is called ambiguous.

31. (b) A person who is very polite is called humble.

32. (c) If Chennai is to India then Brisbane is to Australia.

33. (c) If tiger is to cub then deer is to fawn.

34. (c) Worry

35. (b) Surprise

MOCK TEST 4

ANSWER KEY									
1	(b)	8	(c)	15	(c)	22	(d)	29	(a)
2	(c)	9	(b)	16	(c)	23	(a)	30	(a)
3	(d)	10	(a)	17	(a)	24	(a)	31	(b)
4	(c)	11	(a)	18	(c)	25	(c)	32	(b)
5	(b)	12	(b)	19	(a)	26	(b)	33	(a)
6	(a)	13	(b)	20	(c)	27	(a)	34	(d)
7	(c)	14	(c)	21	(a)	28	(c)	35	(a)

1. (b) Steve's mother is in the garden.

2. (c) What did he see in the water?

3. (d) Noun of 'Happy' is 'Happiness'.

4. (c) Gold is a material noun.

5. (b) This is a pronoun.

6. (a) Delhi is the capital of India. It is a beautiful city.

7. (c) He saw a girl. The girl was beautiful.

8. (c) If hockey is to goal, then cricket is to run.

9. (b) If grain is to kilogram, then milk is to litre.

10. (a) I congratulate you on the occasion of your birthday.

11. (a) He has been playing for two hours.

12. (b) secular

13. (b) buildings

14. (c) He bought a laptop yesterday.

15. (c) She lives in London at Hudson Avenue.

16. (c) She is wise as well as a beautiful girl.

17. (a) He will not play in the next match because he is injured.

18. (c) Request

19. (a) Hunt

20. (c) Freedom

21. (a) Extrinsic

22. (d) Civilised is the correct spelling.

23. (a) Rumour is the correct spelling.

24. (a) Goose

25. (c) Poetess

26. (b) They trap heat and increase temperature.

27. (a) Because of human activities.

28. (c) Yes, I am quite tired; I'll go home and rest.

29. (a) I know it was very tough.

30. (a) Even I want to go, I like his singing.

31. (b) Ok, I will manage on my own.

32. (b) Snake

33. (a) Rabbit

34. (d) People go to temple, mosque, gurudwara, church, etc., to worship the God.

35. (a) A baby who has no one to take care is called orphan.

MOCK TEST 5

ANSWER KEY									
1	(c)	9	(a)	17	(a)	25	(b)	33	(a)
2	(c)	10	(c)	18	(b)	26	(b)	34	(b)
3	(b)	11	(a)	19	(a)	27	(a)	35	(a)
4	(c)	12	(a)	20	(a)	28	(c)	36	(b)
5	(b)	13	(a)	21	(b)	29	(b)	37	(a)
6	(c)	14	(c)	22	(c)	30	(c)	38	(c)
7	(a)	15	(c)	23	(c)	31	(b)	39	(a)
8	(b)	16	(a)	24	(c)	32	(c)	40	(c)

1. (c) Musician is the befitting professional with others.

2. (c) The degree of superlative is appropriate.

3. (b) Fled modifies threw down both in the past.

4. (c) Through

5. (b) To visit someone in the place where they are, especially their house.

6. (c) Sight-- The area or distance within which someone can see or something can be seen; Site-- An area of ground on which a town, building, or monument is constructed.

7. (a) Berth-- A fixed bunk on a ship, train, or other means of transport.

Birth--- The emergence of a baby or other young from the

body of its mother; the start of life as a physically separate being.

8. (b) Used to refer to one or some of a thing or number of things, no matter how much or how many

9. (a) Overcome a difficulty

10. (c) Both the qualities are described.

11. (a) Monday, Wednesday and Friday

12. (a) Both reading and Math

13. (a) Frequently; many times

14. (c) Indicating a division, choice, differentiation involving three or more participants.

15. (c) A place set aside for special use, in particular.

16. (a) A structure carrying a road, path, railway, etc., across a river, road or other obstacle.

17. (a) Here the of essor performs action

18. (b) A group of players forming one side in a competitive game or sport.

19. (a) Around that period of time.

20. (a) Having the thing mentioned as a target, aim or focus.

21. (b) Common means occurring, found or done often; prevalent

22. (c) Other two are associated with action.

23. (c) All are related with play.

24. (c) Indicating location of a physical object beside a place or object.

25. (b)

26. (b) Take hold of so as to seize or restrain or stop the motion of

27. (a) Vet----A veterinary surgeon

Wet----Covered or saturated with water or another liquid.

28. (c) Piece------A written, musical or artistic creation.

Peace------A state or period in which there is no war or a war has ended.

29. (b) Keep under careful observation

30. (c) Piglet is the baby of a pig.

31. (b) The word means a large natural elevation of the earth's surface rising abruptly from the surrounding level; a large steep hill.

32. (c) Turmeric is a spice, rest are flowers.

33. (a) The teacher's name is in feminine gender. A pronoun should be used here.

34. (b) Father is in singular form so the verb will follow singular form.

35. (a) The bird lives in Mumbai, Maharashtra.

36. (b) Two bags full of favourite seedmix, lots of green chillies, another baby parrot to play with.

37. (a) Seedmix and Green Chillies

38. (c) He does not keep the parrot in cage.

39. (a) Both are introductory statements.

40. (c) A person who is in charge of a worker or organisation.

MATHEMATICS

MOCK TEST-1

ANSWERS KEY									
1.	(a)	9.	(c)	17.	(a)	25.	(b)	33.	(c)
2.	(c)	10.	(b)	18.	(b)	26.	(c)	34.	(c)
3.	(a)	11.	(a)	19.	(c)	27.	(a)	35.	(c)
4.	(b)	12.	(c)	20.	(d)	28.	(b)	36.	(c)
5.	(c)	13.	(b)	21.	(c)	29.	(a)	37.	(b)
6.	(a)	14.	(a)	22.	(a)	30.	(a)	38.	(b)
7.	(b)	15.	(c)	23.	(a)	31.	(b)	39.	(c)
8.	(b)	16.	(a)	24.	(a)	32.	(a)	40.	(c)

1. **(a)** $765 + 65 + 70 - 45 - 35$

$= 830 + 70 - 45 - 35$

$= 900 - 45 - 35$

$= 855 - 35$

$= 820$

2. **(c)** $5 \times 300 = 1500$

$(5 \times 3) \times 100 = 15 \times 100$

$= 1500$

3. **(a)** $\frac{5}{7}$ of $49 = \frac{5}{7} \times 49$

$= 35$

4. **(b)** Two digit smallest number = 10

Smallest even number = 2

Division = $\frac{10}{2}$

Quotient = 5

5. **(c)** Total parts = 8

Unshaded part = 3

Fraction = $\frac{3}{8}$

6. **(a)** Given number = 45,632

Face value of 5 = 5

Place value of 5 = 5,000

Difference = 5000 – 5 = 4995

7. **(b)**

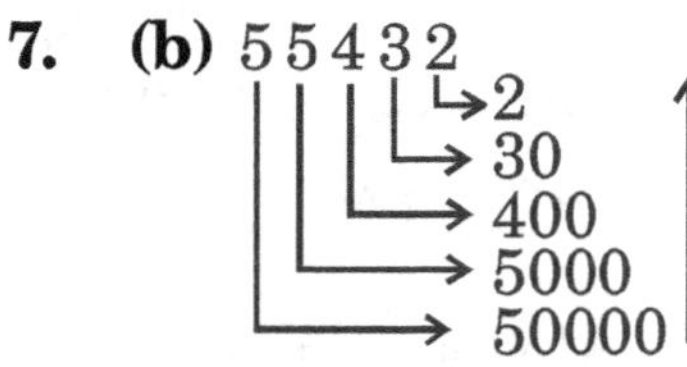

expanded form of 55432 = 50000 + 5000 + 400 + 30 + 2

8. **(b)** Line extends in both directions without end.

9. **(c)** $\because$ 1 kilometre = 1000 metres

$\therefore$ 5km 60m = 5 × 1000 m + 60 m

= 5060 m.

10 **(b)** Cost of a bag = ₹ 145.75

Cost of an instrument = ₹ 23.25

Total money paid by peter =

₹ (145.75 + 23.25) = ₹169.00.

11. **(a)** $\because$ Rotation of second hand of a watch in 1 minute = 1

$\therefore$ Rotation of second hand of a watch in 30 minutes

= 1 × 30 = 30.

12. **(c)** $\because$ The cost of 19 pens = ₹ 247

$\therefore$ The cost of 1 pen = $\frac{247}{19}$ = ₹13

$\therefore$ The cost of 30 pens

= ₹ 13 × 30 = ₹ 390.

13 **(b)** 2735 + 5237 – 3756

= 7972 – 3756

= 4216

14. **(a)** A square has four vertices and four equal sides.

15. **(c)** Given, 56 + 47 – 23 = 89 + 5 – ?

103 – 23 = 89 + 5 – ?

80 = 94 – ?

Subtracting 14 from 94, we get 80.

16. **(a)** A point does not have height, width and length but it has a place.

17. **(a)** $\because$ 1 centimetre = 10 millimetres

$\therefore$ 734 centimetres = 734 × 10

= 7340 millimetres.

18. **(b)** Total parts of pizza = 5

Parts eaten by Priya = 2

Parts left = 3

$\therefore$ Fraction of the pizza left $= \frac{3}{5}$

19. **(c)** (A) → 4, (B) → 1, (C) → 2, (D) → 3

20. **(d)** Length of red ribbon = 3m 5 cm

Length of blue ribbon = 2m 13cm

Total length of ribbons =

	m	cm
	3	05
+	2	13
	5 m	18 cm

21. **(c)** 4 7 8 6 2 3 9

9 → 9
3 → 30
2 → 200
6 → 6000
8 → 80000
7 → 700000
4 → 4000000

Place value of digit 6 is 6000.

Face value of 6 is 6

$\therefore$ Sum = 6000 + 6 = 6006

22. **(a)** Sum of place value of digits of a number is its expanded form.

23. **(a)** Figure which has a starting point and extends in one direction is called ray.

24. **(a)**

25. **(b)** We cannot compare as litre is a unit of volume and kilogram is a unit of weight.

26. **(c)** $\frac{2}{7}$ and $\frac{3}{7}$ have same denominator.

27. **(a)** $\because$ Cost of 4 pens = ₹ 64

$\therefore$ Cost of 1 pen $= \frac{67}{4}$

$\therefore$ Cost of 5 pens

$= \frac{67}{4} \times 5 =$ ₹ 83.75

28. **(b)** Cost of 1 note book = ₹ 13.25

Cost of 9 note books

= 9 × 13.25 = ₹ 119.25

29. **(a)** $\because$ Cost of 6 balloons = ₹ 9

$\therefore$ Cost of 1 balloon = ₹ $\frac{9}{6}$

$\therefore$ Cost of 2 balloons

$= \frac{9}{6} \times 2 =$ ₹ 3

Again,

$\because$ Cost of 9 kites = ₹ 12

$\therefore$ Cost of 1 kite = ₹ $\frac{12}{9}$

$\therefore$ Cost of 3 kites $= \frac{12}{9} \times 3 =$ ₹ 4

Total money paid to the shopkeeper = ₹ 3 + ₹ 4 = ₹ 7.

30. **(a)** Third angle = $180° - (45° + 56°)$

$= 180° - 101° = 79°$

31. **(b)** There are 8 triangles in the given figure.

32. **(a)** The figure is divided into 8 equal parts.

Fraction for shaded part = $\frac{3}{8}$.

33. **(c)** Total questions = 40

Marks for questions carry 2 marks = 30 × 2 = 60

Marks for questions carry 4 marks = 10 × 4 = 40

Total marks = 60 + 40

= 100 marks.

34. **(c)** JKL

35. **(c)** $\frac{3}{9} = \frac{1}{3}, \frac{2}{6} = \frac{1}{3}, \frac{4}{12} = \frac{1}{3}$

But $\frac{8}{10} = \frac{4}{5}$

36. **(c)** If David's game starts at 10:00 a.m. in the morning, then by 2:25 p.m. he would have played for four hour twenty five minutes.

37. **(b)** Capacity of mug = 500 mℓ

Capacity of bucket = 5ℓ

= 5000 mℓ

Number of mugs needed

= 5000 ÷ 500 = 10

38. **(b)** Ritu ate sweets = $\frac{3}{7}$

Priya ate sweets = $\frac{2}{7}$

They ate together = $\frac{3}{7}+\frac{2}{7}=\frac{5}{7}$

(Sol. 39-40):

39. **(c)** Since, 𝍸||| = 8

He used 8 roses.

40. **(c)** Since, Lily was used the most times, i.e.,12 times.

MOCK TEST-2

ANSWERS KEY									
1.	**(c)**	**8.**	**(c)**	**15.**	**(a)**	**22.**	**(b)**	**29.**	**(a)**
2.	**(b)**	**9.**	**(b)**	**16.**	**(c)**	**23.**	**(a)**	**30.**	**(a)**
3.	**(b)**	**10.**	**(a)**	**17.**	**(c)**	**24.**	**(b)**	**31.**	**(b)**
4.	**(b)**	**11.**	**(c)**	**18.**	**(a)**	**25.**	**(c)**	**32.**	**(b)**
5.	**(c)**	**12.**	**(b)**	**19.**	**(c)**	**26.**	**(a)**	**33.**	**(c)**
6.	**(c)**	**13.**	**(b)**	**20.**	**(c)**	**27.**	**(b)**	**34.**	**(b)**
7.	**(c)**	**14.**	**(b)**	**21.**	**(b)**	**28.**	**(b)**	**35.**	**(c)**

1. **(c)** Given

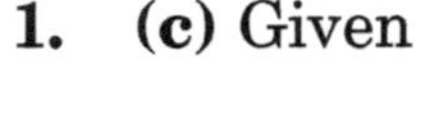

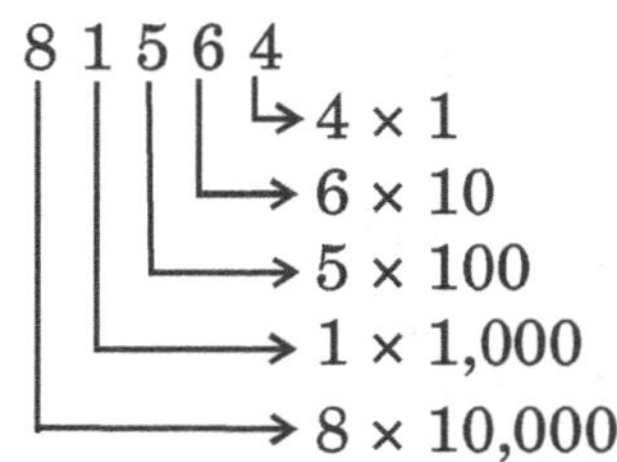

2. **(b)** Expanded form of 648345 = 600,000 + 40,000 + 8,000 + 300 + 40 + 5.

3. **(b)**

A ● —————— ● B

President house India gate

The length between two fixed points is called a line segment.

4. **(b)** There are 8 triangles in the figure.

5. **(c)** 65 kg = 65000 g

Difference = 65000 g – 62450 g

= 2550 g

= 2kg 550 g

6. **(c)** 52367mℓ = 52000mℓ + 367mℓ

= 52ℓ 367mℓ

7. **(c)** Greatest five digit number

= 99999

Smallest five digit number

= 10000

Difference = 99999 – 10000

= 89999

8. **(c)** $\because$ Distance covered in one hour

= 12 km

$\therefore$ Distance covered in 6 hours

= 12 × 6 = 72 km

9. **(b)** $\because$ 1 km = 1000 m

$\therefore$ 4 km = 4 × 1000 = 4000 m

4 km 5 metre = 4000 + 5 = 4005 m

10. **(a)** A sphere has only one curved face.

11. **(c)** The figure given is a hexagon and it has six vertices.

12. (b) 2 is the smallest even number.

13. (b) Product of a number by 0 is 0.

14. (b) A year has 12 months.

There are 100 cm in 1 metre.

15. (a) ∵ The cost of 12 toffees = ₹ 6

= 600 paise

∵ ₹ 1 = 100 paise

∴ The cost of 1 toffee

$= \frac{600}{12} = 50$ paise

16. (c) A cube has length, width and height, eight corners and all sides are equal.

17. (c) The correct descending order is $\frac{13}{9} > \frac{11}{9} > \frac{7}{9} > \frac{4}{9}$.

(Sol. 18 to 20) :

18. (a) Given

= 500 number of vehicles

number of scooters is parking

= 3 × 500 = 1500

19. (c) Number of cars in parking

= 2 × 500 = 1000

20. (c) Number of auto in parking

= 3 × 500 = 1500

Thus, number of scooters = Number of auto

21. (b) 1980 – 1890 = 90.

22. (b) Short form of 50000 + 4000 + 300 + 20 + 8 is 54328

23. (a) 1524 + 12 = 1536

24. (b) Cody had green apples = 1230

Red apples = 8270

Total number of apples

= 1230 + 8270 = 9500

Apples sold = 6783

Apples left

= 9500 – 6783 = 2717

25. (c) ∵ In 1 minute a tap dispense water = 5 litres

∴ In 1 hour (60 minutes) it dispense water = 5 × 60 = 300 litres

26. (a) The cost of 1 rice plate = ₹ 230

The cost of 1 plate of green vegetables = ₹ 175

The cost of 1 cup of curd = ₹ 35

Cody paid = ₹ 230 + ₹ 175 + ₹ 35 = ₹ 440

27. (b) The largest 4 digit number

= 9999

The smallest 2 digit number = 10

The sum of largest 4 digit number and smallest 2 digit number =

9999 + 10 = 10009

28. (b) Total number of voters = 34765

Total number of women voters = 25621

Then, total number of men voters

= 34765 – 25621 = 9144

29. (a) $12 \div 4 = 3$

30. (a) The total number of people in train = 880

Number of coaches = 8

Number of people in each coach

$= \frac{880}{8} = 110.$

31. (b) $\because$ Cost of 1 packet of toffees

= ₹75.20

$\therefore$ Cost of 5 packets of toffees

= ₹75.20 × 5 = ₹376.00

32. (b) Total sheets of paper in bundles

= 3960

Number of sheets in one bundle

= 18

Number of bundles

$= 3960 \div 18 = 220$

$$\begin{array}{r} 220 \\ 18\overline{)3960(} \\ -36 \\ \hline 36 \\ -36 \\ \hline 0 \\ \hline \end{array}$$

33. (c) Difference $= \frac{7}{4} - \frac{3}{4} = \frac{4}{4} = 1$

34. (b) Maximum time for English test paper = 45 minutes

The test starts at 10 : 00 a.m.

So, the test ends =

Hour	Minute
10	00
+	45
10	45

$\therefore$ 10 h 45 min = 10 : 45 a.m.

35. (c) $(A) \to 3, (B) \to 4, (C) \to 1, (D) \to 2$

(A) $\frac{2}{7} + \frac{3}{7} = \frac{2+3}{7} = \frac{5}{7}$

(B) $\frac{6}{7} - \frac{2}{7} = \frac{6-2}{7} = \frac{4}{7}$

(C) $\frac{9}{10} - \frac{3}{10} = \frac{9-3}{10} = \frac{6}{10} = \frac{3}{5}$

(D) $\frac{2}{10} + \frac{3}{10} = \frac{2+3}{10} = \frac{5}{10} = \frac{1}{2}$

MOCK TEST-3

ANSWERS KEY							
1	(b)	9	(d)	17	(d)	25	(b)	33	(c)
2	(d)	10	(b)	18	(b)	26	(a)	34	(b)
3	(c)	11	(d)	19	(d)	27	(a)	35	(c)
4	(b)	12	(d)	20	(c)	28	(c)	36	(b)
5	(b)	13	(d)	21	(d)	29	(a)	37	(b)
6	(d)	14	(c)	22	(c)	30	(c)	38	(b)
7	(b)	15	(b)	23	(c)	31	(b)	39	(c)
8	(a)	16	(c)	24	(c)	32	(a)	40	(b)

1. **(b)** The given numbers in the box are all between 10 and 100.

2. **(d)** 987 rounded off to nearest 100 is 1000.

3. **(c)** 15 25 ?=30 35 45

4. **(b)** 80850 comes between 80849 and 80851.

5. **(b)** 300 – 198 = 102

6. **(d)** XXXIX = 30 + 9 = 39

7. **(b)** 5 thousands + 6 tens = 5060

Now, 5060 – 4 = 5056

8. **(a)** There are 12 balloons in the picture.

The number sentence is

3 + 3 + 3 + 3 = 12

9. **(d)** Number of alphabets = 26

Number of vowels = 5

Number of consonants

= 26 – 5 = 21

Fraction of consonants = $\frac{21}{26}$

10. **(b)** 372 rounds upto 400

313 rounds down to 300

Estimated sum

= 400 + 300 = 700

11. **(d)** 985 × 8 = 7880

= 7000 + 800 + 80

12. **(d)** 275 × 8

= 2200

= 22 × 100

13. **(d)** 52037 mℓ = 52000 mℓ + 37mℓ

= 52ℓ 37mℓ

14. **(c)** When 497 is divided by 9.

```
9)497(55
  45
  ---
   47
   45
   ---
    2
```

Thus, the remainder is 2.

15. **(b)** $\frac{1}{3}$ of 18 = 6

16. (c) Samiksha has cream roles

= 644

Number of friends = 14

Each friend will get = $\frac{644}{14} = 46$

17. (d) $\left(\frac{1}{5} - \frac{1}{5}\right) + \frac{1}{5}$

$= 0 + \frac{1}{5}$

$= \frac{1}{5}$

18. (b) Total parts = 12

Shaded parts = 5

Fractional part of the design is shaded = $\frac{5}{12}$

19. (d) The cost of each stamp = ₹5.15

The cost of 40 stamps

= ₹ 5.15 × 40 = ₹ 206

20. (c) Number of weeks = $\frac{210}{7} = 30$

21. (d) Six thousand eight hundred two rupees = ₹6802.

22. (c) (A) → 4, (B) → 1, (C) → 2, (D) → 3

(A) 5 hours 20 minutes

= (5 × 60) minutes + 20 min.

= 300 + 20 = 320 minutes

(B) 3 minutes 40 seconds

= (3 × 60) minutes + 40 seconds

= 180 + 40 = 220 seconds

(C) 2 years = 2 × 365 = 730 days

(D) 9 months = 9 × 30 = 270 days

23. (c) Rani starts studies at 5: 30 p.m.

Rani finishes at 7 p.m.

She studies = 7 p.m. – 5:30 p.m.

= 1 hour 30 minutes

She studies for 1 hour 30 minutes.

24. (c) Quarter past 4 = 4 : 15

Half past 4 = 4 : 30

Time will be taken from quarter past 4 to be half past 4

= 4 : 30 – 4 : 15 = 15 minutes.

25. (b) Raj runs 2 minutes more on everyday from previous day. So, he would have been running on the tenth day = 14 + 2 (fourth day) + 2 (fifth day) + 2 (sixth day) + 2 (seventh day) + 2 (eight day) + 2 (ninth day) + 2 (tenth day) = 28 minutes.

26. (a) 1980

27. (a) Balance is used to measure the weight of a rock.

28. (c) ∵ 1 hand = 4 inches

∴ 14 hands = 14 × 4 = 56 inches.

29. (a)

x 1000	x 100	x 10	Metre(m)	x1/10	x1/100	x1/1000
kilo	hecta	deca		deci	centi	milli

Thus, 1 milimetre is the shortest length.

30. (c) The pair of shapes given in option (c) can be put together to form the rectangle.

31. (b) Figure in option (b) is not symmetrical.

32. (a) Each represents 5 babies.

So, Srikanth needs to add 3 more to finish the graph.

33. (c) Maximum number of ice-creams were sold on Sunday.

34. (b) According to pictograph daisies is chosen by 4 mothers.

35. (c) Most of Mrs. Keertana's friends have dog.

36. (b) 4 beads should be removed from the hundred's place in the abcacus to represent a number between 500 and 600.

37. (b) 2 burgers cost = ₹10

1 burger cost = ₹ 5

1 burger and 1 cake cost = ₹15

1 cake cost = ₹15 – ₹ 5 = ₹10.

1 cake and 1 icecream cost = ₹18

1 icecream cost = ₹18 – ₹10

= ₹ 8

38. (b) The cost of videogame = ₹2205

Radhika saved money = ₹2147

She need to save money

= ₹2205– ₹2147 = ₹58.

39. (c) $19-18+17-16+15-14+13-12$

$= 1 + 17 - 16 + 15 - 14 + 13 - 12$

$= 18 - 16 + 15 - 14 + 13 - 12$

$= 2 + 15 - 14 + 13 - 12$

$= 17 - 14 + 13 - 12$

$= 3 + 13 - 12$

$= 16 - 12$

$= 4$

40. (b) A cube has six faces.

MOCK TEST-4

ANSWERS KEY									
1	(a)	8	(a)	15	(d)	22	(a)	29	(d)
2	(c)	9	(b)	16	(c)	23	(d)	30	(d)
3	(c)	10	(a)	17	(d)	24	(a)	31	(a)
4	(d)	11	(c)	18	(c)	25	(d)	32	(b)
5	(a)	12	(a)	19	(c)	26	(a)	33	(b)
6	(b)	13	(b)	20	(a)	27	(c)	34	(c)
7	(a)	14	(d)	21	(b)	28	(b)	35	(c)

1. (a) The abacus represents 1 × thousands + 9 hundreds + 9 tens + 9 ones

$= 1 \times 1000 + 9 \times 100 + 9 \times 10 + 9 = 1999.$

2. (c) Given number = 5843

$= 5 \times 1000 + 8 \times 100 + 4 \times 10 + 3$

The number 5843 has 5 thousands.

3. (c) The greatest three digit number is 999.

4. (d) The number sentence

8540 – ? = 6324

? = 8540 – 6324

? = 2216.

5. (a) Number of balloons Kashi has = 4888

Number of balloons Vivek has = 4777

Total number of balloons

= 4888 + 4777 = 9665.

6. (b) Complement of $65° = 90° - 65° = 25°$

7. (a) △4 + [6] = 10

[6] – △4 = 2

8. (a) Number of bowls = 3

Number of apples in each bowl = 7

So, number sentence = $7 \times 3 = 21$.

9. (b) $1000 \div 20 = 50$

10. (a) $165 \div 5 = 33$

and $165 \times 0 = 0$

$33 > 0$.

11. (c) $1978 \div 8$ = quotient is 247 and remainder is 2.

12. (a) Numerator of the fractions is same.

So, the correct arrangement is

$\frac{1}{8} < \frac{1}{4} < \frac{1}{2}$.

13. (b) 13 + 7 = 20, 20 + 7 = 27, 27 + 7 =34, 34 + 7 = 41

14. (d) Since, numerator of the fractions is same. So, the larger is the denominator, the smaller is the number.

Here, 9 > 7 > 5 > 2.

The correct option is (d).

15. (d) Saumya saves every month

= ₹ 225

She saves in 12 months

= ₹ 225 × 12 = ₹ 2700

16. (c) In India, the unit of currency is rupee.

17. (d) $\because$ cost of 5 pens = ₹ 425

$\therefore$ cost of 1 pen = ₹ $\frac{425}{5}$ = ₹ 85

18. (c) 11 : 25 a.m. $\xrightarrow{\text{1hour}}$ 12:25p.m. $\xrightarrow{\text{1hour}}$ 1 : 25 p.m. $\xrightarrow{\text{1hour}}$ 2: 25 p.m.

19. (c) Both statements are true.

20. (a) 1 day = 1 × 24 hours

= 1 × 24 × 60 minutes

= 1440 minutes.

21. (b) (A) → 3,(B) → 1,(C) → 4,(D) → 2

22. (a) The minutes hand takes 1 rotation to complete 1 hour. So, it will take 6 rotations to move hour hand from 3 to 9.

23. (d) Weight of each □ = 1 kg

So, 9 kg + 16 kg = 25 kg.

24. (a) 1 litre = 1000 ml

So, 1000 ml + 250 ml

= 1250 ml.

25. (d) A cuboid has 6 faces and 8 vertices.

26. (a) Circle is made of curved line only.

27. (c) According to pictograph 60 students played soccer. So, the most popular sport is soccer.

28. (b) House - 2 has number of fish = 13

House - 3 has number of fish = 10

Number of fish in house - 2 more than house - 3

= 13 – 10 = 3

29. (d) Purple is the most favorite colour of class III students.

30. (d) 104 × 50 = (100 + 4) × 50

= (100 × 50) + (4 × 50).

31. (a) The correct check is quotient × divisor + remainder = dividend.

32. (b) There are 5 triangles in the given drawing.

33. (b) The standard unit of measuring weight is kilogram. millilitre is written as ml.

34. (c) 2050 m*l* = 2000 m*l* + 50 m*l*

= 2 *l* 50m*l*

35. (c) 18 faces of the 4 cubes were painted red.

MOCK TEST-5

ANSWERS KEY									
1	(c)	8	(a)	15	(a)	22	(b)	29	(a)
2	(d)	9	(c)	16	(c)	23	(b)	30	(a)
3	(b)	10	(b)	17	(b)	24	(c)	31	(c)
4	(d)	11	(b)	18	(c)	25	(c)	32	(c)
5	(b)	12	(a)	19	(d)	26	(c)	33	(b)
6	(b)	13	(b)	20	(a)	27	(a)	34	(d)
7	(a)	14	(c)	21	(b)	28	(c)	35	(b)

1. (c) The greatest four digit number can be formed using 7, 0, 6, 5 without repeating the digits is 7650.

2. (d) Ritu jogged on Monday = 350 m

She jogged on Tuesday = 350 m + 170 m = 520m

She jogged altogether = 350 m + 520 m = 870 m

3. (b) Abacus in option (b) shows 5231 which is greater than 4321.

4. (d) The biggest number made using defferent digits is 689.

5. (b) Gopal and Raju said the truth and the 2-digit number is 99.

6. (b) Number of eggs produced in March is 5,879 and May is 5,164.

5, 164 < 5, 879

7. (a) The distance yet to be covered

$\frac{1000}{2}$ km.

8. (a) Given, 2467 + $\square$ = 7121

$\square$ = 7121 –2467 = 4654.

9. (c) $\because$ Ticket to the dolphin show costs for 1 adult = ₹ 999

Estimated cost of a ticket

= ₹1000

$\therefore$ A ticket for 3 adults will cost

= 1000 + 1000 + 1000

= ₹ 3000

10. (b) 43 = 40 + 3 = XL + III = XLIII

11. (b) Number sentence = 14 × $\square$

224 = 14 × $\square$

$\square = \frac{224}{14}$

$\square$ = 16

12. (a) Figure given in option (a) shows $\frac{1}{6} < \frac{4}{6}$

13. (b) Total numbers in the given box = 11

Number of zeroes at the unit's place = 5

Fraction of such numbers in the given box = $\frac{5}{11}$.

14. (c) The flight takes off at 3 : 30 p.m.
Flight duration is 5 hours 30 minutes.
∴ The flight will land at 9 : 00 p.m. (3 : 30 + 5 : 30).

15. (a) Fraction of circle painted by Jai
$= \frac{2}{8}$
Fraction of circle painted by Nihal $= \frac{3}{8}$
Fraction of circle will be painted by both of them
$= \frac{2}{8} + \frac{3}{8} = \frac{5}{8}$.

16. (c) Rahul has money = ₹ 1120.50
The cost of Robot = ₹ 2080.75
Rahul needs
=₹2080.75 – ₹ 1120.50
= ₹ 960.25

17. (b) ∴ The cost of 16 packets of icecream bricks = ₹ 6400
∴ The cost of 1 ice-cream brick
= ₹$(6400 \div 16)$.

18. (c) XLIX = XL + IX = 40 + 9 = 49

19. (d) Cost of 2 ice creams = 2 × 55
= ₹ 110
Cost of 2 milky bars = 2 × 25 = ₹ 50
Cost of 1 pen = 1 × 75 = ₹ 75
Cost of 1 burger = 1 × 110 = ₹ 110
Total money spent = 110 + 50 + 75 + 110 = ₹ 345
Money left = ₹ 500 – ₹ 345
= ₹ 155.

20. (a) Dia saves money in one day
= ₹ 51.50
She saves in 9 days = 9 × ₹ 51.50
= ₹ 463.50.

21. (b) Total length of rope = 45 m
Number of piece cut by Simran = 5
Length of one piece $= \frac{45}{5} = 9$m

22. (b) Lalita read on Wednesday
= 31 pages
She read on Tuesday = 17 pages
Now,
Difference 31 – 17 = 14 pages
Lalita read 14 pages more on Wednesday than on Tuesday.

23. (b) Numerator of the fractions are same.
$\therefore \frac{11}{9} > \frac{11}{13} > \frac{11}{15}$

24. (c) 12 cuboids [cuboid] are needed to make the given figure.

25. (c) Circle is the base of cylinder.

26. (c) [figure]

Alphabet '[I]' has 2 lines of symmetry.

27. (a) The difference between the minutes of practicing per day = 15 minutes.
So, she will spend 105 minutes in practicing on Saturday.

28. (c) 4

29. (a) 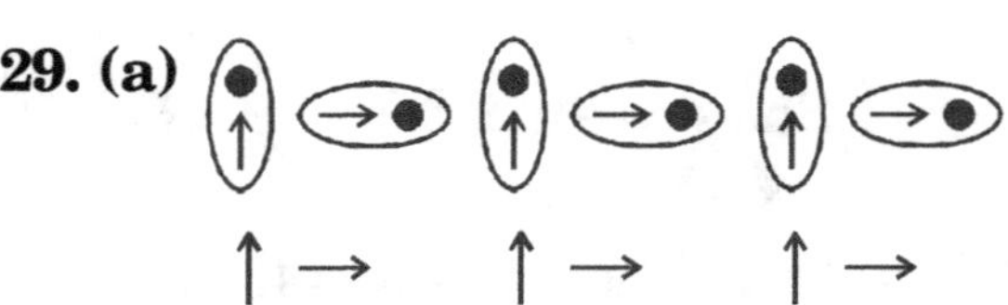

30. (a) (A) → 4, (B) → 3,(C) → 1,(D) → 2

31. (c)

125 $\xrightarrow{-20}$ 105 $\xrightarrow{-20}$ 85 $\xrightarrow{-20}$ 65 $\xrightarrow{-20}$ 45 $\xrightarrow{-20}$ 25

32. (c) Both statements 1 and 2 are true.

33. (b) Number of blue buttons used = 14

Number of pink buttons used = 11

Number of more blue buttons used = 14 – 11 = 3

34. (d) Number of orange buttons used = 8

Number of green buttons used = 13

Number of less orange buttons used = 13 – 8 = 5

35. (b) The number 1000 more than 5529 = 5529 + 1000 = 6529.

SCIENCE

MOCK TEST -1

1	(b)	2	(b)	3	(d)	4	(d)	5	(c)
6	(d)	7	(c)	8	(a)	9	(c)	10	(b)
11	(c)	12	(d)	13	(b)	14	(a)	15	(d)
16	(a)	17	(c)	18	(c)	19	(c)	20	(a)
21	(d)	22	(b)	23	(d)	24	(c)	25	(b)
26	(a)	27	(d)	28	(d)	29	(d)	30	(a)
31	(c)	32	(a)	33	(d)	34	(a)	35	(a)

1. **(b)** Air is a matter as it occupies space and has mass.

2. **(b)** Green plants make their own food, and hence, are called autotrophs.

3. **(d)** 4 is tyre, made up of rubber. We get rubber from plants.

4. **(d)** Touch-Me-Not – living thing
Sunflower – living thing
Water and cloud are non-living things.
(3) and (4) shows movement in living things.

5. **(c)** Taproot is a large, central and most dominant root from which other roots sprout laterally. For example, beetroot, turnip, etc. Fibrous root: It is opposite of taproot and is formed by thin moderately branched roots growing from the stem.

6. **(d)** Water - liquid form, water vapour - gas form, ice - solid form. From the given statement, we can conclude that water is found in all the three states of matter.

7. **(c)** In Summer – you sweat a lot.
In Winters – you need warm clothes.
In Autumn – plants shed their leaves.
In Spring – there are flowers everywhere.
In Rain – it rains heavily.

8. **(a)** Sense organs (ears, nose, eyes and skin) help in obtaining information about the surroundings.

9. **(c)** Turnip plant stores food in the root.

10. **(b)** When you exhale, air moves out from the body, this reduces space in the chest and makes the lung contract. When we inhale lungs expand.

11. **(c)** Water is in liquid state and water vapour is in gaseous state. Evaporation is the process for conversion of a substance (water, etc.) from liquid state to gaseous state.

12. (d) When water boils, we see the water droplets as mist.

13. (b) Uniform motion: A car is said to have uniform Motion, if it travels equal distance in equal interval of time. For example,

A |—1 hr / 30 km—|—1 hr / 30 km—|—1 hr / 30 km—| B

Non-Uniform motion: If a car travels unequal distance in equal interval of time: Example:

A |—1 hr / 30 km—|—1 hr / 31 km—|—1 hr / 30 km—| B

14. (a) Woodpecker has chisel shaped beak.

Crows have sharp pointed triangle-shaped beak.

Parrot has stout red-coloured beak.

Eagle has large hooked beak.

15. (d) Weathering is the breaking down of rocks by physical and chemical process into soil.

16. (a) Males have more diet than females.

17. (c) Industrialization, deforestation are causes of pollution and pollution causes depletion of ozone layer. Thus, by preventing pollution we can prevent depletion of ozone layer.

18. (c) We are able to see the Moon because it reflects light from the Sun.

19. (c) Population is a boon because we cannot do everything on our own but over population is a bane because there will be shortage of food and other resources.

20. (a) Parrot, Kiwi and Ostrich are all birds but all birds can't fly, only parrot can fly.

21. (d) Plants are living organisms, they require air, water and sunlight to make their food. Man requires food, air and water to live.

22. (b) Seeds do not germinate until three needs are met : water, correct temperature (warmth) and good soil.

23. (d) Birds have hollow, lightweight bones and have strong chest muscles to pull their wings up and down.

24. (c) Our sense organs send signals to our brain and then helps us to act accordingly. So our brain helps us to make decisions.

25. (b) Eye muscles

26. (a) Crust is the outermost part of the Earth and is the coolest part.

27. (d) Diamond is the hardest among coal, chalk and slate. They are soft as compared to diamond.

28. (d) Water in the form of ice in glaciers, groundwater and water vapour in atmosphere are available in the form of fresh water.

29. (d) Giraffe, cat and zebra all live on land.

30. (a) Plant is eaten by deer. Dear is eaten by tiger.

31. (c) Both the statements are true. Seeds grow into plants and buds grow into flowers.

32. (a) The food made by the leaves travel through the stem to all parts of the plant.
The food made by the leaves is stored in leaves, root, stem, fruits and seeds.

33. (d) Excretory system removes the waste material from the body.

34. (a) Vultures – strong & sharp beak
Woodpecker – long and sharp beak.
Kingfisher – long and scissors like beak.
Parrot – red coloured beak.

35. (a) Jill and Jane.

MOCK TEST -2

1	(b)	2	(d)	3	(c)	4	(c)	5	(b)
6	(b)	7	(c)	8	(b)	9	(d)	10	(b)
11	(c)	12	(d)	13	(d)	14	(a)	15	(b)
16	(d)	17	(a)	18	(b)	19	(a)	20	(a)
21	(b)	22	(a)	23	(c)	24	(a)	25	(a)
26	(a)	27	(c)	28	(b)	29	(a)	30	(d)
31	(b)	32	(c)	33	(b)	34	(b)	35	(d)

1. (b) 2

2. (d) Cabbage and mint store food in their leaves.

3. (c) Sunlight + Carbon dioxide + Water → Glucose + Oxygen. Thus, photosynthesis needs carbon dioxide gas.

4. (c) A person can become sick from germs and not practicing good hygiene.

5. (b) Public transport is a shared passenger transport service which is available for use by large number of people. Buses, trains, etc, are example of public transport.

6. (b) Sandy soil is found at the beaches.

7. (c) Loamy soil is a combination of sand, silt and clay. Thus, this soil combines the benefits of multiple type of soils that make it up and is considered the best for growing plants.

8. (b) 71% of the Earth is covered by the oceans.

9. (d) Glass is used for making windowpanes.
Plastic is used for making television.
Fibre is used for making cloth.
Rubber is used for making tubes.

10. (b) Statement A is wrong because only living things breathe in oxygen. Elements are non-living.

11. **(c)** Banana tree has soft green stem.
12. **(d)** Nose, windpipe and lungs constitute our breathing system.
13. **(d)** Digestion starts from mouth where food is broken into smaller units with the help of teeth, then tongue helps to push the food into food pipe from where it enters the stomach. After leaving stomach, food enters into small inestine where body absorbs nutrients from the food.
14. **(a)** Mercury, Venus, Earth
15. **(b)** Moon is the nearest celestial body to the Earth.
16. **(d)** Humus is black or dark brown in colour. It is an organic material that is formed in soil when plant and animal matter decay.
17. **(a)** Animals can feel changes around them because they have sense organs. Plants feel changes but do not have sense organs.
18. **(b)** Birds don't have teeth to eat.
19. **(a)** The surface of the Moon has craters. Moon revolves around the Earth.
20. **(a)** Asteroids are smaller than planets which revolve around the Sun.
21. **(b)** Moon is a natural satellite.
22. **(a)** The movement of air from the sea towards the land is known a sea breeze.
23. **(c)** Polythene bags are non-biodegradable so they are not degraded by the help of micro organisms and cause environmental pollution. That is why, government advice to discard the use of polythene bags.
24. **(a)** Flowers give rise to fruits. Fruits bear seeds which give rise to a new plant.
25. **(a)** After running, oxygen requirement of the body increases. That is why, we breathe fast to fulfill the oxygen requirement of our body.
26. **(a)** Herbivores eat only plants and plant products.
27. **(c)** Climbers require support for their growth.
28. **(b)** Production of food is carried out by leaves and other green parts of the plant.
29. **(a)** The image shown is a monkey which is an arboreal animal. Arboreal animals live on trees.
30. **(d)** Lion is a carnivore which eats other animals, goat is a herbivore, frog is an amphibian and snake is a reptile.
31. **(b)** This is a turnip which has tap root.
32. **(c)** Silk and cotton both are natural fibres. Silk is obtained from silk worm and cotton is obtained from cotton plant.
33. **(b)** Mushroom is a non-green plant.
34. **(b)** Figure (b) is dog which has a very good sense of smelling.
35. **(d)** Lava

MOCK TEST -3

1	(a)	2	(b)	3	(c)	4	(d)	5	(b)
6	(d)	7	(b)	8	(a)	9	(a)	10	(b)
11	(c)	12	(a)	13	(a)	14	(c)	15	(c)
16	(a)	17	(b)	18	(a)	19	(b)	20	(c)
21	(b)	22	(d)	23	(a)	24	(b)	25	(d)
26	(d)	27	(a)	28	(a)	29	(b)	30	(c)
31	(a)	32	(a)	33	(b)	34	(b)	35	(d)

1. **(a)** Birds have wings to fly.

2. **(b)** Protozoa are parasites because they live on the body of other organisms.

3. **(d)** Ludo, carrom, badminton, table tennis and chess are indoor games whereas football is an outdoor game.

4. **(d)** Some bacteria are useful for human beings.

5. **(b)** Milk is converted into curd due to bacteria.

6. **(d)** Antibacterial antibiotic kills bacteria in our body.

7. **(b)** Exchange of gases takes place through the process of respiration.

8. **(a)** Plains are most suitable for human beings to live.

9. **(a)** Desert area has less rainfall.

10. **(b)** The area near the mountain is called hilly area.

11. **(c)** Rabbit eats plants & plant parts by gnawing.

12. **(a)** Producers are the organisms that make their own food.

13. **(a)** In solid, the molecules are tightly packed.

14. **(c)** In a liquid form of a substance, volume is measured.

15. **(c)** Sodium reacts with chlorine to form sodium chloride. This is a chemical reaction.

16. **(a)** The digested food is oxidised to form energy.

17. **(b)** No displacement means no work done.

18. **(a)** Force of gravity is the force naturally applied to everything on the earth.

19. **(b)** The iron ball will fall fast because it is heavier than plastic ball.

20. **(c)** The force between a magnet and a piece of iron is called magnetic force.

21. **(b)** Grass reflects green light back to your eyes.

22. **(b)**

23. **(a)** When a ball is placed between a torch & a wall, the shadow of ball can be seen on the wall.

24. **(b)** Glass is the smallest, then bottle followed by tub and tank has the highest capacity.

25. **(d)** Both statements are true.

26. **(d)** Recycling means reusing a resource to make something new.

27. (a) A seed germinates to give rise to a baby plant.

28. (a) Sublimation is the process of changing solid directly into gas.

29. (b)

30. (c) Anything which occupies space and has mass.

31. (a) Individual bones combine together to form skeletal system.

32. (a) Birds lay eggs, rest are mammals giving birth to young ones.

33. (b) Wood is not a mineral.

34. (b) Low fat diet can control the possibility of heart attack.

35. (d) Tiger cannot be tamed.

MOCK TEST -4

1	(c)	2	(a)	3	(c)	4	(a)	5	(a)
6	(c)	7	(d)	8	(a)	9	(a)	10	(a)
11	(b)	12	(c)	13	(b)	14	(c)	15	(d)
16	(d)	17	(b)	18	(c)	19	(b)	20	(a)
21	(b)	22	(b)	23	(a)	24	(c)	25	(d)
26	(a)	27	(c)	28	(d)	29	(a)	30	(d)
31	(d)	32	(d)	33	(a)	34	(b)	35	(c)
36	(c)	37	(a)	38	(b)	39	(d)	40	(c)

1. (c) Very tiny and light droplets of water float in the air (forming clouds). Water droplets that are too heavy to float make rain.

2. (a) Liquid is having a property of taking the shape of the container in which it is kept. Oil, water and milk are liquid they will take the shape of the container in which they are poured in. Pencil is solid and solids have a definite shape.

3. (c) Sand is insoluble, it does not dissolve in water. It settles down in the water.

4. (a) The skull is a bony structure, the head in the skeleton. It protects the brain and supports the other soft tissues of the head.

5. (a) Cuckoo lays its eggs in the nest of other birds.

6. (c) An important function of soil is to store and supply nutrients to the plants or trees. This ability of soil is known as soil fertility.

7. (d) Umbrella cloth must not allow liquids to pass through.

8. (a) A green substance in plants called chlorophyll traps the energy from the Sun needed to make food. Chlorophyll is mostly found in leaves. So, green leaves are known as food factories of a plant.

9. (a) The Sun provides the energy that causes Earth's weather.
10. (a) Fat layer under bear skin keeps them warm.
11. (b) Heat
12. (c) In soil, the grasses grow in the top layer.
13. (b) Dams are build by people to stop flooding.
14. (c) Making scrambled eggs.
15. (d) Femur is the longest and strongest bone of the human body, extending from the hip to the knee.
16. (d) Plant A, B and C will not survive. Any plant without root and leaves cannot survive. Root provides nutrients to the plant and leaves store food for the plants.
17. (b) Bark of the tree protects the trunk. It's an outer protective layer that makes the trunk, branches and roots grow thicker overtime.
18. (c) Desert plants like cactus has leaves modified into thorns. These thorns protect the plant from being eaten by animals.
19. (b) The animal shown in the picture is chameleon, it changes its skin colour to protect itself from its enemies.
20. (a) Based on the given information it's true that the lost animal is a carnivore as it feeds on insects only.
21. (b) Water boils at 100°C and freezes at 0°C.
22. (b) Conservation of water means protecting water from pollution and being wasted. Water used for washing vegetables can be used for watering plants. This conserves some water.
23. (a) The given figure shows a raddish. It is an edible root vegetable.
24. (c) Food with lots of sugar and starch are rich in carbo-dydrates. Carbohydrates are natural compounds of carbon, hydrogen and oxygen. Carbohydrates are present in simple form such as sugar and in complex form such as starch and fibre.
25. (d) We should keep our house clean, sweep the floor of all the rooms and the floor should be mopped with phenyl everyday.
26. (a) A chemist sells medicines in a medicine shop. Doctor and surgeon treats patients. Nurse takes care of the patients.
27. (c) Braille script, a system of raised dots made on a thick paper, which can be read by running the fingers on them. It is used by the blind people.
28. (d) PCO (Public call Office) service is used for the local calls, this facility is located at public places within a country.

STD (Subscriber Trunk Dialling) service is used for local and long distance calls within the country.

ISD (International Subscriber Dialling) service is used for international calls world wide (outside the country)

29. **(a)** Tractor is odd one. It is used in agriculture by farmers.

Car, bus and autorickshaw are used to travel from one place to another by anyone in the city.

30. **(d)** Sense of sight helps in seeing that baby sister wakes up and sense of hearing helps in hearing the sound of her cry.

31. **(d)** Nostril is a part of respiratiory system.

Heart is a part of circulatory system.

32. **(d)** Digestion starts when you put food in your mouth where food is chopped and chewed into smaller pieces by your teeth for easy digestion of food.

33. **(a)** Sun is the source of energy. It provides heat to enable living things to survive on the Earth and provides light and energy which is used by green plants to make their food.

34. **(b)** Table Tennis ball.

35. **(c)** A ball is supposed to bounce. Good material for making a ball is rubber.

36. **(c)** Newspaper is made up of paper only and muffler is made up of wool only. Specs is made up of plastic and glass. Pen is made up of plastic and metal-like steel.

37. **(a)** 'A' represents the Earth, it's a planet and revolves around the sun. Stars, cloud and moon do not revolve around the Sun. 'E' represents another planet. All 8 planets revolve around the Sun.

38. **(b)** Solar system consists of a Sun and 8 planets in the order Mercury, Venus, Earth, Mars, Jupiter, Saturn, Uranus and Neptune. Mercury is closest to the Sun, therefore, the hottest of all other members.

39. **(d)** A woman making and baking cookies uses her sense of smell, taste, touch and sight at the same time.

40. **(c)** A frog is an amphibian and can live on land and in water. All other are insects and live on land.

MOCK TEST -5

1	(b)	2	(c)	3	(a)	4	(a)	5	(d)
6	(d)	7	(b)	8	(d)	9	(d)	10	(c)
11	(b)	12	(d)	13	(c)	14	(c)	15	(d)
16	(c)	17	(a)	18	(a)	19	(a)	20	(c)
21	(b)	22	(a)	23	(a)	24	(c)	25	(c)
26	(d)	27	(d)	28	(c)	29	(b)	30	(c)
31	(d)	32	(a)	33	(b)	34	(d)	35	(b)
36	(c)	37	(a)	38	(d)	39	(c)	40	(c)

1. **(b)** Sense of smell works for a tiger in the night.
2. **(c)** Mushroom is a vegetable and vulture is a scavenger.
3. **(a)** Duck, mouse and fish can be grouped together because they eat both plants and animals.
4. **(a)** Dog lives in kennel, fish lives in aquarium, hen lives in coops, rabbit lives in burrows.
5. **(d)** Nervous system is in charge of the senses.
6. **(d)** Only statement-The duck is an aquatic bird is true.
7. **(b)** A parrot uses its beak to climb branches of tree.
8. **(d)** Shadows
9. **(d)** Weaver bird's nest is very attractive.
10. **(c)** These droplets come out from stomata of the leaf by the process of transpiration.
11. **(b)** Water from roots → stem → water in leaves
12. **(d)** A microscope is used to observe the cells of a leaf.
13. **(c)** When you are eating sugar-cane, you are actually eating the stem of sugarcane.
14. **(c)** In this experiment air bubbles were seen rising. This shows soil contains air.
15. **(d)** Loamy soil can hold both water and air in adequate amounts. That is why, this soil is said to be the best soil for growing plants.
16. **(c)** Nerve receptors provides information to your brain about external conditions.
17. **(a)** If a puddle of water on a marble floor is left untouched for some hours, it will become smaller, due to evaporation.
18. **(a)** The days are longer in summer season.
19. **(a)** Molecules
20. **(c)** Equator of the Earth will receive almost the same amount of sunlight throughout the year.

21. (b) In human body
A: Circulatory system helps in the movement of blood.
B: Skeletal system helps the body to move.
C: Reproductive system helps in the production of offspring.
D: Respiratory system helps in the exchange of air.

22. (a) Lungs are a pair of organs in human body which belongs to both the respiratory and the excretory system.

23. (a) The figure represents a man crossing the road using pedestrian crossing.

24. (c) A house made up of clay and thatch or coconut branches is most effective in a place that is very hot and dry.

25. (c) Only air is renewable all others are non renewable.

26. (d) Cotton clothes are preferred during summers because they are light, do not absorb heat and allow the body heat to escape.

27. (d) Early man produced fire with the help of stones. Match box was invented much later.

28. (c) Wood catches fire quickly.

29. (b) Policeman and army people works in very far places so wireless communication is very useful in communication for them.

30. (c) In this experiment, by tuesday the level of water has decreased because it has been absorbed by the roots.

31. (d) Rock is not a living organism, therefore it will not grow.

32. (a) Touch-me not plant has the sense of touch.

33. (b) Some animals like snake, squirrel, etc., swallow the food without chewing it and after sometime they bring this food back into their mouth from stomach. These animals are called cud-chewing animals.

34. (d) Snake is a carnivore.

35. (b) Flight feathers help the bird fly in the air.

36. (c) Veins in plants transport water, food and minerals in a leaf.

37. (a) Humus, a dark brown material in soil that is formed when plants and animals decay, is the most helpful material present in the soil for the growth of plants.

38. (d) Top soil, Sub soil and Bed rock is the correct arrangement of layers of the soil from top to bottom.

39. (c) Swallowing the food without chewing it is not a good habit. Because chewing mix the food with saliva and helps in digestion.

40. (c) Plant is eaten by goat, goat is eaten by lion.

GENERAL KNOWLEDGE

MOCK TEST 1

ANSWER KEY									
1	(a)	6	(a)	11	(a)	16	(b)	21	(b)
2	(a)	7	(c)	12	(b)	17	(a)	22	(c)
3	(a)	8	(c)	13	(b)	18	(a)	23	(a)
4	(c)	9	(c)	14	(b)	19	(a)	24	(a)
5	(c)	10	(d)	15	(c)	20	(c)	25	(a)

1. (a) Astronomers are scientists who study the Earth and other objects in the solar system.

2. (a) A dermatologist is the medical expert you should consult, if you have any significant problem with your skin.

3. (a) Only plants have green-coloured substance called chlorophyll, which is required for producing food through photosynthesis.

4. (c) Jews celebrate Hanukkah festival to dedicate Holy Temple in Jerusalem.

5. (c) Kiwi is a flightless bird native to New Zealand.

6. (a) Bald Eagle is a native to the North America and is facing extinction due to environmental pollution.

7. (c) Money Plant is a climber because it needs support to grow.

8. (c) Each year September 8th marks UNESCO's International Literacy day

9. (c) Pitcher Plant has a pitcher-like structure to trap insects. This plant eats insects, hence called insectivorous plant.

10. (d) Crocodile is a carnivore animal which eats other animals. Deer is an herbivore animal because it eats only plants. Mango is a tree because it has well-defined thick and woody stems. Blood contains red pigment called haemoglobin.

11. (a) A hundred dollar note of the United States shown has the photo of Benjamin Franklin, who was one of the Founding Fathers of the United States.

12. (b) Zeus

13. (b) The President of India lives in Rashtrapati Bhavan, Delhi and is located at the Western end of Rajpath in New Delhi, India.

14. (b) Sun is a renewable source of energy which is available in abundant amount. Coal, petrol and natural gas are non-renewable energy sources which are present in limited amount and are lost after use.

15. (c) Barometer is an instrument which is used to measure atmospheric pressure.

16. (b) Padma Shri (also Padma Shree) is the fourth highest civilian award in the Republic of India, after the Bharat Ratna, the Padma Vibhushan and the Padma Bhushan. Awarded by the Government of India, it is announced every year on India's Republic Day. Shri Karimul Hak was the recipient of Padam Shri Award 2017 in Social work.

17. (a) World Youth Skills Day is celebrated on 15th July every year. This day is celebrated to expand awareness on the importance of investing in youth skills development.

18. (a) Shabana Azmi played the role of 'Makri' who lives in a mansion that was said to be haunted.

19. (a) Leonardo Di Caprio is an American actor who played the role of 'Jack' in the hit film 'Titanic'.

20. (c) The given sign is generally seen in public places and means 'do not eat'.

21. (b) Compass is generally used on ships to find the direction of navigation.

22. (c) Sachin is the first Indian cricketer to have a waxwork at Madame Tussaud's wax museum.

23. (a) Deshna Jain (20), who is from Tikamgarh in Madhya Pradesh, has been crowned the 2018 Miss Asia (Deaf) title and was the 3rd runner-up in the 2018 Miss International (Deaf) contest held in Taipei, Taiwan, from July 8 to July 16. At 20, she is also the youngest contestant to take part in the event.

24. (a) Zabivaka - "the one who scores" (in Russian) is a wolf who radiates fun, charm and confidence was the Official mascot of FIFA World Cup 2018. It has brown and white fur, wearing a T-shirt emblazoned with the words "RUSSIA 2018" and orange sports goggles. This was designed by Ekaterina Bocharova.

25. (a) Smartphone company Vivo has become the official sponsor of FIFA World Cup 2018 and 2022.

MOCK TEST 2

ANSWER KEY									
1	(d)	6	(c)	11	(d)	16	(a)	21	(a)
2	(a)	7	(d)	12	(a)	17	(b)	22	(b)
3	(a)	8	(c)	13	(a)	18	(b)	23	(a)
4	(b)	9	(a)	14	(b)	19	(b)	24	(d)
5	(a)	10	(d)	15	(a)	20	(d)	25	(a)

1. (d) Stomata are circular structures in plants used for respiration, whereas heart, lungs and kidney are the organs of our body.

4. (b) Fish contains lot of protein. Apple contains minerals and vitamins. Noodle is rich in fat and chocolate has sugar in it.

5. (a) Heart helps in blood circulation in our body. Urine formation takes place in kidneys. Stomach and liver contains substances for food digestion.

6. (c) Touch-me-not is a plant which wilts after being touched by hands and reopens after some time.

7. (d) Bats are nocturnal and produce sound to locate insects they eat.

8. (c) Mangroves are a group of plants growing in coastal area and have tube-like aerial roots for breating.

9. (a) These were flightless birds. They became extinct by the 17th or 18th century. Its closest living relatives are emus.

10. (d) Water and carbon dioxide are used by plants to produce food and oxygen is used for breathing.

11. (d) The President is the supreme commander of the defense forces of India. Depending upon the approval of the Parliament, the President can declare war or peace. He appoints the chief of Army, Navy, and Air Force.

12. (a) Bharatanatyam is a popular classical dance from Tamil Nadu.

13. (a) The Sun is a star and is closer to Earth (93 million miles away,) while other stars are much further away.

14. (b) Jupiter has no volcanoes, craters, and lakes.

15. (a) Bees collect flower nectar and store them in their honeycomb in the form of honey.

17. (b) The Gandhi Sagar Dam is built on Chambal river and is located in the Mandsaur & Neemuch district of Madhya Pradesh. It is a masonry gravity dam, standing 62.17 metres (204.0 ft) high, with a gross storage capacity of 7.322 billion cubic metres from a catchment area of 22,584 km^2.

18. (b) The name of the alien in the film is 'Jaadoo'.

19. (b) Volleyball was declared the national game of Nepal in May 2017.

20. (d) C.K. Nayudu was the first test captain of India who led the team in four matches against England in 1932.

21. (a) Viswanathan Anand

22. (b) The Government of India (GOI) has invited US President Donald Trump to be chief guest at the 2019 Republic Day Parade.

23. (a) The Nobel Prize in Literature, 2016 was awarded to Bob Dylan for creating new poetic expressions within the great American song tradition.

24. (d) India won 8 medals in the 2018 Junior Asian Wrestling Championship (JAWC) which concluded in New Delhi on July 22. The medals comprised 2 gold, 3 silver and as many bronze. Here, Indian wrestler Sachin Rathi won gold in 74 kg freestyle category by defeating Bat-Erdene of Mangolia in the final on July 22.

25. (a) Maharashtra

MOCK TEST 3

ANSWER KEY									
1	(a)	6	(b)	11	(b)	16	(b)	21	(a)
2	(b)	7	(a)	12	(a)	17	(a)	22	(b)
3	(b)	8	(d)	13	(a)	18	(b)	23	(c)
4	(b)	9	(c)	14	(b)	19	(b)	24	(d)
5	(b)	10	(a)	15	(c)	20	(a)	25	(b)

1. (a) Pediatrics is the branch of medicine that deals with medical care of children. Psychiatry is the medical branch related to the treatment of mental disorders. Geriatrics is the branch of medicine that treats diseases of old persons. Ophthalmology is the branch that deals with eye diseases.

2. (b) Neurons are the cells of nervous system which help in sending and receiving brain information to and from the body parts.

4. (b) Tear-producing glands are called lacrimal glands and are located in the upper region of each eye orbit.

5. (b) Bats are nocturnal animal Cassowary is a bird that cannot fly. Crocodiles have breathing system similar to mammals. They have trachea connected to the lungs. Sharks are carnivores because they eat smaller fish and other aquatic animals.

7. (a) The hanging thread-like structures in banyan tress are aerial roots that mature into thick, woody trunks.

8. (d) Plants are very important to our life. It produces food and oxygen for us. Without plants, it would be difficult for us to survive.

10.(a) Haemoglobin is a red colour pigment that provides red colour to blood. It helps in the transportation of oxygen in blood.

11.(b) The Eiffel Tower is one of the famous towers in Paris, France, named after the engineer Gustave Eiffel. It was constructed from 1887 to 1889.

12.(a) Ashna Chauhan designed the structure of the Red Fort in Delhi.

13.(a) In solar eclipse, the Moon passes between the Sun and Earth, and the Moon fully or partially blocks the Sun.

14.(b) C.V. Raman was the great Indian physicist who made new discoveries in the field of light.

15. (c) Astronomy, Botany, Zoology and Physics are the study of outer space, plants, animals and nature of materials, respectively.

16. (b) Abhimanyu was the son of Arjuna and Subhadra.

20. (a) Mary Kom is the only Indian woman boxer to have qualified for the 2012 Summer Olympics.

21. (a) Bidhya Devi Bhandari; born on 19 June, 1961) is a Nepalese politician who is the current President of Nepal and Commander-in-Chief of Nepalese Army. She is the first woman to hold the office.

22. (b) January 15 is celebrated as the Army Day in recognition of Lieutenant General K. M. Cariappa's taking over as the first Commander-in-Chief of the Indian Army from General Sir Francis Butcher.

23. (c) The 2018 Asian Games, officially known as the 18th Asian Games and also known as Jakarta Palembang 2018, is a pan-Asian multi-sport event scheduled to be held from 18th August to 2th September, 2018 in the Indonesian cities of Jakarta and Palembang.

24. (d) Mahamana Pandit Madan Mohan Malaviya was an Indian educationist and politician. Atal Bihari Vajpayee was former Prime Minister of India and A.P.J. Abdul Kalam was the former President of India and a nuclear scientist.

25. (b) HDFC is a private Indian Bank. Punjab National Bank, Indian Bank and State Bank of India are government banks.

MOCK TEST 4

ANSWER KEY															
1	(d)	6	(d)	11	(a)	16	(b)	21	(b)	26	(d)	31	(b)	36	(a)
2	(b)	7	(c)	12	(a)	17	(d)	22	(d)	27	(b)	32	(d)	37	(a)
3	(b)	8	(d)	13	(c)	18	(a)	23	(a)	28	(c)	33	(d)	38	(a)
4	(a)	9	(b)	14	(a)	19	(b)	24	(b)	29	(a)	34	(a)	39	(c)
5	(d)	10	(c)	15	(d)	20	(a)	25	(b)	30	(b)	35	(a)	40	(b)

2. (b) Canines are sharp conical teeth used for tearing food. Ophthalmologist checks eyes. Milk contains vitamins, minerals and proteins. Plant leaves have circular openings called stomata used for breathing.

3. (b) Kidney is a bean-shaped organ which removes waste and excess water from the body in the form of urine.

4. (a) Gorkha district of Nepal was the epicenter of earthquake. It killed nearly 9,000 people and injured nearly 22,000.

6. (d) Fried foods are not healthy and cause heart diseases. Butter is prepared from milk. Foods can be stored either by freezing or heating which kills the microbes.

7. (c) An aardvark is an animal which eats termite and lives in Africa. It has strong claws with which it opens termite nests and a very long sticky tongue which it uses to slurp the termites up out of their tunnels.

8. (d) Ostriches, rheas and emus are all egg-laying birds which cannot fly.

9. (b) Plants has roots to absorb water and minerals from the soil. Water and minerals are used to carry out the process of photosynthesis for the production of food.

12. (a) Blue Whale is the largest of all animals, which grows to a maximum length of 30 metres and weighs about 150 tonnes. It spends its summers in the polar waters and during winters, it moves to the equator. It lives on sea food.

13. (c) Hedgehogs are medium-sized spiny animals, with a round body, small head, pointed face, and little or no tail. Their sizes vary from 4 to 17 inches. They are omnivorous but prefer animal food.

14. (a) Statue of Unity is a statue of freedom fighter and first Home Minster of India Sardar Vallabhbhai Patel. The statue is 182 metres high.

15. (d) Singapore is an island city-state that is located along southern Malaysia. Other neighbouring countries of India are Pakistan, Nepal, China and Bangladesh.

16. (b) Abraham Lincoln was born on February 12, 1809 in Kentucky and belonged to an extremely poor family.

17. (d) The original portrait is on display in Paris in Louvre Museum and it has been there since 1797. Mona Lisa's portrait has remained for as long as 500 years.

18. (a) AR Rahman is an Indian classical music composer and singer. He has received two Academy Awards, two Grammy Awards, a BAFTA Award, a Golden Globe, four National Film Awards, fifteen Filmfare Awards and sixteen Filmfare Awards South.

19. (b) Antarctic Polar Desert covers the continent of Antarctica and has a size of about 5.5 million square miles. The second-largest desert is the Arctic Polar Desert. It extends over parts of Alaska, Canada, Greenland, Iceland, Norway, Sweden, Finland, and Russia.

20. (a) Carrot is rich in vitamin A which is good for eye vision. Fish, milk and meat are good source of proteins. Ghee is rich in fat. Rice and cereals have carbohydrates.

21. (b) A light-year is the distance that light can travel through space in a year. It is equivalent to 9.4607×10^{15} meters.

22. (d) A satellite is an object that moves around a larger object. Earth is a satellite because it moves around the Sun. The Moon is a satellite because it moves around Earth. Earth and the moon are called "natural" satellites.

23. (a) Har Gobind Khorana became the first to synthesize an artificial gene in a living cell. His work became the foundation for much of the later research in biotechnology and gene therapy.

24. (b) Hydrogen is a light gas which when filled in a balloon causes it to rise in the sky.

27. (b) Medicine is the branch of science that deals with the study of diagnosis, treatment and prevention of diseases.

28. (c) Shahid Afridi was appointed as the ambassador of Blind Cricket World Cup. The 2018 Blind Cricket World Cup was the fifth Blind Cricket World Cup tournament, and was held from 8 to 20 January 2018 in Pakistan and the United Arab Emirates

29. (a) Pluto, also called Pluto the Pup, is a cartoon character created in 1930. He is a yellow-orange colour, medium-sized, short-haired dog with black ears.

30. (b) Smee is Hook's humorous firstmate.

31. (b) One should never cross a road, if the traffic signal shows green light. It is safe to cross a road when the traffic light is red in colour.

32. (d) Ambulance, fire brigade, and police van have emergency lights so that they get a clear road and reach the destination on time.

33. (d) Tour de France is a bicycle race held in France while also occasionally making passes through nearby countries.

34. (a) Naukasana is comprised of two words-Nauka means Boat and Asana indicates Yoga pose. Since, the body posture is having the shape of boat, the asana is called Naukasana.

35. (a) 'Me-Dam-Me-Phi' is festival of the Tai Ahom community of Assam.The Tai-Ahoms extend offerings to their departed ancestors and offer sacrifices to Gods in a traditional manner..

36. (c) The 2018 Nelson Mandela International Day (NMID) is marked as the 100th birth anniversary of Nelson Mandela, the former South African President & Nobel Peace Prize winner on July 18. The Nelson Mandela Foundation (NMF) dedicated this year's Mandela Day to 'Action Against Poverty', honouring Nelson Mandela's leadership and devotion to fighting poverty and promoting social justice for all.

37. (a) 25th April is celebrated as the World Malaria Day to recognize global efforts to control malaria.

38. (a) Ahmedabad is known for peace and as a landmark city where Mahatma Gandhi began India's freedom struggle.

39. (c) Gopal Das Neeraj, the Doyen of Hindi poetry, has passed away in New Delhi on July 19, 2018. Neeraj, who was awarded Padma Shri (1991) and Padma Bhushan (2007), was born in Purvali village of Uttar Pradesh's Etawa district.

40. (b) 'Worlds of Wonder' is a water park opened in mid 2007 and includes over 20 rides, a water park and a go-kart.

MOCK TEST 5

ANSWER KEY

1	(d)	6	(b)	11	(c)	16	(c)	21	(c)	26	(d)	31	(d)	36	(c)
2	(a)	7	(a)	12	(a)	17	(b)	22	(d)	27	(a)	32	(c)	37	(a)
3	(a)	8	(d)	13	(b)	18	(c)	23	(b)	28	(d)	33	(c)	38	(d)
4	(c)	9	(d)	14	(b)	19	(a)	24	(c)	29	(d)	34	(c)	39	(c)
5	(b)	10	(c)	15	(a)	20	(b)	25	(a)	30	(a)	35	(c)	40	(a)

1. (d) Bunnies, rabbits and lambs are often associated with Easter because most babies of the animals are born in spring around Easter time.

2. (a) The deficiency of iodine in food causes goiter disease which is characterized by swelling in the neck region. Salt we buy at stores is rich in iodine.

3. (a) The inner part of our ear has a fluid which helps in maintaining balance of the body.

5. (b) An ophthalmologist is an eye specialist who treats eye diseases. Cardiologist treats heart diseases. Dentists checks teeth. Zoologist studies animals.

6. (b) Clones are those organisms that have identical genes.

7. (a) Baobab is an endangered plant which stores water in its broad and twisted trunk. The people of Madagascar, Africa and India often build their homes among its roots to survive the dry seasons

8. (d) There are lots of strange animals in the deepest parts of the oceans. For example, some communities live around undersea hot-springs called 'black smokers'. They don't need light at all. Some of these animals even make their own light.

9. (d) All the parts of a plant can be used as medicine. For example, the leaves of maidenhair tree, roots of stinging nettle, and seeds of Juniper berries can be used as medicinal preparations.

10. (c) Dodo is a flightless bird. Whale is an aquatic mammal which gives birth to young ones. Dolly was first successful cloned animal. Rat does not show camouflage as it cannot change its body colour.

11. (c) Rice is not cultivated on hill slopes, whereas tea and cocoa are grown of the slopes of hills as they cannot tolerate stagnant water along their roots.

12. (a) Moon flowers, as the name suggests, only blooms at night.

13. (b) A baby deer is called a cub. A baby dog is called pup. Fawn is a baby deer.

14. (b) Christ the Redeemer is a symbol of Christianity across the world and was constructed between 1922 and 1931. Statue of Liberty is in New York City. Statue of Unity is being constructed at Near Sardar Sarovar Dam in Gujarat. Statue of Freedom is in Washington, D.C.

15. (a) Lake Kariba is the world's largest man-made lake which lies 1300 kilometres upstream from the Indian Ocean, along the border between Zambia and Zimbabwe.

16. (c) The currency of Belgium is Euro. Krone, Dollar and Pound are the currencies of Norway, United States and Great Britain, respectively.

17. (b) Rabindranath Tagore gave the title of 'Mahatma' to Gandhi.

18. (c) Navroz is the name of the Iranian New Year, also known as the Persian New Year, which is celebrated worldwide by the Iranians, as the beginning of the New Year.

19. (a) The first Rajdhani Express left New Delhi station for Howrah station to cover a distance of 1,445 km in 17 hours 20 mins.

20. (b) Buzz Aldrin was the first man to urinate on the moon.

21. (c) Water freezes at zero degree celsius. Freezing changes water into ice. It starts boiling at 100 degree celsius.

22. (d) Diamond, lead pencil and coal are all made of carbon.

23. (b) Rotation of the Earth around its axis causes day and night. Revolution of the Earth around the Sun causes seasons.

24. (c) Neptune is the farthest planet from the Sun. The distance between the Neptune and the Sun is 4.498 billion km.

25. (a) Stethoscope is a medical device used to listen to lung and heart sounds.

26. (d) Lata Mangshkar is a Great Indian singer who has been given the title of 'Nightingale of India'. She has been honoured with Bharat Ratna in 2001.

27. (a) Red is sent for an anger management class after his temper causes a "premature hatching" of a customer's egg. The voice of Red has been given by actor Daniel Jason Sudeikis.

28. (d) Submarines can travel under the water and are often used by military personnel.

29. (d) Kharagpur railway station has the third longest railway platform in India, located in the state of West Bengal and the length of the platform is 1,072.5 meters.

30. (a) The opening ceremony of the 2010 Commonwealth Games was held at the Jawaharlal Nehru Stadium in New Delhi, India, on 3 October, 2010.

31. (d) The umpire in the picture is signaling leg bye which is equivalent to a run scored by the batting team, if the batsman or batswoman has not hit the ball with his or her bat, but the ball has hit the batsman's body or protective gear.

32. (c) Archery is the national sport of Bhutan. National game of Japan, India, and Afghanistan is sumo, hockey, and buzkashi, respectively.

33. (b) Dr. Seuss

34. (c) The given traffic sign means no U-turn.

35. (c) Dhanak features Hetal Gadda and Krrish Chhabria as the two children, playing brother and sister, in the leading roles, with supporting performances from Chet Dixon, Vipin Sharma, and Gulfam Khan.

36. (b) The Government of India has declared 29th August as Sports Day in honour of Major Dhyan Chand.

37. (a) The Government of Union Territory of Puducherry has nominated its capital city for inclusion in the Union Government's flagship 100 Smart Cities Mission.

38. (b) Journalist Carlos Alvarado has been sworn-in as the new President of Costa Rica on May 8, 2018

39. (b) The 2018 International Children's Theatre Festival will be held at the Academy of Fine Arts in Kolkata, West Bengal from June 17 to 21. Children of various theatre groups from eight countries besides host India will take part in fest.

40. (b) The World Water Day (WWD) is observed every year on 22nd March to raise awareness about the importance of water. The 2018 theme 'Nature for Water' is exploring nature-based solutions to the water challenges the world faces in the 21st century. The day is about focusing on the importance of water and the need to preserve it.

LOGICAL REASONING

MOCK TEST-1

ANSWERS KEY									
1	(d)	6	(b)	11	(a)	16	(b)	21	(c)
2	(b)	7	(c)	12	(c)	17	(a)	22	(b)
3	(d)	8	(b)	13	(a)	18	(d)	23	(a)
4	(a)	9	(c)	14	(c)	19	(a)	24	(c)
5	(c)	10	(d)	15	(d)	20	(c)	25	(a)

1. **(d)** Except fish, all others live both on land and water.

2. **(b)** Shaded parts move one step forward and faces inside the square change.

3. **(d)** Word formed from the given letters is 'TUESDAY'.

4. **(a)** As, P A I N T ↓ ↓ ↓ ↓ ↓ 7 4 1 2 8 and E X C E L ↓ ↓ ↓ ↓ ↓ 9 3 5 9 6

So, A C C E P T ↓ ↓ ↓ ↓ ↓ ↓ 4 5 5 9 7 8

5. **(c)** Cricket is played with a 'bat' and 'bat' is called 'racket'. So, 'cricket' is played with a 'racket'.

6. **(b)** The sequence of a day is Morning, Afternoon, Evening, and Night.

7. **(c)** Today is 3rd day from Tuesday and 3rd day from Tuesday is Thursday [Tuesday, Wednesday, Thursday]. So, Today is Thursday.

8. **(b)**

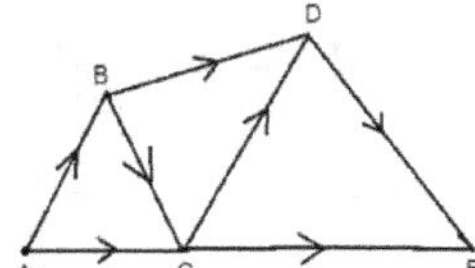

Different possible ways are:

ACE, ABDE, ABCE, ABCDE, ACDE

9. **(c)** Observe the pattern in each segment.

10. **(d)** The correct mirror image is as shown below:

Mirror

11. **(a)**

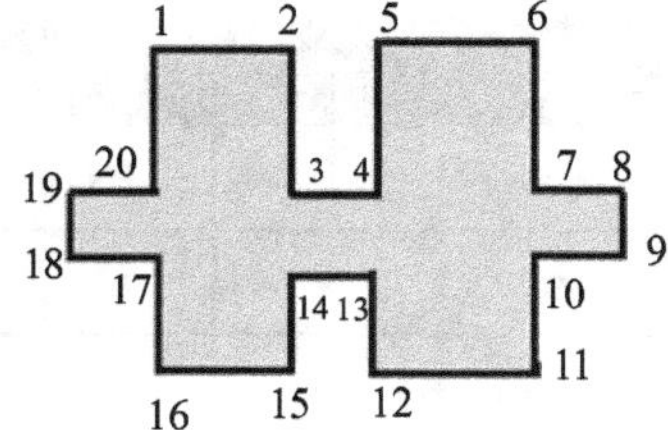

Number of corners in the figure is 20.

Sol. (12-13)

12. (c) If one more butterfly is added on the left of butterfly 1, then 7 butterflies are on the left of butterfly 7.

13. (a) If two butterflies 2 and 3 are removed, then 7th butterfly is 3rd from the right end.

14. (c)

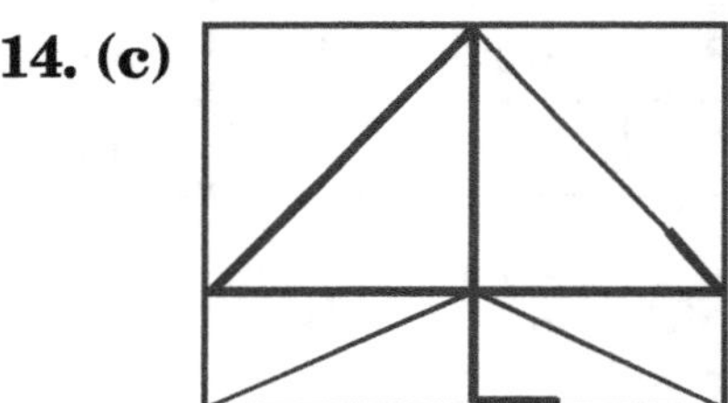

15. (d) 'C' is not in the given word.

16. (b) According to the first two statements,
Lily > Maya > Gautam
Lily runs fastest. So, the third statement is false.

17. (a) Soap is heavier than feather.

Sol. (18-20) The sitting arrangement of five friends is as shown below:

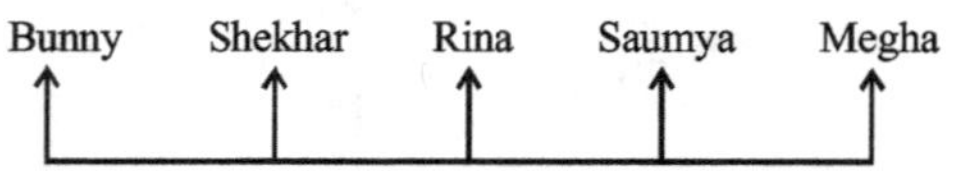

18. (d) Rina is sitting immediate right to Shekhar.

19. (a) Shekhar is 2nd from the left.

20. (c) Rina is sitting in the middle of a bench.

21. (c) Oranges in pattern 1 = 4
Oranges in pattern 2 = 8
Oranges in pattern 3 = 12
So, the pattern is as follows:

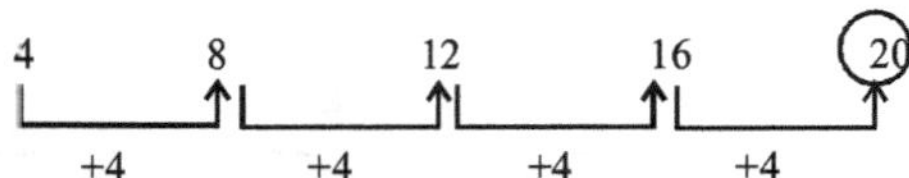

Hence, in pattern 5 there are 20 oranges.

22. (b) 3,2,1,4 is the correct logical sequence.

23. (a) The arrangement of four students according to their marks is as follows:
Nandy > Purvi > Tushar > Anusha
So, Nandy scored the highest marks.

24. (c) The code for 🍒🎼💎🧊 is EVRM.

25. (a) The code for ⏰🎂🐱🐧 is HGAP.

MOCK TEST-2

ANSWERS KEY									
1	(b)	6	(d)	11	(d)	16	(c)	21	(a)
2	(a)	7	(c)	12	(d)	17	(d)	22	(d)
3	(d)	8	(d)	13	(b)	18	(c)	23	(a)
4	(a)	9	(c)	14	(a)	19	(b)	24	(c)
5	(c)	10	(b)	15	(b)	20	(d)	25	(b)

1. **(b)** The correct mirror image is as shown below:

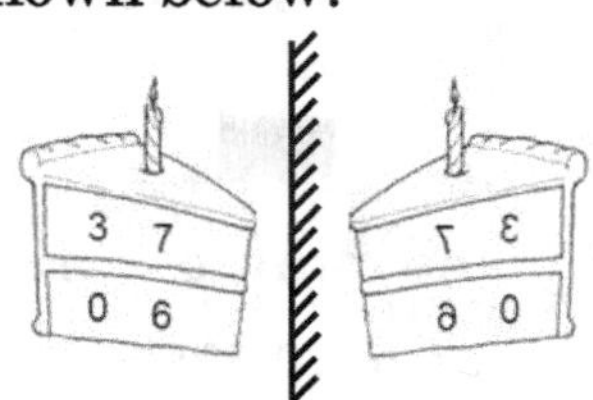

2. **(a)** The arrangement of three books is as following:

Books

Hindi
Maths
English

So, English is the last book from the top.

3. **(d)** 'O' is not in the given word.

4 **(a)** As, In 1st figure,
$(12 - 3) + (9 - 1) = 9 + 8 = 17$
In 2nd figure,
$(20 - 10) + (15 - 5) = 10 + 5 = 15$
Similarly,
In 3rd figure,
$(8 - 4) + (7 - 6) = 4 + 1 = 5$

5. **(c)** Figures (a),(b) and (d) have triangle inside the outer figure.

6. **(d)** In group (X), all elements are the mirror images of English alphabets.

7. **(c)** Number of rectangles in the figure is 14.

8. **(d)** Number of circles – Number of triangles = 11 – 2 = 9.
So, number of circles is 9 more than number of triangles.

9. **(c)** Letter in first figure is represented for an animal. So,C for camel. Similarly, T for tiger.

10. **(b)** If yesterday was 2nd day after Wednesday, then today is Saturday.

Second Day	First Day	Yesterday	Today
Wednesday	Thursday	Friday	Saturday

11. **(d)** The number pattern followed in series is:

6,7,1,2 ; 6,7,1,2 ; 6,7,1, [2]
↓
Barbie Doll 2

12. **(d)** February has 29 days but February is called August.

13. **(b)** Train B is the third train to the left of fifth train from left train.

14. **(a)** If train D is removed from the row, then train E is in the middle of the row.

15. **(b)** 'K' of the word BANKS is not in the given word.

16. **(c)** Letters of word are written in reverse order to get the decoded word. So, code for PAPER is REPAP.

17. **(d)** 49 comes in table of 7.

18. **(c)** is used to draw the shape (X).

19. **(b)** The given numbers are arranged in ascending order,
158 283 321 438 467 641 764 952
So, 438 is fourth from the left.

20. **(d)** One [pentagon] = 9 Strawberries

One [square] = 6 Guavas

Raghav brought two [pentagon]
= 9 × 2 = 18 Strawberries

Raghav brought three [square]
= 6 × 3 = 18 Guavas

So, there is no difference between the number of strawberries and guavas.

21. **(a)** According to Robin : 17, 18, (19), 20

According to his father : (19)

According to both common days is 19th October.

Hence, Ritika's birthday was on 19th October.

22. **(d)** As, 6 × 6 = 36
9 × 4 = 36
And, 12 × 3 = 36
But, 15 × 2 = 30

23. **(a)** One minute = 60 seconds
12 minutes = 60 × 12
= 720 seconds

24. **(c)** 580 is closet to 583.

25. **(b)**

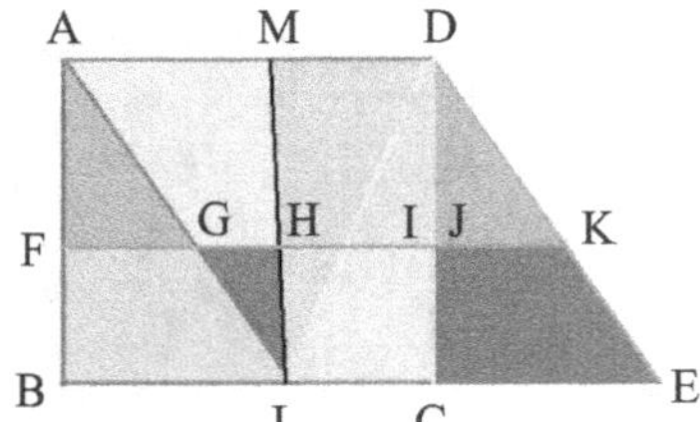

Number of triangles = AFG, GLH, LHI, IDJ, DJK, ABL, ALM, MLD, LDC, DCE, ALD, DLE, GIL and DIK

So, total number of triangles = 14

MOCK TEST-3

ANSWERS KEY									
1	(d)	6	(b)	11	(c)	16	(a)	21	(c)
2	(b)	7	(d)	12	(c)	17	(c)	22	(b)
3	(b)	8	(b)	13	(b)	18	(b)	23	(c)
4	(a)	9	(b)	14	(a)	19	(d)	24	(a)
5	(d)	10	(c)	15	(c)	20	(a)	25	(b)

1. **(d)** As, 6 + 3 + 1 = 10
8 + 2 + 0 = 10
And, 7 + 1 + 2 = 10
But, 4 + 4 + 3 = 11

2. **(b)** Here, unshaded rectangle becomes shaded circles and shaded circles becomes unshaded rectangles in the first pair. Similarly, unshaded hexagon becomes shaded rectangles and shaded rectangles becomes unshaded hexagon.

3. **(b)** The pattern is as follows:

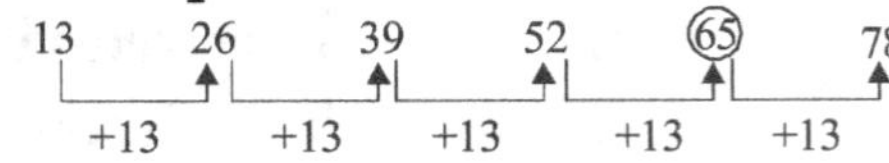

4. (a) SPRQ is the proper sequence.
5. (d) Word formed is LIPS.
6. (b) If one more seahorse is added on right of seahorse 10, then 5 seahorse are on right of seahorse 6.
7. (d) If three seahorses 2,4 and 6 are removed, then seahorse 8 is 5th from the left end.
8. (b) We used to read time by watch, but watch is called bag. So, bag is used to read time.
9. (b) Saumya will stay 6 nights in the resort.

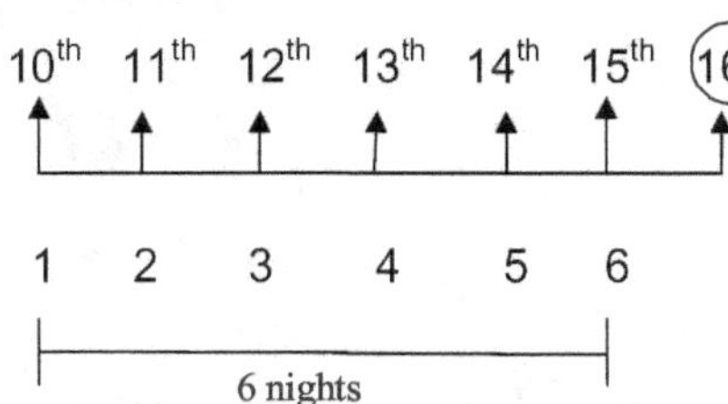

So, Saumya will checkout the resort on 16th November.
10. (c) There are 15 triangles in the dotted line.
11. (c)

12. (c) The correct mirror image is as follows:

Mirror

13. (b) Number of sectors in the picture of pizza is 10.
14. (a) Number of black circles in the picture of pizza is 26.
15. (c) Number of white circles in the picture of pizza is 4.
16. (a) Shoes of a boy, Shirt of a boy and top of a girl are missing in picture-B.
17. (c) Number of bananas has = 12
Number of bananas Ekta has = 5 more than Jenny
= 5 + 12 = 17
18. (b) As, C ⟶ 3 (positional value of C)
D ⟶ 4 (positional value of D)
C + D = 3 + 4 = 7
Similarly, D ⟶ 4 (positional value of D)
G ⟶ 7 (positional value of G)
And, A ⟶ 1 (positional value of A)
Then, D+G+A = 4+7+1 = 12
19. (d) Except duckling, all others are birds.
20. (a) The pattern is as follows:

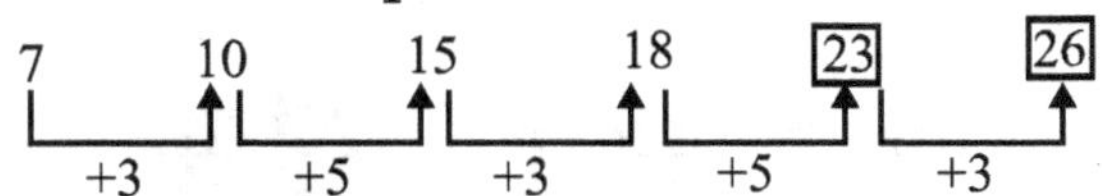

21. (c) As, 7 + 2 = 9 Similarly, 6 + 4 = 10
22. (b) The meaningful word is CYCLE. So, the correct order is 1,3,5,2,4.
23. (c) ESTATE can be formed from the given combination of letters.
24. (a) The correct mirror image is as follows:

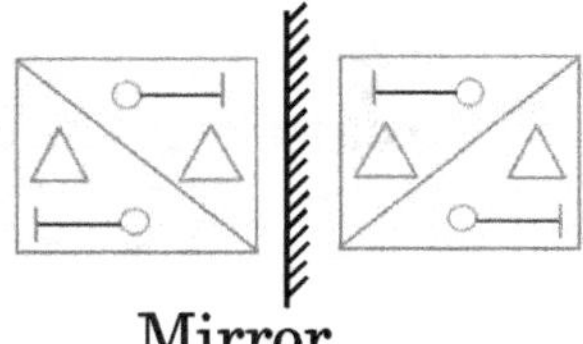

Mirror

25. (b) If yesterday was Friday, then day after tomorrow will be Monday.

MOCK TEST-4

ANSWERS KEY									
1	(d)	6	(c)	11	(c)	16	(a)	21	(c)
2	(a)	7	(d)	12	(a)	17	(b)	22	(d)
3	(b)	8	(a)	13	(b)	18	(a)	23	(a)
4	(c)	9	(d)	14	(b)	19	(b)	24	(d)
5	(b)	10	(a)	15	(c)	20	(a)	25	(a)

1. **(d)** As, $2 \times 6 = 12$
$3 \times 4 = 12$
And, $6 \times 2 = 12$
But, $5 \times 4 = 20$

2. **(a)** The correct mirror image is as shown below:

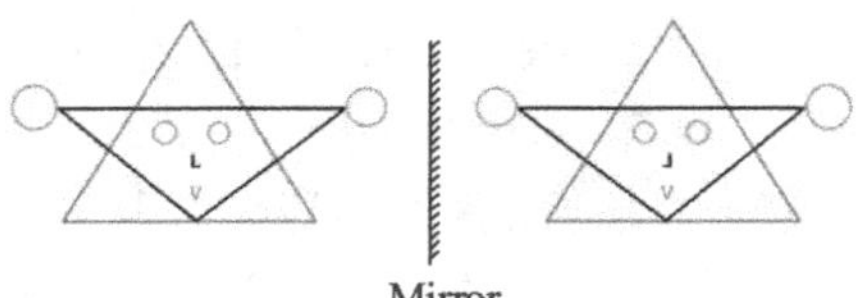

3. **(b)** Word formed is APRIL.

4. **(c)** DONE cannot be formed from the given letters.

5. **(b)** As,
R E N T → 4 6 2 8 and L E A S T → 1 6 5 9 8
so, E A S T → 6 5 9 8

6. **(c)** P at top, Q and R below.
The pattern followed: P = Q × R

7. **(d)** As, A D : B E (A +1 → B, D +1 → E)
Similarly, P S : Q T (P +1 → Q, S +1 → T)

8. **(a)** After excluding 2nd, 4th Fridays and 4 Sundays, the working days in the month of November are 24.

9. **(d)**

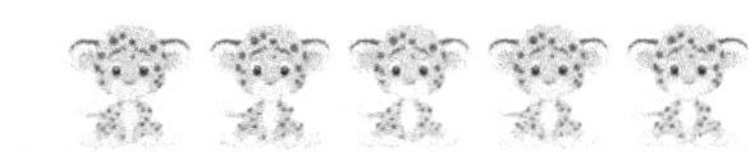

10. **(a)** Lady finger is the lightest vegetable among them.

11. **(c)** A cow has 4 legs and a horse has also 4 legs.
Number of cows = 2
Number of legs of 2 cows
$= 4 + 4 = 8$
Number of horses = 2
Number of legs of 2 horses
$= 4 + 4 = 8$
Total number of legs
$= 8 + 8 = 16$

12. **(a)** There are total 4 triangles in the given diagram.

13. **(b)** There are total 5 circles in the given diagram.

14. **(b)** There are total 3 shapes in the given diagram, i.e., circles, triangles and rectangles.

15. (c) Number of different ways: ACE, ABCDE, ABCE and ACDE

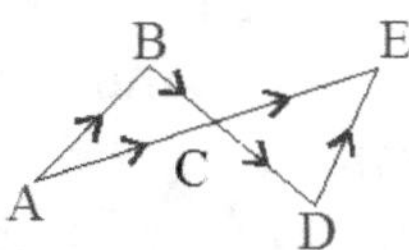

16. (a) Strawberry 5 is the third strawberry to the right of eighth strawberry from right end.

17. (b) Strawberry 5 is in the middle of strawberry 3 and 7.

18. (a) The given numbers are arranged in descending order,

986 768 732 685 406 329 119 103

6th from the right end

19. (b)

20. (a) There are 12 straight lines in the given figure.

21. (c) The correct sequence is 3,2,1,4.

22. (d) The arrangement of four students according to their marks is as follows:

Neha > Gunjan > Sapna > Kanak

So, Kanak scored lowest marks among them.

23. (a) Two circles are increasing in each step.

24. (d) Red Fort is situated in Delhi and Delhi is called Agra. So, Red Fort is situated in Agra.

25. (a) The p attern is as follows:

3 → 6 → 8 → 16 → 18

×2, +2, ×2, +2

MOCK TEST-5

ANSWERS KEY									
1	(b)	6	(a)	11	(c)	16	(b)	21	(c)
2	(c)	7	(c)	12	(d)	17	(a)	22	(b)
3	(d)	8	(d)	13	(a)	18	(b)	23	(d)
4	(b)	9	(a)	14	(d)	19	(c)	24	(b)
5	(d)	10	(b)	15	(a)	20	(d)	25	(c)

1. **(b)** As, 2 + 4 = 6 (middle number)
3 + 6 = 9 (middle number)
And, 4 + 3 = 7 (middle number)
But, 8 + 2 = 10

2. **(c)** Observe the pattern in each segment.

3. **(d)** The correct mirror image is as follows:

BASKET | ꓭAƧKET (mirror image)
Mirror

4. **(b)** 1,4,3,2 is the correct logical order.

5. **(d)** TENTION can be formed from the letters of the given word.

6. **(a)** As,

N → P (+2), O → Q (+2), S → U (+2), E → G (+2)

Similarly,

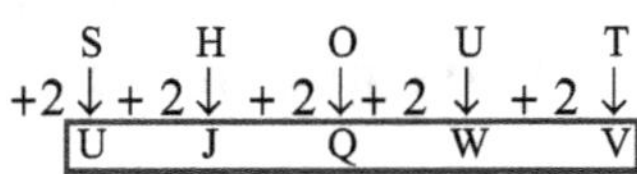

7. **(c)** Letter H in the middle of

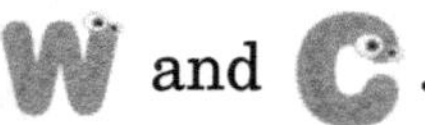

8. **(d)** 8 : 10 + 25 minutes = 8 : 35 p.m.

9. **(a)** Number of boats = 25
Number of people held by 1 boat = 30
Total people in all boats
= 25 × 30 = 750 people.

10. **(b)** The pattern is as follows:

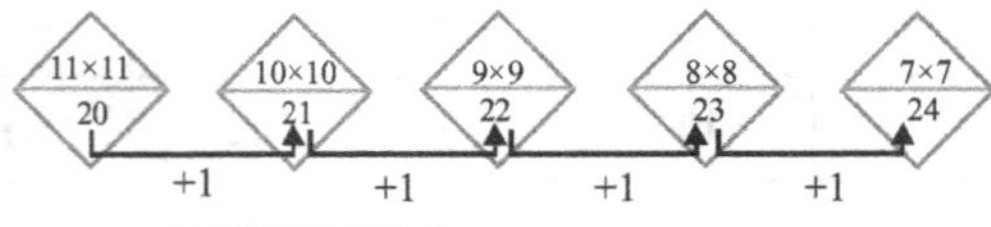

11. **(c)**

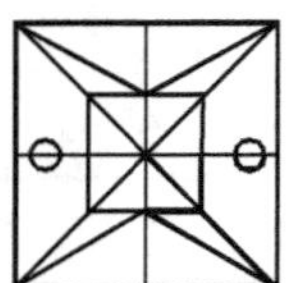

12. **(d)** The weight of a butterfly around 10 g.

13. **(a)** There are total 9 straight lines in the given diagram.

14. **(d)** Ritesh is 2 months older than Naman.

15. **(a)** The code for 7916 is BKWL.

16. **(b)** The code for 3825 is APYN.

17. **(a)** The arrangement of pictures is as follows:

1 2 3 [4] 5 6 7
↑
Prettiest picture

So, Ritu have 7 pictures altogether.

18. **(b)** Boots, Belt and Rope are missing in the second picture.

19. **(c)** The king of flowers is Lotus, but Lotus is called Lily. So, Lily is the king of flowers.

20. **(d)**

21. **(c)** The pattern of the series is as follows:

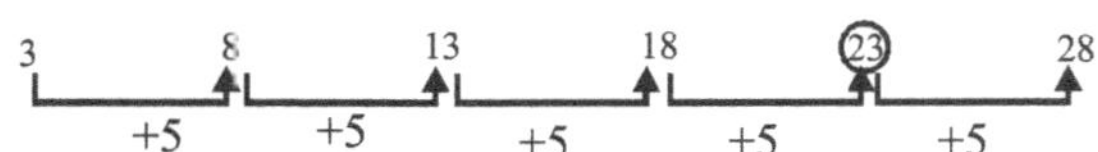

22. **(b)** Except squirrel, all others animals are taller.

23. **(d)** As, 2 × 3 × 2 = 12
Then, 3 × 4 × 3 = 36

24. **(b)** The meaningful word is CHAIR.

25. **(c)** Number of apples kritika has
= 20
Number of apples Mohita has
= 8 more than Kritika
= 8 + 20 = 28

CYBER

MOCK TEST 1

ANSWER KEY									
1	(d)	6	(c)	11.	(c)	16	(c)	21	(b)
2	(c)	7	(a)	12.	(c)	17	(a)	22	(b)
3	(a)	8	(d)	13	(b)	18	(a)	23	(a)
4	(d)	9	(d)	14	(c)	19	(a)	24	(c)
5	(b)	10	(a)	15	(d)	20	(b)	25	(b)

3 (a) Blu-ray or Blu-ray Disc (BD) is a digital optical disc data storage format. It was designed to supersede the DVD format.

5 (b) Only (b) is the input device, which can be used to putting the input into the computer system.

6 (c) Only (c) is an output device and all other given options are input devices so monitor is the odd term.

7 (a) A trackball is a computer cursor control device used in many notebook and laptop computers.

8 (d) A GPS is a navigation system that provides the geographical information based on the data received by satellites.

9 (d) Option (d) is not matched correctly because name of image  is watercolour brush and calligraphy brush 1 is denoted by image.

13 (b) Facebook is not a search engine because it is an American for-profit corporation and an online social media or social networking service.

14 (c) Windows Explorer is not a web browser because it displays the hierarchical structure of files, folders, and drives on your computer. It also shows any network drives that have been mapped to drive letters on your computer.

15 (d) All of these

16 (c) It is basically a system of Internet servers that support specially formatted documents.

18 (a) Android "Nougat" (codenamed N in-development) is the major 7.0 release of the Android operating system. It was first released as a developer preview on March 9, 2016.

22 (b) Micro SD card is used as a storage medium in portable hand-held smartphone device.

23 (b) The equivalent number of spaces used to create a tab is usually five or eight spaces depending on the program being used.

25 (b) Android is a mobile operating system developed by Google, based on the Linux kernel and designed primarily for touch-screen mobile devices such as smartphones and tablets.

MOCK TEST 2

ANSWER KEY									
1	(b)	6	(d)	11	(a)	16	(a)	21	(d)
2	(d)	7	(a)	12	(a)	17	(d)	22	(a)
3	(d)	8	(d)	13	(d)	18	(b)	23	(d)
4	(c)	9	(a)	14	(a)	19	(a)	24	(d)
5	(c)	10	(d)	15	(a)	20	(d)	25	(b)

2. (d) Printer

5. (c) Dot matrix printer. Dot matrix printing is a type of computer printing which uses a print head that moves back-and-forth, or in an up-and-down motion, on the page and prints by impact, striking an ink-soaked cloth ribbon against the paper, much like the print mechanism on a typewriter, so continuous stationery paper is used in this type of printer.

6. (d) Option (D) is a scanner, it is used for capturing data from a page directly and it converts them into digital form to store them in the computer.

11. (a) Set as desktop background option is used to change the windows desktop background picture.

Option 1: Go to File tab, select Set as desktop background

Option 2: Select File tab and press the key "b".

14 (a) A URL (Uniform Resource Locator), as the name suggests, provides a way to locate a resource on the web, the hypertext system that operates over the internet. The first part of a URL identifies what protocol to use. The second part identifies the IP address or domain name where the resource is located.

17 (d) Microsoft word 2016 with an office 365 subscription is the latest version of word.

18 (b) Use the rulers in Word to align text, graphics, tables, and other elements in your document horizontally or vertically. The horizontal ruler shows across the top of your Word document and the vertical ruler shows along the left side of your document.

19 (a) The given image is a format painter; format painter is used on the Home tab to quickly apply the same formatting, such as colour, font style and size, and border style, to multiple pieces of text or graphics. The format painter lets you copy all of the formatting from one object and apply it to another one – think of it as copying and pasting for formatting.

20 (d) The given image is a Google Play. It is a digital distribution service operated and developed by Google. It serves as the official app store for the Android operating system, allowing users to browse and download applications developed with the Android software development kit (SDK) and published through Google.

24 (d) FarmVille is a farming simulation social network game developed by Zynga in 2009.

25 (b) Playstation4 is a gaming brand that consists of four home video game consoles, as well as a media center, an online service, a line of controllers, two handhelds and a phone, as well as multiple magazines.

MOCK TEST 3

ANSWER KEY									
1	(b)	6	(d)	11	(a)	16	(c)	21	(c)
2	(a)	7	(d)	12	(b)	17	(d)	22	(b)
3	(a)	8	(a)	13	(d)	18	(a)	23	(d)
4	(c)	9	(a)	14	(a)	19	(b)	24	(a)
5	(a)	10	(a)	15	(b)	20	(c)	25	(b)

1 (b) CPU is called the brain of the computer because it processes all the instructions given to the computer to perform its tasks.

2 (a) The given image in option (a) is an abacus and it is also called a counting frame. It is a calculating tool that was in use in Europe, China and Russia centuries before the adoption of the written Hindu–Arabic numeral system.

7 (d) The colour 1 box represents the foreground colour in paint program, so after clicking the colour1 box, if any colour is selected from the colour palette then the new colour is set as the foreground colour.

8 (a) Wikipedia is a free online encyclopedia created and edited by volunteers around the world and hosted by the Wikimedia Foundation.

10 (a) When we pressing (Ctrl + o) keys, the open dialog box is displayed, from here you can select as many files as you want to open, hold ctrl key while selecting more than one file.

12 (b) To change the margins of the document, you should use the

(1) Click the Page Layout tab on the Ribbon, and then select the Margins command.

(2) Select the desired margin size from the drop-down menu.

15 (b) A hard drive is fixed inside the CPU cabinet in desktops and laptops computers.

22 (b) Microsoft One-Drive launches worldwide; free cloud storage service provides one place for everything in your life.

24 (a) Except Option (a), all are the digital payment services and option (a) is Google play and it is used for downloading apps.

www.ingramcontent.com/pod-product-compliance
Lightning Source LLC
LaVergne TN
LVHW080041170826
845677LV00024B/1341
* 9 7 8 9 3 8 8 2 4 0 5 3 6 *